Advancing Global Bioethics

Volume 11

The book series Global Bioethics provides a forum for normative analysis of a vast range of important new issues in bioethics from a truly global perspective and with a cross-cultural approach. The issues covered by the series include among other things sponsorship of research and education, scientific misconduct and research integrity, exploitation of research participants in resource-poor settings, brain drain and migration of healthcare workers, organ trafficking and transplant tourism, indigenous medicine, biodiversity, commodification of human tissue, benefit sharing, bio-industry and food, malnutrition and hunger, human rights, and climate change.

More information about this series at http://www.springer.com/series/10420

Dónal P. O'Mathúna • Vilius Dranseika
Bert Gordijn
Editors

Disasters: Core Concepts and Ethical Theories

COST
EUROPEAN COOPERATION IN SCIENCE & TECHNOLOGY

Funded by the Horizon 2020 Framework Programme of the European Union

Springer Open

Editors
Dónal P. O'Mathúna
School of Nursing and Human Sciences
Dublin City University
Dublin, Ireland

College of Nursing
The Ohio State University
Columbus, Ohio, USA

Bert Gordijn
Institute of Ethics
Dublin City University
Dublin, Ireland

Vilius Dranseika
Vilnius University
Vilnius, Lithuania

This publication is based upon work from COST Action IS1201, supported by COST (European Cooperation in Science and Technology).

COST (European Cooperation in Science and Technology) is a funding agency for research and innovation networks - www.cost.eu. Our Actions help connect research initiatives across Europe and enable scientists to grow their ideas by sharing them with their peers. This boosts their research, career and innovation.

ISSN 2212-652X ISSN 2212-6538 (electronic)
Advancing Global Bioethics
ISBN 978-3-030-06501-0 ISBN 978-3-319-92722-0 (eBook)
https://doi.org/10.1007/978-3-319-92722-0

This Springer imprint is published by the registered company Springer Nature Switzerland AG
The registered company address is: Gewerbestrasse 11, 6330 Cham, Switzerland

Contents

Contributors

Ayesha Ahmad Lecturer in Global Health, Institute for Medical and Biomedical Education, St George's University of London, UK; aahmad@sgul.ac.uk. Ayesha Ahmad is a philosopher specialising in ethics and working in Global Health. Particular areas of expertise are cross-cultural mental health and trauma in the context of gender-based violence and conflict.

Andrew Crabtree Adjunct Associate Professor, Department of Management, Society and Communication, Copenhagen Business School, Denmark; ac.msc@cbs.dk. Andrew Crabtree works primarily on ethics and sustainability issues related to the human development paradigm and contractualism. Particular interests include, justice, climate change, human development and environmental indicators, disasters, mental health and culture.

Robert DeLeo Assistant Professor, Department of Global Studies, Bentley University, USA; rdeleo@bentley.edu. Rob DeLeo is an assistant professor of public policy. Research focus is on the political dynamics of policy change in anticipation of emerging hazards, including novel diseases and other public health issues, technological dangers, and the various risks associated with climate change.

Vilius Dranseika Lecturer, Institute of Philosophy, Vilnius University, Lithuania and Researcher, Faculty of Social Sciences, Arts and Humanities, Kaunas University of Technology, Lithuania; vilius.dranseika@gmail.com. His main academic interests are research ethics, moral psychology, and experimental philosophy.

Bert Gordijn Professor and Director, Institute of Ethics, School of Theology, Philosophy, and Music, Dublin City University, Ireland; bert.gordijn@dcu.ie. Bert Gordijn has served on Advisory Panels and Expert Committees of the European Chemical Industry Council, the European Patent Organisation, the Irish Department of Health and UNESCO. Bert is Editor-in-Chief of two book series: The International Library of Ethics, Law and Technology and Advances in Global Bioethics as well as a peer reviewed journal: Medicine, Health Care and Philosophy, all published by

Springer Nature. He is Secretary of the European Society for Philosophy of Medicine and Healthcare and President of the International Association of Education in Ethics.

Eleni Kalokairinou Associate Professor of Philosophy, Department of Philosophy and Education, Aristotle University of Thessaloniki, Greece; ekalo@edlit.auth.gr. Eleni Kalokairinou studied philosophy and her research interests focus on moral philosophy, applied ethics, bioethics, Ancient Greek ethical theories with an emphasis on Aristotle and the Hellenistic Ethical Theories, the origins of bioethics in classical antiquity, on Kant's ethical theory, and political philosophy with an emphasis on liberalism and communitarianism.

Kristian Cedervall Lauta Associate Professor, Center for International Law, Conflict and Crisis, Faculty of Law and Copenhagen Center for Disaster Research (COPE), University of Copenhagen, Denmark; klau@jur.ku.dk. He is the author of *Disaster Law* (Routledge 2015) and of numerous international peer-reviewed articles on law and disaster risk.

Lars Löfquist Senior Lecturer, Theology Department, Uppsala University, Sweden; lars.lofquist@teol.uu.se. Lars Löfquist's research background is in the field of ethics in which he obtained his PhD. His current research focuses on how humanitarian workers can cultivate moral character traits and especially how organizations can support these traits.

Veselin L. Mitrović Senior Research Associate, Faculty of Philosophy, University of Belgrade, Serbia; mitrove@gmail.com. Research activities focus on bioethics, disaster study, sociology of culture and social action. He has published on resilience in marginal groups and his last book in Serbian is *Apathetic Society* (2015).

Ilan Noy Chair in the Economics of Disasters, School of Economics and Finance, Victoria University of Wellington, New Zealand; ilan.noy@vuw.ac.nz. Ilan Noy is a Professor of Economics at Victoria University and the founding Editor-in-Chief of *Economics of Disasters and Climate Change*, published by SpringerNature. He also consulted for the World Bank, the Asian Development Bank, the Inter-American Development Bank, UNISDR, and ASEAN.

Dónal P. O'Mathúna Associate Professor, School of Nursing and Human Sciences, Dublin City University, Ireland and College of Nursing, The Ohio State University, USA; donal.omathuna@dcu.ie. Dónal O'Mathúna has degrees in pharmacy and bioethics. His research interests are in systematic reviewing and the ethics of disasters, particularly around disaster research ethics and humanitarian healthcare ethics.

Vojin Rakić Full Professor, Center for the Study of Bioethics, University of Belgrade, Serbia; vojinrakic@hotmail.com. Vojin Rakić is the Head of the European Division of the UNESCO Chair in Bioethics and Chair of the Cambridge Working Group for Bioethics Education in Serbia. He has a PhD in Political Science and his publications include books, edited collections, and articles in the domain of (bio-) ethics, and political philosophy.

Per Sandin Senior Lecturer in Bioethics and Environmental Ethics, Department of Crop Production Ecology, Swedish University of Agricultural Sciences, Sweden; per.sandin@slu.se. Per Sandin received his PhD in and his research is concerned about applied ethics, the philosophy of risk and the precautionary principle, and the ethics of biotechnology in agriculture.

Jan Helge Solbakk Professor, Centre for Medical Ethics, Institute of Health and Society, Faculty of Medicine, University of Oslo, Norway; j.h.solbakk@medisin.uio.no. Solbakk is a physician and theologian and holds a PhD in ancient Greek Philosophy. His research interests are in international research ethics, bioethics and human rights and human development, and bioethics and Ancient Greek literature.

Siri Tellier Course Leader, Health in Emergencies and Refugee Health, School of Global Health, University of Copenhagen, Denmark; stellier@sund.ku.dk. Siri Tellier has 40 years' experience in international health, humanitarian work and development. She also has 10 years' experience teaching and conducting research, particularly public health demography, reproductive health, and humanitarian medicine including non-communicable diseases.

Henk ten Have Professor of Healthcare Ethics, Center for Healthcare Ethics, Duquesne University, USA; tenhaveh@duq.edu. Henk ten Have worked as professor of healthcare ethics in Maastricht and Nijmegen, The Netherlands, and as Director of the Division of Ethics of Science and Technology at UNESCO in Paris.

Paul Voice Professor, Philosophy Department, Bennington College, USA; pvoice@bennington.edu. Paul Voice's research interests include problems of justice, focusing in particular on the work of John Rawls, and issues of applied political philosophy. Recent publications focus on a Rawlsian account of what states owe victims of disasters and Hannah Arendt's view on the politics of the environment.

Naomi Zack Professor, Philosophy Department, University of Oregon, USA; nzack@uoregon.edu. Recent books include *Ethics for Disaster* (Rowman & Littlefield, 2009), *Philosophy of Race: An Introduction* (Palgrave, 2018), and *Reviving the Social Contract* (Rowman & Littlefield, 2018).

Chapter 1
Conceptualizing and Assessing Disasters: An Introduction

Dónal P. O'Mathúna and Bert Gordijn

Abstract This introduction explains the rationale behind the volume at hand against the backdrop of the existing state of the art in research related to disasters and disaster bioethics. The volume offers an overview of how disasters are conceptualized in different academic disciplines relevant to disaster bioethics (Part I), and addresses normative issues that arise in responding to disasters from the perspective of a number of fundamental normative approaches in moral and political philosophy (Part II). Part I aims at identifying and exploring the dominant approaches to basic concepts and categorization criteria of disasters in different academic disciplines, including Philosophy, Theology, Law, Economics, Public Health, Literature Studies, Political Science, and Gender Studies. The eight chapters in Part I provide an introduction to conceptual research in disasters and aim to stimulate further work. It thereby contributes to enhanced awareness and recognition of the real-world importance of basic concepts and disaster criteria. Part II provides a broad range of normative perspectives (Consequentialism, Virtue Ethics, Kantian virtue ethics, Capabilities approach, Deontology, Human Rights and Communitarianism). These chapters are offered as a starting point, not a final conclusion on the topic of disaster ethics. Ethical justification for actions taken in the face of disasters needs recourse to normative traditions and this book aims at setting the stage for more focused normative debates.

Keywords Ethics · Disaster · Consequentialism · Virtue ethics · Capabilities approach · Deontology · Human rights

D. P. O'Mathúna (✉)
School of Nursing and Human Sciences, Dublin City University, Dublin, Ireland

College of Nursing, The Ohio State University, Columbus, Ohio, USA
e-mail: donal.omathuna@dcu.ie

B. Gordijn
Institute of Ethics, School of Theology, Philosophy, and Music, Dublin City University, Dublin, Ireland
e-mail: bert.gordijn@dcu.ie

D. P. O'Mathúna et al. (eds.), *Disasters: Core Concepts and Ethical Theories*, Advancing Global Bioethics 11, https://doi.org/10.1007/978-3-319-92722-0_1

The book here presented[1] offers an overview of how disasters are conceptualized in different academic disciplines relevant to disaster bioethics (Part I), and addresses ethical issues that arise in responding to disasters from the perspective of a number of fundamental normative approaches in moral and political philosophy (Part II). In this introduction, we explain the rationale behind the volume at hand against the backdrop of the existing state of the art in research related to disasters and disaster bioethics.

1.1 Part I: Conceptualization of Disasters in Different Disciplines

Disasters are typically viewed as overwhelmingly negative events. However, more thorough analysis reveals that they do not always have exclusively negative consequences. Disasters can provide the impetus for change that brings positive outcomes, such as changes in building practices or regulations when previous ones are shown to be inadequate. Disasters can expose injustice and be the stimulus for reform. They can trigger deeper philosophical and societal reflection that has positive impact. Rebuilding after destruction can have long-term gains, such as how the 1931 earthquake in Napier, New Zealand led to Art Deco architecture that is enjoyed by contemporary tourists. In spite of such examples, the term *disaster* more typically has a negative connotation, and one that is at the extreme end of negativity.

At the same time, it is not immediately obvious which events qualify as disasters and which incidents should be deemed to be ineligible. Lack of a consistent definition is not just a challenge for those who seek conceptual clarity. While academics debate different views, the concern is not just academic. Different concepts and definitions are used in identifying and forecasting disasters, and humanitarian agencies make response decisions based on different concepts. If international aid is predicated on an event fitting a certain definition of a disaster, that definition and the concepts it is based on, have very practical implications. Equally, different notions are used to track the impact of disaster responses. But if disasters are seen as events that primarily arise suddenly and unexpectedly, the chronic conditions that precede them or the long-term impact of the disaster and its response, may not be examined. Finally, little conceptual unity exists across legal documents, policy guidelines and disaster scholarship. And yet, stipulating the necessary and sufficient requirements for an event to be counted as a disaster is crucial, to ensure those laws and guidelines are implemented appropriately.

[1]The editors and authors are grateful to the European Cooperation in Science & Technology (COST) for funding provided to COST Action IS1201: Disaster Bioethics (http://DisasterBioethics.eu). COST is funded through the European Union Horizon 2020 research and innovation programme within the frame of the COST H2020 Framework Partnership Agreement. This funding allowed the authors to gather at a workshop in Vilnius University in Lithuania in 2016. Funding was also provided by COST to made this book available as an open access publication.

Hence Part I of this book aims at identifying and exploring the dominant approaches to basic concepts and categorization criteria of disasters in different academic disciplines, including Philosophy, Theology, Law, Economics, Public Health, Literature Studies, Political Science, and Gender Studies. Other disciplines could have been included, such as History, Sociology, and Medicine. A balance had to be found between being all-encompassing and providing a manageable overview of a number of fields. Many other topics could be addressed, and subsequent scholarship should fill these gaps. The eight chapters in Part I provide an introduction to conceptual research in disasters and aim to stimulate further work. It thereby contributes to enhanced awareness and recognition of the real-world importance of basic concepts and disaster criteria.

As conceptualization is a philosophical enterprise, it is fitting to start with Per Sandin's chapter on philosophical perspectives. He contends that while disasters have been defined, relatively little philosophical analysis has occurred. At the same time, disasters have triggered much philosophical reflection since at least the ancient Greek philosophers. Sandin reviews some contemporary philosophical work on disasters, particularly that linked to ethics and political philosophy. Sandin concludes by proposing a number of areas in which disaster research could gain profitably by further engagement with philosophy. Particular areas include reflection on risk, social psychology, typologies of disasters, and environmental apocalypse.

Just as disasters have led to philosophical reflection, they have led to much theological analysis. This field is examined by Dónal P. O'Mathúna, who limits his analysis mainly to Christian theology. Disasters have led to much theological reflection as they raise the practical question of why God would allow such things. The occurrence of events of such largescale destruction appear to clash with theological notions that a loving God cares for humans. Hence, disasters are particularly challenging for religions that invoke a personal and loving God, such as Christianity. O'Mathúna applies theological reasoning on the problems of evil and suffering to disasters, and reviews some of the proposals developed within the field of theodicy. He concludes that theology has provided ways to sustain belief in God in spite of the existence of disasters, which links into the possibility that good can come even from things as terrible as disasters.

Kristian Cedervall Lauta takes as his starting point the move away from theological reflection on disasters to legal perspectives. Rather than questioning why God allowed a disaster, recent legal perspectives have focused on human responsibility for disasters. Lauta notes the increasing number of legal cases around the world involving disasters, with a particular focus on compensating victims. He sees three characteristics in the trend. One is the serious losses involved for victims, the second is the complexity of these events, and the third are what he calls 'the tricky distinctions' that must be made. Lauta holds that these distinctions are peculiar to legal cases involving disasters, and they generate controversy because of ambiguity in our understanding of central concepts like science, agency and culture. He uses the case involving the 2009 L'Aquila earthquake in Italy to illustrate his perspective. Disasters thus challenge society to address the lack of conceptual clarity on categories central to how wealth and justice are distributed in society.

Ilan Noy addresses economics and disasters, noting that economics as a discipline gives relatively little attention to language and terminology. A clear definition of what is meant by a disaster is not usually found in economic analyses, nor have the ethical issues behind such analyses been examined broadly. However, Noy holds that the way forward is to examine those areas where disagreement exists among economists when they address disasters and their ethical issues. Noy examines controversies around two issues, price gouging and post-disaster economic recovery, to show different approaches to disasters within the economics literature. Price gouging involves inflating prices during periods of scarcity and explicitly involves ethical perspectives on distributing scarce resources. While many find price gouging inherently unethical, Noy reviews economic arguments both supporting and rejecting such practices. He finds little empirical evidence to support either perspective, and then examines the practical challenges for laws concerning price gouging. Noy then addresses economic perspectives on long-term recovery after disasters. Many of the approaches are based on consequentialist assumptions, and yet these have serious limitations. However, few alternatives are available, pointing to the need for further conceptual research on economic perspectives on disasters.

The political dimensions of disasters have arisen in earlier chapters, but are examined in detail by Robert DeLeo. He reviews some historical examples of the inextricable link between politics and disasters. In some cases, smart governance helped to put in place good strategies that mitigated the consequences of disasters, but examples abound of political failures also. As with other fields, disasters are conceived conceptually in different ways across the political sciences, and within its subfields. What is widely recognised is that disasters are social constructs. As such, political decisions impact the vulnerability and resilience of communities towards disasters. At the same time, disasters impact the electoral process and can either strengthen or weaken political power and shape policy change. DeLeo explores these interconnections within three streams of political science research: the policy implications of disasters, the electoral implications of disasters, and disaster risk management. Within each area, political scientists have used disasters to advance prominent political science theories and at the same time informed practical debates on how to apply political theory to all phases of disaster preparation and response. Gaps remain, particularly around the challenges and opportunities for approaches to policy-making regarding anticipated events. In addition, further attention needs to be given to the importance of language in shaping policy debates and the narrative dimensions of disasters.

Narratives have conceptualised disasters since ancient times. Jan Helge Solbakk explores how this occurred in ancient Greek tragedy, finding that the ethical dimensions of disasters were at the centre of this genre. Solbakk uses Greek tragedy as a paradigm for recurrent patterns of attitudes and behavior that come to life when disasters are caused by humans or gods. He finds a number of patterns in several tragedies set in the aftermath of war. Frequently, mention is given of moral degradations and crimes committed by victors on the vanquished. At the same time, homecoming for the veteran soldier can be very difficult, often with tragic consequences. Another pattern seen in Greek tragedy is the deep impact of war on women and children, both on and off the battlefield. The violence committed against women and children in Greek tragedy reads just like contemporary news headlines. In this way, Solbakk argues that such narratives continue to offer much to our understanding of ethics and disasters. A narrative approach to disaster ethics has much more to contribute than has not yet been explored.

Ayesha Ahmad focuses on the analysis of disasters and women. The field of gender studies views disasters as gender-constructed processes. It brings to the fore the backdrop of gender inequalities and their impact on how disasters are conceptualised. Given the level of violence, injury and death inflicted on women during and after disasters, this perspective argues that gender must be considered an integral factor in conceptualising and responding to disasters. This brings an explicitly ethical dimension as it informs humanitarian responses and policies that aim to protect individuals in disaster situations. When such policies do not mediate the risks to women in disaster contexts, particularly refugee or internally displaced camps, pre-existing injustices and inequalities can be reinforced. Ahmad concludes that disasters, even when conceptualised from a gender perspective, require a more all-encompassing theoretical framework to account for the lived experiences of individuals in disasters. The aim is to provide more sustainable and long-term approaches to disasters that take appropriate account of gender in societies.

Siri Tellier examines public health in disasters and humanitarian action. The objectives of humanitarian action are rooted in its origins with the foundation of the International Committee of the Red Cross. Given its origin in providing healthcare for soldiers, saving lives continues to be a central objective and ethical mandate. Over the last two centuries, many measures of global health and mortality have improved. Tellier examines how this has led to changing conceptualisations of public health and with that, differing approaches to ethical issues. Public health has traditionally relied on utilitarian approaches with its emphasis on the goal of improving the health of the population as much as possible. Tellier finds a number of ethical challenges remain for public health in disasters, particularly decisions about prioritising actions, the limits of humanitarian action within complex social settings, global differences in practice standards, exit strategies, gaining access to various groups, and effective coordination. These issues require substantial further ethical analysis.

1.2 Part II: Basic Moral Theories and Response to Disasters

The above-mentioned conceptual and definitional issues feed into discussions about how normative issues that arise in responding to disasters should be addressed. Nevertheless, supposing we had a broadly accepted definition of disaster, it would obviously not determine how we ought to react from a normative point of view. Being able to answer the question "what is a disaster?" does not imply a specific take on the way in which we should relate to the phenomenon. So what, if any, are our ethical obligations in relation to people struck by disasters? This question has gained importance because of globalisation. Whereas for most of human history we have been blissfully unaware of the disasters that struck others who did not live in our immediate vicinity, this naïve ignorance has definitely disappeared as a result of the fast development of transportation, information and communication technologies. On the one hand, we seem not to have been provided with a natural inclination to empathise with strangers far away. And yet, nowadays disasters at the other end of the world appear on our television screens as they happen, and we can go anywhere in the world to help within a few days. The resulting normative questions confuse us.

In Part II, therefore, this volume provides a broad range of normative perspectives (Consequentialism, Virtue Ethics, Kantian virtue ethics, Capabilities approach, Deontology, Human Rights and Communitarianism). No volume could hope to include all normative perspectives and still remain a manageable size. While we attempted to include all major approaches, our final selection was determined to some degree by the availability of authors to provide material. In no way do we claim that the perspectives included here are the only relevant ones, or even the most important ones. These chapters are offered as a starting point, not a final conclusion on the topic of disaster ethics. Ethical justification for actions taken in the face of disasters needs recourse to normative traditions and this book aims at setting the stage for more focused normative debates.

Since disasters often involve making decisions for the good of many, Part II opens with a chapter on consequentialism by Vojin Rakić. He argues that consequentialist ethics is often the preferred moral approach in disaster settings where decisions are taken that affect larger numbers of people, not just individuals. This approach is suited to political decision making, especially in the domain of international relations and also in disaster settings. Rakić begins with an historical overview of various approaches to consequentialism. He concludes that in such large-scale contexts, consequentialism is most adequate as a moral theory. However, other situations require different approaches to ethics. He provides case examples, some of which point to situations in which consequentialism is the preferred ethical approach, and others which point out the limitations and problems with consequentialist approaches.

Henk ten Have affirms the importance of saving more lives in disasters, but notes that emergency ethics will accept that not everyone can be saved. This approach can lead to a neglect of other important values, including human dignity, justice, and human rights. Disasters have a way of leading to the neglect and violation of human rights. While some have criticised the adequacy of a human rights approach, ten Have provides reasons to redefine humanitarianism in terms of rights. Ten Have next turns to the concept of vulnerability, a core notion in continental philosophy. Vulnerability has emerged as a key principle in global bioethics, and is especially salient in the context of global disasters. Its usefulness arises in part because it highlights the conditions that produce vulnerability and how these might be ameliorated, rather than focusing on the emergency decisions needed in disasters. The combination of human rights approaches, humanitarianism and vulnerability is advocated by ten Have. He claims this would require a critical reformulation of human rights discourse, since it often shares the vision of neoliberal approaches and policies of globalization, rather than questioning the negative relationships between social context, trade and human flourishing. Global bioethics, ten Have concludes, can redirect human rights discourse towards the protection of the vulnerable and the prevention of future disasters.

The broader and longer view of disasters is continued by Andrew Crabtree as he applies Amartya Sen's capabilities approach to disasters. Crabtree sees a clear connection between Sen's work and disasters because Sen emphasises the social context in which hazards occur. Sen's early work on famines explored their social dimension, particularly how famines arise not because there is no food, but because certain people in society lack entitlements to food. Sen's early work has been criticised as incomplete, but it overlaps with ten Have's chapter in pointing to the importance of poverty and vulnerability in causing disasters. Crabtree notes that in developing his capabilities approach, Sen moved into a normative framework. Sen points to weaknesses in resource-based approaches, such as Rawlsian views of justice, and end-state approaches, such as consequentialism. Crabtree examines these arguments as he describes the capabilities approach. He finds much to commend this approach to disasters, particularly because of its emphasis on freedoms and agency. However, he notes that Sen has contributed little to reflection on disasters since the 1980s, something Crabtree explores, particularly the relevance of his approach to sustainability. He concludes by examining how the capabilities approach could contribute to normative discussions with disasters, while acknowledging the challenges in such an endeavour.

Paul Voice takes up another perspective which has received relatively little application to disasters: communitarian ethical theory. His chapter aims to philosophically examine the contribution that communitarian ethics might make to disaster ethics and at the same time reflect on its philosophical difficulties and weaknesses. Voice does not present a communitarian ethics template to apply in disasters, but rather uses a communitarian lens to identify ethical issues that other ethical perspectives might underemphasise. Voice begins by describing the main features of communitarianism and its roots in critiquing John Rawls's theory of justice. Instead of Rawls's impartial moral stance, communitarian ethical theory emphasises the social and cultural roots that all people have and which they bring to their ethical decision-making. Voice then focuses on one strand of communitarian thinking: political communitarianism. This approach is sceptical about the value of the state and its agencies, preferring instead local community autonomy. Little has been written on how communitarian ethics applies to disasters, something Voice finds odd given the emphasis on community in disaster literature. He reviews some of these contributions and develops a communitarian perspective on justice and disasters. He then points out several criticisms of this approach, noting that more philosophical work remains to be done in this area.

Virtue ethics has undergone a revival in recent years, which Lars Löfquist argues adds a distinctive and thought-provoking perspective on disasters. His chapter begins with a short introduction to non-religious Western virtue ethics, beginning with Aristotle, and moving through Hume, MacIntyre and Slote. He then provides a historical overview of the connection between virtues and disasters. He finds two important links, one exploring the morally excellent response we might have in the face of a disaster, and the other being our moral response to a disaster experienced by others. The former is developed by Löfquist in an exploration of the virtue of resilience, and includes perseverance with this. The latter virtue that responses to others is called humanity by Löfquist. By this he means a response to the suffering of others which has variously been called beneficence, benevolence and fellow feeling. Turning then to how virtue ethics is examined in the context of disasters, Löfquist sees three themes. The first consists of general writings that explore the connection between virtue ethics and disasters. Various cases and examples are provided to demonstrate the virtues that are important in disasters. The second theme explores the professional virtues that should exist in humanitarian workers to allow them to meet the moral challenges they face. The third theme concerns the virtues of those suffering a disaster, with a particular emphasis on resilience as a virtue. Löfquist concludes with suggestions for future work, finding that the virtues are as yet untapped in their potential for contributing to disaster ethics.

Eleni Kalokairinou continues the exploration of virtue ethics and disasters, although she starts from Immanuel Kant's discussion of virtues. She argues that Kant's deontological account is not just a formally ideal ethical theory, but that it also possesses an ethical account of virtues. Kantian deontological virtues are directly applicable to the problems caused by disasters in the real world. Kalokairinou reviews some of the debate over ideal and nonideal moral theories in ethics, and concludes that Kant examined this debate much earlier and concluded that ideal theories were compatible with nonideal approaches. Kalokairinou demonstrates how Kant supplemented his ideal ethical theory with a nonideal one, his theory of virtues. She argues that Kant's explorations in the area of helping those in need and in poor conditions are applicable to contemporary disasters. Kalokairinou shows how Kant developed two duties of virtue, namely the duty of justice and the duty of beneficence. She shows that these are very applicable to the real-world ethical dilemmas in disasters. Kalokairinou concludes that Kant's account is very carefully worked-out and is the right one for dealing with disasters.

The final chapter by Veselin Mitrović and Naomi Zack also examines deontology. Their argument is that many similarities exist between the ethical issues arising during disasters and violent conflicts, and other issues in bioethics that are rarely connected to disasters. Their argument is that all of these bioethical issues involve a failure on the part of some to respond with indignation and therefore lead to apathy towards change. Underlying both of these, they claim, is an absence of deontology. Mitrović and Zack develop two case studies in support of their argument. One involves a picture of social apathy and loss of care towards homeless people in society. The second case involves a group of people pursuing infertility treatment and the changes they undergo in terms of altruism and solidarity. In both cases, there is a loss of altruism which Mitrović and Zack claim leads people into apathy and then to a lack of any sense of obligation to perform their duties to help others. They view apathy as a lack of indignation at an unjust or unethical situation, resulting in indifference towards one's duties. They claim that a more appropriate response to the suffering of another should lead to an expression of solidarity with the sufferer which then leads to action on the basis of one's duties. In this way, Mitrović and Zack argue that by taking deontology seriously, people will be motivated to respond to those who suffer, including those suffering after disasters.

We trust the chapters in this book will make a valuable contribution to the field of disaster ethics. However, their authors all agree that much more work needs to occur in this area as a whole, and on the specific topics addressed in each chapter. Ethical dilemmas are increasingly recognised as a major element of disaster preparedness and disaster response. It will take careful research and engagement with affected communities to ensure this is done well.

Part I
Conceptualization of Disasters in Different Disciplines

Chapter 2
Conceptualizations of Disasters in Philosophy

Per Sandin

Abstract This chapter provides an overview of how disasters have been conceived of in philosophy, starting with Plato, with focus on the analytic tradition. Philosophers have been surprisingly little concerned with disasters. Some works where philosophers, and some non-philosophers, explicitly define disasters are surveyed and discussed. Works by philosophers who have discussed philosophical issues pertaining to disasters and disaster-like situations without offering much discussion of the definition of the term are also treated. Those have mainly been ethicists, normative as well as applied, and political philosophers dealing with the Hobbesian tradition's problems of state authority and exceptions. The use of imagined disasters in philosophical thought experiments, typically in ethics, is also discussed. The chapter concludes by offering tentative suggestions of some possible future developments in disaster philosophizing. Among them are that we might expect philosophers to devote increased attention to empirical work, for instance from behavioural science, and increased exploration of the intersection between disaster philosophizing and environmental ethics.

Keywords Threshold deontology · Hobbes · Disaster · Ethics · Emergencies · Philosophy

2.1 Introduction

How have philosophers defined and conceptualized disasters? The short answer is: surprisingly little. They have hardly defined it explicitly, and they have provided implicit definitions pretty much like everyone else who has attempted it; that is, they have defined it in ways that suit their own purposes. That is the short answer, and of course it is too short. In what follows I will present a slightly longer one.

P. Sandin (✉)
Department of Crop Production Ecology, Swedish University of Agricultural Sciences, Uppsala, Sweden
e-mail: per.sandin@slu.se

D. P. O'Mathúna et al. (eds.), *Disasters: Core Concepts and Ethical Theories*, Advancing Global Bioethics 11, https://doi.org/10.1007/978-3-319-92722-0_2

Approaching the question of conceptualization of disasters in philosophy requires an idea of what philosophy is. Does the term refer to the activities carried out by people working from within academic philosophy departments? That characterization would be unsatisfactory, since it would leave out very significant parts of the historical philosophical canon—there were no philosophy departments in antiquity, for instance. And a lot of what is regarded as philosophy today would not fit the bill either. For instance, important contributions to political philosophy have come from political scientists or people working in government departments, and theologians have made important contributions to ethics. A more plausible characterization would be to say that 'philosophy' refers to a set of topics, including but not limited to ethics (including political philosophy), epistemology (including logic), and metaphysics, all very broadly conceived. Philosophy in this sense is about searching for answers to the questions—and I am paraphrasing Kant here—'What is there? What can we know? What ought we to do?' I take this to be a rather conventional characterization and will employ it in the present paper. I will, however, emphasize contributors who are identified by themselves and others as philosophers. The reason for this is simply that conceptualizations of disasters in other fields have been examined by others, who are no doubt more knowledgeable about those fields than I am.

In this paper I attempt to give an overview of how disasters have been conceived of in philosophy. My focus will be on the analytic tradition. I will summarize and discuss some works where philosophers have explicitly engaged in defining disasters, and devote some more space to philosophers who have discussed philosophical issues pertaining to disasters and disaster-like situations without so much discussion of the definition of the term. Those have mainly been ethicists, normative as well as applied, and political philosophers. I also highlight how imagined disasters have been employed in philosophical thought experiments. I conclude by sketching some possible future developments.

2.2 Defining Disaster

To begin with, there is at least one non-philosopher whose efforts must be mentioned: E.L. Quarantelli. There are at last two reasons for this. First, Quarantelli has an analytic philosophical approach to the definitional issue, and his work is an eminent example of Carnap's idea of explication, 'the transformation of an inexact, prescientific concept, the *explicandum*, into a new exact concept, the *explicatum*' (Carnap 1950, 3). Second, philosophers discussing disasters refer to Quarantelli (Voice 2016; Zack 2009). In his introduction to the seminal volume *What is a Disaster?* Quarantelli recounts how he asked a number of scholars to 'put together a statement on how they thought the term "disaster" should be conceptualized *for social science research purposes*' (Quarantelli 1998, 2). The emphasis is in the original and it is important. Quarantelli continues by saying that while '[a] minimum rough consensus on the central referent of the term "disaster" is necessary', he emphasizes that at the same time 'for legal, operational, and different organizational purposes, there is a need for and there will always continue to be different definitions/conceptions' (Quarantelli 1998, 3). However, he also argues that 'for *research* purposes aimed at developing a theoretical superstructure for the field, we need greater clarity and relative consensus' (Quarantelli 1998, 3, emphasis in original).

Despite the surprising scantiness of academic philosophical discussions of the topic, disaster—or the potential of disaster—has been a looming presence in Western philosophy since its early days. For instance in the *Timaeus* and *Critias*, Plato recounts the myth of Atlantis where disaster befalls the once-mighty kingdom:

> But at a later time there occurred portentous earthquakes and floods, and one grievous day and night befell them, when the whole body of your warriors was swallowed up by the earth, and the island of Atlantis in like manner was swallowed up by the sea and vanished; wherefore also the ocean at that spot has now become impassable and unsearchable, being blocked up by the shoal mud which the island created as it settled down (Plato 1925, 25c–25d)

Similar eschatological myths prevail over the millennia in Christianity as well as in other religious traditions. A pivotal point in this development, and one which perhaps marks the beginnings of modern philosophical engagement with disasters, is the Lisbon earthquake of 1755. It struck in the morning of November 1st, at a time when many of the city's inhabitants were attending mass. The city centre, where the nobility dwelled, was particularly badly damaged (Dynes 2000).

The Lisbon earthquake figures in the interchange between Rousseau and Voltaire (Cassidy 2005). Philosophically, the occurrence of the disaster prompted Voltaire's questioning of the optimistic world view of Leibniz, Pope and others (Dynes 2000), a view Voltaire subsequently ridiculed in *Candide*. Rousseau replied and the ensuing discussion concerned Providence and God's place (if any) in a world containing evil, or at least apparent evil. The theodicy is apparently still discussed in the context of disasters, e.g. volcanic eruptions (Chester 2005).

However, Rousseau's reply is also interesting from a more secular point of view for several reasons. One is that it points to a conceptualization of disasters that recognizes that 'natural' disasters do not strike blindly—the way buildings are located and constructed affects the outcome, as do to some extent the actions of the victims (if they postpone evacuation in order to collect their belongings or not, for instance; Cassidy 2005, p. 9). The Lisbon earthquake was also the first disaster that occurred in a nascent modern nation-state, and it was 'the first disaster in which the state accepted the responsibility for mobilizing the emergency response and for developing and implementing a collective effort for reconstruction' (Dynes 2000, 112). The Lisbon earthquake thus in more than one respect can be said to have been the first modern disaster.

2.3 Disaster Conceptualizations in Philosophy

In a recent paper, Paul Voice (2016) offers a relevant categorization of areas where philosophers might be concerned with disasters. First, there is a set of metaphysical and, in some cases, theological issues. This is what concerned Rousseau and Voltaire in the wake of the Lisbon earthquake, and it would be expected that here is where you could find statements at least purporting to be the true answer to Quarantelli's question 'what is a disaster?' Second, there is the ethical approach, which is concerned mainly with individuals and their actions. Here belong also applied ethical issues such as responsibilities of health care workers in disaster situations, questions of triage, and so on. Third, there is the political-philosophical perspective, which is concerned primarily with institutions rather than individuals, with questions such as what coercive measures the state is justified in taking in a post-disaster situation. In this category we will find the heritage from Hobbes and also materials from discussions about just wars and warlike situations (Sandin 2009a). However helpful, it appears that at least one field of philosophy that could and arguably should be concerned with disasters is missing from Voice's categorization: epistemology, and its close relative, philosophy of science. In fact, the discussion of some of the issues treated in Quarantelli's (1998) volume would likely benefit from such approaches, and indeed some of the authors in that volume touch upon them, for instance Dombrowsky (1998). Oliver-Smith (1998) uses another standard item from the toolbox of analytical philosophy, W.B. Gallie's notion of essentially contested concepts.

Voice discusses some existing definitions of disasters, for instance those of the US Federal Emergency Management Agency (FEMA), and some more academic authors like Quarantelli, Donald W. Perry, and Naomi Zack. He notes that they typically emphasize harm and breakdown of life in a community. Since these criteria are not unique to disasters, the amount of harm is what sets disasters aside from non-disastrous events involving harm. '[A] high degree of harm often (but not always) in a spatially confined place and in a brief period of time combine as rules of thumb for identifying a disastrous event' (Voice 2016, 397). He points out that such a 'definition' hinges on others and that there are demarcation problems, for instance how much harm is required in order for the disaster label to be applied, and so on. Voice argues that '[m]ore academic definitions of disasters are mostly constructed from a sociological perspective' (Voice 2016, 397), referring to the Quarantelli tradition.

Voice's own definition is that a disaster is 'an event that destroys or disables the institutions required for moral agency and effective citizenship' (Voice 2016, 399). He argues that a disaster is something more than aggregated individual harm and that it is not necessary that anyone be actually physically harmed for a disaster to occur, nor does any property have to be damaged, 'although nearly all disasters are violent events of some kind' (Voice 2016, 399). It is not entirely easy to envisage what such a non-violent disaster would be, and Voice does not provide examples. Perhaps a breakdown of communication systems might fit such a definition? However, it would perhaps be more natural to say that such a situation is a crisis, which might result in a disaster (if harm occurs). Voice however emphasizes that disasters in this sense need not be sudden, but that 'the slow erosion of dignity and citizenship in a case like Zimbabwe is a disaster' too (Voice 2016, 399). Voice's position implies that states owe disaster victims not only emergency relief, but also longer-term rebuilding, for instance provision of schools and other things required to restore citizen capacities. However, the state does not owe the victims to restore the level of well-being that they had before disaster struck.

Another of the few philosophers who have treated disasters at any length is Naomi Zack, in her 2009 book, *Ethics for Disaster*. She clearly recognizes that the very term 'disaster' carries normative implications. 'To call an event a "disaster" is to signal that it is worthy of immediate, serious human attention and purposive corrective activity" (Zack 2009, 7). However, the definition of disaster she presents contains elements that point in different directions.

She contrasts her approach to the one of 'disaster-research specialists' represented in the Quarantelli volume and writes that as an ethicist, amateur observer, and potential disaster victim, her job is 'after the fact', paying attention to 'disruptive events that will have already been designated "disasters"' (Zack 2009, 7). She defines a disaster as

> ...an event (or series of events) that harms or kills a significant number of people or otherwise severely impairs or interrupts their daily lives in civil society. Disasters may be natural or the result of accidental or deliberate human action. (Zack 2009, 7)

She goes on to enumerate a number of examples including earthquakes, floods, pandemics, and, notably, terrorist attacks, and 'other events that officials and experts designate "disasters"' (ibid). She also writes that

> Disasters always occasion surprise and shock; they are unwanted by those affected by them, although not always unpredictable. Disasters also generate narratives and media representations of the heroism, failures, and losses of those who are affected and respond. (Zack 2009, 7)

It might appear that Zack's definition is a purely lexical one, describing actual use of the term among a particular group of language users, in this case disaster researchers and officials. It is unclear what she takes to be defining characteristics of disasters and characteristics that are accidental but typical. She also includes terrorist acts, but explicitly excludes war. The reasons for this appear to be twofold. First, the insight among crisis researchers that disasters typically generate prosocial behavior rather than the opposite, while this is not the case for conflict situations, i.e. war. Secondly, wars 'are structured', according to Zack. Even though the effects of war might be disasters from the point of view of civilians, from the point of view of the military, wars 'have deliberate agency, systematic planning, and the active involvement of legitimate government, all of which distinguish them from disasters' (Zack 2009, 7.) However, it is not difficult to see that at least the first two of these characteristics apply also to acts of terrorism. Zack's definition offers very little in the way of clarification.

2.3.1 Ethics and Political Philosophy

Zack is an ethicist, and applied ethics is a field where considerable philosophical work involving disasters has been carried out, and even in cases where no explicit definitions of disasters are given, the discussions nevertheless involve conceptual choices that are of importance for the understanding of how disasters might be conceived of. This is particularly the case within the sub-field of medical ethics. (Here the question of whether philosophy is defined by its topics or by its disciplinary home recurs. Medical ethics is a field spanning several disciplines, in addition to academic philosophy.) Arguments from medical ethics have also been transferred to other professions with obvious roles in disasters, such as fire and rescue personnel (Sandin 2009b).

Arguably, the most disaster-relevant contribution from medical ethics is the idea of *triage*. Triage involves sorting and prioritizing between victims in emergency situations. Who should receive treatment first, who must wait, and who, if any, is beyond rescue? In what can be labelled the classic work on triage, Gerald R. Winslow distinguishes between *utilitarian* and *egalitarian* triage principles, and discusses five utilitarian and five egalitarian principles for triage. His starting point, however, is the following observation:

> The principle [of doing the greatest good for the greatest number] obviously has a strong intuitive appeal in triage situations. [...] Moreover, appealing to the utilitarian principle receives hefty support from the prevailing moral spirit of the age. One or another brand of utilitarianism has tended to dominate moral thought in modern times. (Winslow 1982, 22)

It is questionable whether 'the moral spirit of the age' is utilitarian, and indeed whether it was when Winslow wrote in the early 1980s. However, he is entirely right that the idea of the greatest good for the greatest number is the default approach in disaster medical ethics generally (cf. Zack 2009, Chap. 1). Anecdotally, many conversations I have had with rescue professionals indicate that if you propose any other triage principle than the utilitarian one of saving the greatest number, they will look at you with disbelief. And according to James F. Childress, all systems of triage have a utilitarian rationale, whether explicit or implicit (Childress 2003). There is, however, some opposition to this claim. For instance, Baker and Strosberg (1992, 103) argue that 'the logic of triage is not primitive utilitarianism, but theoretically sophisticated egalitarianism'. And Winslow himself offers a triage rationale claiming that Rawlsian rational contract agents, deciding behind a veil of ignorance, would opt for the principle of *usefulness under the immediate circumstances* According to this principle, priority should be given to those individuals who are likely to be most useful in the immediate circumstances, such as nurses and paramedics. He takes this principle to be similar to Rawls' difference principle. It is important, Winslow claims, 'to distinguish the contract justification for the difference principle, which has been identified here with the principle of immediate usefulness, from a basically utilitarian rationale' (Winslow 1982, 153). Winslow admits that a straightforward utilitarian approach and the difference principle may recommend strategies that are identical, but holds that they nevertheless 'clearly exemplify different perspectives' (Winslow 1982, 153).

Kenneth Kipnis (2013), working within medical ethics, introduces a scalar taxonomy of calamities. Kipnis offers narrow, or domain-specific, characterizations of the concepts of disasters and catastrophes. They concern the healthcare system, not society in general. (It is not uncommon that when philosophers discuss disasters, they are actually not treating disasters in general, but rather some particular instance of disaster, but Kipnis is explicit about this.) His taxonomy has four levels in addition to Level 0, ordinary clinical practice. Those levels are characterized based on (i) what resources are likely to be insufficient and (ii) what the appropriate response by the healthcare system would be. They are (1) local patient surges and staff shortages, requiring diversion of patients to other facilities, (2) disasters—where triage applies, (3) Physical and Medical Catastrophes, where a healthcare system collapses, and (4) Mega-Pandemics, requiring planning ahead for measures such as social distancing, i.e. large-scale isolation of people in order to prevent the disease from spreading. They are also in part geographical. Thus, he writes, a disaster in his terminology is 'a large-scale disruptor that creates a burden of patient need that exceeds the *region's* clinical carrying capacity (Kipnis 2013, 299, emphasis added), and '"catastrophe" refers narrowly to the collapse of a previously functional healthcare institution' (Kipnis 2013, 301).

In these discussions, two issues stand out: First, does consideration of ethics 'scale up' to politics? Second, are the considerations from one type of mass casualty situation generalizable to other situations?

The problem of generalizability applies to natural disasters versus conflict situations, i.e. war. Let us begin with the latter question, which is a central one and which involves a dividing line between philosophers who conceive of disasters as like war, in relevant aspects, and those who do not.

Examples of arguments by philosophers in the first category are ones related to disease control: Can self-defence justify compulsory disease-control measures that restrict individuals' liberty? So has sometimes been thought. Wilkinson (2007) discusses such arguments. (Protective but liberty-infringing disease control measures might be quarantine, isolation, screening of airline passengers for fever, travel restrictions, compulsory prophylaxis, and various social distancing measures.) Wilkinson argues for the justifiability of such public health compulsion in cases when it involves the state acting as a third-party defender of individuals' rights. He also recognizes limits to the justificatory force. There are plenty of historical examples of draconian measures in times of contagious disease. Ngalamulume (2004) writes about forced removals and enforcement of sanitation rules by means of draconian punishment in late nineteenth and early twentieth century colonial Senegal. Kallioinen (2006) discusses measures to combat plagues in medieval and early modern Finland (then part of the Swedish realm). Kallioinen points out how disease prevention and enforcement of preventative measures also serve to strengthen and legitimize government authority:

> The actions of the authorities had, besides the prevention of plague, another dimension, too. Although the purpose of the public actions was to stop outbreaks, behind them there was a more or less unconscious aim to make the subjects more disciplined to the authorities' power. (Kallioinen 2006, 45)

Interestingly, General Ehrensvärd who was in charge of ordering the harsh disease control measures during the 1770 plague gave an explicitly utilitarian justification of those measures: 'in similar situations this takes place everywhere in the world, because there is no other solution, and a single life cannot be compared with the lives of thousands' (cited in Kallioinen 2006, 44).

In this sense, disasters and similar events do the political-philosophical work of providing justification for government authority in general or for extraordinary measures.[1] This is of course the thrust of Hobbes' arguments, and we might refer to this approach as the *Hobbesian tradition*.

A recent discussion in the *Journal of Medical Ethics* illustrates how some applied ethics issues of disasters might have implications for normative ethics. In the feature article of the discussion, Kodama (2015) argues for *tsunami-tendenko*—a rule taught to school children, that when a tsunami hits, everyone should run for safety without wasting time on attempting to help others.[2] (Kodama's offered justification for *tsunami-tendenko* is straightforwardly rule-consequentialist.) Here, the basic insight is that everyday morality might not work in extreme situations. 'Ordinary moral rules and virtues can be found seriously inadequate in circumstances where natural catastrophes afflict large numbers of people,' writes Justin Oakley (2015).

Also in more theoretical discussions, the idea that rule-consequentialism might have a place in disaster ethics is prominent. Rule-consequentialism basically amounts to the idea that an action is right if it is in accordance with a rule that would lead to the best outcome if the rule were accepted by everyone. However, some actions or omissions might lead to disastrous outcomes. Discussing rule-consequentialism, Leonard Kahn (2013) argues that every ethical theory needs to contain some sort of 'disaster clause'. It is interesting that Kahn shuns real disasters, instead preferring a thought experiment involving a demon who will torture everyone in London unless a person tells a lie to another person (Kahn 2013, 222). His reason for doing so is that 'more realistic thought experiments of this sort are possible, but they require much more qualification and take up considerably more room as a result' (Kahn 2013, 222n).

An idea related to rule-consequentialism, and based on the same insights, is *threshold deontology*. Threshold deontologists maintain the view that 'when consequences become extremely grave, what would otherwise be categorically forbidden becomes morally possible' (Hurd 2002, 405). Heidi M. Hurd distinguishes between two versions of threshold deontology. The first is the gappy version. According to this version, once the threshold is crossed, morality ends. Beyond the threshold, anything goes, and someone's actions cannot be morally evaluated at all—this is the 'gap'. Hurd describes this position as saying "all is fair in love and war" (Hurd 2002, 406). A version of this view is to be found in the *realist* position on the ethics of war. Realists hold that it is not possible to judge warlike activities morally at all. The second version of threshold deontology is the non-gappy version. According to this view, when the threshold is crossed, deontology is simply replaced by consequentialism. In this vein, Kantians have also dwelt on the problem of how adherence

[1] We should of course be aware that plagues, or to use modern terms, outbreaks of infectious disease including pandemics, might be very different from disasters that are more localized in time and space (May et al. 2015).

[2] Comments are by Oakley (2015) and Asai (2015); see also response from Shortridge (2015).

to some moral absolute undermines the very institution of morality (Hill 1992; Korsgaard 1986). Notably, threshold deontologists have mostly been concerned with situations that involve antagonistic threats, such as acts of terrorism or war, even though some arguments might plausibly be transferred to non-antagonistic threats as well. In particular, disease control has been conceived of in terms of self-defence (Wilkinson 2007; cf. Sandin 2009a), and the potential for threshold deontology to contribute to disaster policy is occasionally recognized (Hosein 2016). Threshold deontology also immediately moves to the field of political philosophy rather than (individual) ethics.

In his recent book-length treatment of emergency, Tom Sorell (2013) approaches the topic from an explicitly Hobbesian perspective. He accepts the distinction between 'natural disasters and emergencies arising from political disorder' (Sorell 2013, 23).[3] Sorell is aware that this distinction might overlook important aspects and that many emergency-relevant questions cut across the distinction (Sorell 2013, 23, footnote) and that other distinctions might be more important. He mentions mild versus severe emergencies, and emergencies facing weak states versus those facing strong ones. Sorell notes that Hobbes does not use the word emergency. Hobbes' starting point is war (Sorell 2013, 29). This is significant for a lot of political philosophy dealing with exceptional situations. (For one example involving an earthquake, see La Torre 2012.)

2.3.2 *Real and Imagined Disasters*

Even though philosophers have not engaged that much with *real* disasters, there is no shortage of *imaginary* ones. Those disasters figure in thought experiments, usually in ethics (Dancy 1985). One example is the 'Last Man' arguments employed by Richard Routley (Sylvan) and others (Routley 2009; Peterson and Sandin 2013). Routley asks us to imagine that,

> [t]he last man (or person) surviving the collapse of the world system lays about him, eliminating, as far as he can, every living thing, animal or plant (but painlessly if you like, as at the best abattoirs). (Routley 2009, 487)

His purpose is to elicit intuitions about anthropocentrism. The disaster scenario does the work of isolating certain factors that he is interested in. Sometimes these disaster scenarios are described very generally (as in Routley). Other authors are more detailed. Mary Ann Warren (1983), for instance, varies Routley's example with a virus "developed by some unwise researcher" that has escaped from a laboratory and is about to extinguish animal, or perhaps sentient, life.

However, while common, it is well known that hypothetical, fictional examples might lead to conclusions that are misleading or have unwanted consequences in the

---

[3] This nuances an argument made by Sorell in earlier work (Sorell 2003; see also comments by Sandin and Wester 2009).

real world (Walsh 2011; Davis 2012; cf. Sandin and Wester 2009). For a potentially disaster-relevant example, Bob Brecher's (2007) critical discussion of how torture supposedly can be justified by reference to 'ticking bombs' is illuminating. The argument Brecher takes on is roughly as follows, and is likely to be familiar to most readers: Suppose that an extraordinarily capable terrorist has hidden a nuclear bomb in some metropolis. The terrorist is in custody, but of course refuses to disclose the location of the bomb, which is about to detonate shortly, killing millions. In such situations, would it not be justifiable to torture the terrorist into confessing where the bomb is hidden, assuming that we have reason to believe that the torture is effective? This is a 'lesser evil' argument. One of Brecher's points is that the scenario is based on unrealistic assumptions, and thus does not do the normative work it is supposed to be doing. 'The more closely the real case approximates to the ticking bomb scenario, the closer it is to being too late to prevent the impending catastrophe' (Brecher 2007, 38).

2.4 Conclusion and Looking Forward

In summary, philosophers—at least analytic ones—who have given thought to disasters have typically been either political philosophers dealing with the Hobbesian tradition's problems of state authority and exceptions, or ethicists. Some of those ethicists have been applied ethicists who have pondered the actions, duties and responsibilities of individuals in emergencies, of which disasters constitute a subset, along with wars and other situations. Many of them have been working in medical ethics and discussed issues pertaining to actions of medical professionals such as nurses and physicians in disasters and disaster-like situations. Others have been normative ethicists, who have reasoned around the implications of disasters for a certain normative position. Sometimes the relationship between normative theory and applied disaster ethics is unclear (Mallia 2015). If one wants to ponder what philosophers have contributed to the discussion of disasters, the term 'disaster' itself might not be the most important focal point. Other, related terms may be as relevant: for instance, 'crisis', calamity', and 'catastrophe'. Terminology might be confusing. For instance, writing about global catastrophic risks, including what they call 'existential' risks, Bostrom and Ćircović (2008) do not appear to distinguish between catastrophes and disasters. Perhaps most importantly, the discussions involving 'emergency' may be potentially relevant for disaster philosophizing (Sorell 2013; Walzer 2000, 2004).

So, what is there to do for philosophers? What, if anything, may they contribute to disaster conceptualization, and what are the likely areas where this might happen?

First, in recent years several philosophers have been probing the philosophy of risk (Hansson 2012). One observation in that field is that ethical theory has been focused on situations with outcomes that are certain, while referring situations with non-certain outcomes to decision theory (Hansson 2012, 43, 2013). Disasters, however, include situations where uncertainty prevails. Compare discussions of the closely related term 'crisis'—according to one standard view, crises are characterized by threats to basic values, urgency—and uncertainty (Stern 2003). Some of the concepts developed in this field might also be applicable to disasters, in particular since disasters often result in crises of various kinds.

Second, we can probably expect philosophers to devote increased attention to empirical work, in particular such work as regards human behavior, for instance psychology and social psychology (cf. Sandin and Wester 2009). This is in line with a general trend in contemporary philosophy: Analytic philosophers, now to a greater extent than before, are paying attention to behavioral sciences and their implications for philosophy and ethics, and this might lead to changes in disaster preparation and response.

Third, the discussion about 'natural' disasters and 'man-made' or 'anthropogenic' ones is likely to continue (Shaluf 2007, 705; Coeckelbergh 2016). In philosophy, the idea of the natural is as ancient as it is controversial (Soper 1995).

Fourth, and finally, in recent years, the idea of an 'environmental apocalypse' (due to population growth or chemical pollution) that was prominent in the 1970s but then lay dormant for decades, has resurfaced in the wake of predicted anthropogenic climate change (Skrimshire 2010). Randers and Gilding (2010) call for a 'one degree war plan', the first phase of which involves 'a world war level of mobilisation to achieve a global reduction of 50 per cent in climate gas emissions within five years' (Randers and Gilding 2010, p. 175). In the 1970s, this idea prompted a number of authors to argue that extreme emergency measures were morally justified given the perceived extremity of the situation, e.g. the 'lifeboat ethics' of Garrett Hardin (2015, originally published 1974). As can be seen, this is an argument closely resembling the threshold deontology discussed above. We are likely to have to relate to a number of extreme climate-related and environmental disasters in the coming decades. Thus, there is potential in the intersection between disaster philosophizing and environmental ethics—a hitherto relatively little explored area.

There are notable policy implications here. The distinction between 'natural' and 'man-made' might affect to what part of government the task of preventing, or preparing for, some disaster is given. The arguments of 'apocalytic' situations might lead to calls for suspending democratic processes, and indeed have done so. When interviewed recently, Jorgen Randers, member of the Rome Club and a proponent of the 'climate war plan' cited above, proposes an elite rule in the interest of the common good, since democracy is too short-sighted, and mentions China as a model (Stiernstedt 2017). In times where authoritarian positions seem to be gaining ground, these types of arguments should be cause for concerns among decision makers in democratic societies.

References

Asai, Atsushi. 2015. Tsunami-tendenko and morality in disasters. *Journal of Medical Ethics* 41: 365–366.

Baker, Robert, and Martin Strosberg. 1992. Triage and equality: An historical reassessment of utilitarian analyses of triage. *Kennedy Institute of Ethics Journal* 2: 103–123.

Bostrom, Nick, and Milan M. Ćircović. 2008. Introduction. In *Global catastrophic risks*, ed. Nick Bostrom and Milan M. Ćircović, 1–29. Oxford: Oxford University Press.

Brecher, Bob. 2007. *Torture and the ticking bomb*. Oxford: Blackwell.

Carnap, Rudolf. 1950. *Logical foundations of probability*. London: Routledge and Kegan Paul.

Cassidy, Eoin G. 2005. The problem of evil: The dialogue between Voltaire and Rousseau revisited. *Yearbook of the Irish Philosophical Society* 2005: 1–18.

Chester, David K. 2005. Theology and disaster studies: The need for dialogue. *Journal of Volcanology and Geothermal Research* 146: 319–328.

Childress, James F. 2003. Triage in response to a bioterrorist attack. In *In the wake of terror: Medicine and morality in a time of crisis*, ed. Jonathan D. Moreno, 78–93. Cambridge, MA/ London: MIT Press.

Coeckelbergh, Mark. 2016. Vulnerability to natural hazards: Philosophical reflections on the social and cultural dimensions of natural disaster risk. In *Risk analysis of natural hazards: Interdisciplinary challenges and integrated solutions*, ed. Paolo Gardoni, Colleen Murphy, and Arden Rowell, 27–41. Cham: Springer.

Dancy, Jonathan. 1985. The role of imaginary cases in ethics. *Pacific Philosophical Quarterly* 66: 141–153.

Davis, Michael. 2012. Imaginary cases in ethics: A critique. *International Journal of Applied Philosophy* 26: 1–17.

Dombrowsky, Wolf R. 1998. Again and again: Is a disaster what we call a "disaster"? In *What is a disaster? Perspectives on the question*, ed. E.L. Quarantelli, 19–30. London/New York: Routledge.

Dynes, Russel R. 2000. The dialogue between Rousseau and Voltaire on the Lisbon earthquake: The emergence of a social science view. *International Journal of Mass Emergencies and Disasters* 18: 97–115.

Hansson, Sven Ove. 2012. A panorama of the philosophy of risk. In *Springer handbook of risk theory: Epistemology, decision theory, ethics, and social implications of risk*, ed. Sabine Roeser, Rafaela Hillerbrand, Per Sandin, and Martin Peterson, vol. 1, 27–54. Dordrecht: Springer.

———. 2013. *The ethics of risk: Ethical analysis in an uncertain world*. Houndsmills: Palgrave–Macmillan.

Hardin, Garrett. 2015 [1974]. *Lifeboat ethics: the case against helping the poor*. http://www.garretthardinsociety.org/articles/art_lifeboat_ethics_case_against_helping_poor.html. Accessed 16 Jan 2018.

Hill, Thomas E., Jr. 1992. *Dignity and practical reason in Kant's moral theory*. Ithaca/London: Cornell University Press.

Hosein, Adam. 2016. Deontology and natural hazards. In *Risk analysis of natural hazards: Interdisciplinary challenges and integrated solutions*, ed. Paolo Gardoni, Colleen Murphy, and Arden Rowell, 137–153. Cham: Springer.

Hurd, Heidi M. 2002. Liberty in law. *Law and Philosophy* 21: 385–465.

Kahn, Leonard. 2013. Rule consequentialism and disasters. *Philosophical Studies* 162: 219–236.

Kallioinen, Mika. 2006. Plagues and governments: The prevention of plague epidemics in early modern Finland. *Scandinavian Journal of History* 31: 35–51.

Kipnis, Kenneth. 2013. Disasters, catastrophes, and worse: A scalar taxonomy. *Cambridge Quarterly of Healthcare Ethics* 22: 297–307.

Kodama, Satoshi. 2015. Tsunami-tendenko and morality in disasters. *Journal of Medical Ethics* 41: 361–363.

Korsgaard, Christine M. 1986. The right to lie: Kant on dealing with evil. *Philosophy and Public Affairs* 15: 325–349.

La Torre, Massimo. 2012. The collapse of the rule of law: The Messina earthquake and the state of exception. *Netherlands Journal of Legal Philosophy* 41: 159–176.

Mallia, Pierre. 2015. Towards an ethical theory in disaster situations. *Medicine, Health Care and Philosophy* 18: 3–11.

May, Thomas, Michael P. McCauley, Jessica Jeruzal, and Kimberly A. Strong. 2015. Catastrophic events versus infectious disease outbreaks: Distinct challenges for emergency planning. *Reason Papers* 37: 54–64.

Ngalamulume, Kalala. 2004. Keeping the city totally clean: Yellow fever and the politics of prevention in colonial Saint-Louis-du-Sènègal, 1850–1914. *Journal of African History* 45: 183–202.

Oakley, Justin. 2015. Can self-preservation be virtuous in disaster situations? *Journal of Medical Ethics* 41: 364–365.

Oliver-Smith, Anthony. 1998. Global change and the definition of disaster. In *What is a disaster? Perspectives on the question*, ed. E.L. Quarantelli, 177–194. London/New York: Routledge.

Peterson, Martin, and Per Sandin. 2013. The last man argument revisited. *Journal of Value Inquiry* 47: 121–133.

Plato. 1925. *Timaeus*. Trans. W.R.M. Lamb. Perseus Digital Library. http://www.perseus.tufts.edu/. Accessed 4 Jan 2018.

Quarantelli, E.L. 1998. Introduction: The basic question. In *What is a disaster? Perspectives on the question*, ed. E.L. Quarantelli, 1–7. London/New York: Routledge.

Randers, Jorgen, and Paul Gilding. 2010. The one degree war plan. *Journal of Global Responsibility* 1: 170–188.

Routley, Richard. 2009. Is there a need for a new, an environmental, ethic? In *Encyclopedia of environmental ethics and philosophy*, ed. J. Baird Callicott and Robert Frodeman, vol. 2, 484–489. Farmington Hills: Macmillan Reference USA.

Sandin, Per. 2009a. Supreme emergencies without the bad guys. *Philosophia* 37: 153–167.

———. 2009b. Firefighting ethics: Principlism for burning issues. *Ethical Perspectives* 16: 225–251.

Sandin, Per, and Misse Wester. 2009. The moral black hole. *Ethical Theory and Moral Practice* 12: 291–301.

Shaluf, Ibrahim Mohamed. 2007. Disaster types. *Disaster Prevention and Management: An International Journal* 16: 704–717.

Shortridge, Andrew. 2015. Moral reasoning in disaster scenarios. *Journal of Medical Ethics* 41: 780–781.

Skrimshire, Stefan, ed. 2010. *Future ethics: Climate change and apocalyptic imagination*. London/New York: Continuum.

Soper, Kate. 1995. *What is nature?* Oxford: Blackwell.

Sorell, Tom. 2003. Morality and emergency. *Proceedings of the Aristotelian Society* 103: 21–37.

———. 2013. *Emergencies and politics: A sober hobbesian approach*. Cambridge: Cambridge University Press.

Stern, Eric K. 2003. Crisis studies and foreign policy analysis: Insights, synergies, and challenges. *International Studies Review* 5: 183–202.

Stiernstedt, Jenny. 2017. Demokratin måste pausas för att lösa klimatkrisen. *Svenska Dagbladet*, November 4.

Voice, Paul. 2016. What do liberal democratic states owe the victim of disasters? A Rawlsian account. *Journal of Applied Philosophy* 33: 396–410.

Walsh, Adrian. 2011. A moderate defence of the use of thought experiments in applied ethics. *Ethical Theory and Moral Practice* 14: 467–481.

Walzer, Michael. 2000. *Just and unjust wars: A moral argument with historical illustrations*. 3rd ed. New York: Basic Books.

———. 2004. *Arguing about war*. New Haven: Yale University Press.

Warren, Mary Ann. 1983. The rights of the nonhuman world. In *Environmental philosophy: A collection of readings*, ed. Robert Elliot and Arran Gare, 109–134. Milton Keynes: Open University Press.
Wilkinson, T.M. 2007. Contagious disease and self-defence. *Res Publica* 13: 339–359.
Winslow, Gerald R. 1982. *Triage and justice*. Berkeley: University of California Press.
Zack, Naomi. 2009. *Ethics for disaster*. Lanham: Rowman & Littlefield.

Chapter 3
Christian Theology and Disasters: Where is God in All This?

Dónal P. O'Mathúna

Abstract This chapter examines ways that disasters have led to reflection within Christian theology. Mention will be made of other religious traditions, but because of the volume of material available, the focus will be on biblical accounts of disasters, God's role in them, and discussions about how believers can and should respond to them. First, the chapter will examine accounts where God is stated to have sent disasters as a judgement for human sin. This will require a broad overview of some central theological positions. Then, the chapter will examine historical and contemporary claims that disasters can be blamed on human sin. This will lead to a review of theodicy, theological arguments developed to justify why God could allow evil and suffering, which could include disasters. Then some popular reactions to disasters that blame particular sins will be critiqued. In contrast, the Bible calls for responses that include practical help for those impacted by disasters. A full response must go further, including empathy for those hurt and working to overcome injustice when that has been a contributing factor. The final theological perspective is the belief that God works with believers to bring good out of bad situations, in spite of how bad the disaster can be. The chapter concludes with a discussion of how theological reflection can bring hope in the midst of disasters.

Keywords Bible · Image of God · Injustice · Judgement · Love · Theodicy · Theology

---

D. P. O'Mathúna (✉)
School of Nursing and Human Sciences, Dublin City University, Dublin, Ireland

College of Nursing, The Ohio State University, Columbus, Ohio, USA
e-mail: donal.omathuna@dcu.ie

D. P. O'Mathúna et al. (eds.), *Disasters: Core Concepts and Ethical Theories*, Advancing Global Bioethics 11, https://doi.org/10.1007/978-3-319-92722-0_3

3.1 Religion and Disasters

Theological ideas about disasters are common in English metaphors. We talk about a flood as being of biblical proportions (in reference to Noah's Flood in Genesis), about worldwide disasters being apocalyptic (in reference to the biblical Apocalypse and the Day of Judgment), and insurance companies talk of "acts of God," by which they mean natural disasters[1] that humans did not cause or could not reasonably have prevented (CBS 2015). For insurance purposes, an act of God could be a lightning strike that burns a home to the ground, or a tsunami swamping a city where one had never previously hit. The implicit presumption is that no one is to blame (and can't be sued), other than God (and he's not easily sued), so the insurance company will likely have to pay out (unless acts of God are not covered in the specific policy).

This insurance language links to probably the most common way in which theology is invoked in relation to disasters. Many ancient religions, from Greek and Roman mythology to various tribal religions, are thought to have arisen in response to various natural phenomena, including disasters. The view was that disasters occurred because the gods were angry and sent the disaster to punish guilty humans. Something was needed to appease the gods, and various rituals and sacrifices were developed, along with a priesthood to discern what is needed and carry out the appeasement activities. For example, according to Herodotus, often called "the Father of History," the earliest recorded tsunami, in 479 BC, was sent by the god of the sea, Poseidon, to punish the Persians for their siege of Potidaea. 'Such explanations were more nearly the norm for much of antiquity' (Molesky 2015, 150).

As scientific understandings of the world developed, so-called acts of God came to be viewed as natural phenomena. The world came to be seen as behaving in predictable ways, following natural laws that sometimes lead to destructive events like earthquakes, tsunamis, hurricanes, volcanic eruptions and other disasters. In theology and philosophy, they have been called natural evils, in contrast with moral evils, because natural evils did not involve human choices. Bad things sometimes happen to humans when by chance they are in the path of some colossally powerful forces of nature. Science has no place for angry gods sending disasters as punishments.

And yet, when a village full of humans is incinerated by lava, or a city collapses in an earthquake, or thousands are drowned by a wave, we cry foul. This should not be! What have they done to deserve this? The innocent should not suffer this way. Why do bad things happen to good people? This may be the most common way that theological perspectives arise around disasters. Such reactions may not be very reflective, they may not be informed by much theology, but they happen frequently and reflect recognition of the widespread belief that something is wrong with our world. After the 2004 Indian Ocean Tsunami and the 2010 earthquake in Haiti, different Christian, Jewish, Muslim and Buddhist adherents claimed that the disasters

[1] The term "natural disaster" is increasingly questioned because most disasters are influenced to some degree by human choices. I accept this view, and the issue is addressed here. The term "natural disaster" will be used occasionally in this chapter because the idea of a purely natural disaster arises in some relevant literature.

occurred because of various people's sins—usually those of adherents to other religions (Behreandt 2005; Lutzer 2011). This suggests that the view of disasters as divine punishment continues to be held. At the same time, some survivors give God the credit for saving them from disasters (Lutzer 2011; Molesky 2015).

Critics point out that even a quick examination of the devastation reveals that disasters do not carefully select between the guilty and the innocent. Babies and infants are often among the victims. If God was behind the destruction, could he not discern between the guilty and the innocent, or between adherents of one religion or another? This raises questions about God's role in disasters. 'Surely God can differentiate between those who try to live godly lives and those who spurn both God and man alike' (Behreandt 2005, 32). Or maybe, God judges indiscriminately, which raises more serious theological questions about his character.

3.2 Raising Theological Questions

Disaster responders and the field of disaster risk reduction focus on the many practical and scientific challenges with disasters. But other, deeper questions arise. 'Earthquakes, the New York towers, the barbarity in Afghanistan, the AIDS pandemic make us think and force us to wrestle with ourselves ... such thinking ... challenges us and raises questions that cannot be ignored' (Sobrino 2004, xxvii). Many of these questions are framed and answered in theological language. 'Disasters pull us up sharp and make us face head-on the hard questions of life and death. For atheists and agnostics they challenge humankind's hubris that we can control our environment—or that our cleverness can keep us from suffering. For Christians they raise the hard question of why an all-powerful, all-loving God allows such things to happen' (White 2014, 19).

Such questions are not new. One of the most devastating disasters in modern history hit Lisbon on 1 November 1755. The Great Lisbon Earthquake and its subsequent tsunami and fires killed tens of thousands of people and destroyed most of Lisbon (Molesky 2015). The impact was much deeper. 'Just as earthquakes create aftershocks, natural disasters create religious aftershocks. Believers wrestle with doubts; unbelievers use disasters as justification for their refusal to believe in a loving God' (Lutzer 2011, 5). The Great Lisbon Earthquake led to theological, philosophical and scientific reactions from such renowned thinkers as Voltaire, Jean-Jacques Rousseau, Immanuel Kant, Johann von Goethe, Adam Smith and John Wesley. 'In the 5 years following the disaster, hundreds of books, articles, letters, treatises, poems, reviews, sermons, and scientific tracts on the subject were published across the continent ... Was God solely to blame or had nature or a combination of natural forces played the leading role? And perhaps more importantly: how could a just and all-powerful God have sanctioned the deaths of so many innocent people? The ensuing debate was arguably the most significant of the European Enlightenment' (Molesky 2015, 322). The debate was not restricted to philosophers and theologians, but was a widespread public event. Historian Molesky concludes that, 'It was the Lisbon Earthquake's impact on human history, however, that distinguishes it from all other natural catastrophes, before or since … Once again in its history, the West found its conceptions of God, Nature, and Providence under a barrage of scrutiny' (2015, 19).

3.3 The General Approach

The theological responses elicited by disasters vary widely. This chapter could not possibly address how every religion examines these issues, so it will focus on Christianity. Even developing a Christian perspective on disasters is not straightforward. Differences exist on many theological issues between Roman Catholic, Orthodox, Protestant, and other branches and denominations of Christianity. Just as debates occur over what the founder of every philosophy meant, and different branches develop over time, Christianity is no different. The approach here will be to examine what can be learned from the main theological resource that all branches of Christianity take as authoritative in one way or another: the Bible. What has the Bible to say about disasters, God's role in them, and how humans should respond to them? No doubt my understanding of these issues will be debated, but that may help further these discussions.

3.4 Disasters as God's Judgment

The Bible records many disasters. Some are household names in many parts of the world (Noah's Flood, Sodom and Gomorrah, the Plagues visited on Egypt in Moses' time). God is declared to have sent these events as judgments on human sin (understood as human moral failure, where people fail to live and act according to the ways that God has declared to be best). The explicit nature of such declarations makes it necessary to address how and why the Judeo-Christian God could be justified in using such means to judge human sin.

It should be noted that the Bible mentions many disasters without linking them to judgment. For examine, famines are noted in the stories of Abraham, Joseph, Naomi, David, Elijah and the early Christian church (White 2014 has an extensive table of biblical famines). These events are mentioned in various accounts, some leading to significant people movements and others having little obvious significance. God is not said to have had any role in these and other disasters. The implicit message is that disasters happen, and people respond in practical ways—much like today. The Bible does not claim that God's hand of judgment can be seen in every disaster.

At the same time, holding the Bible to be theologically authoritative in any way requires an examination of the disasters declared to be God's judgment. To do so, raises some central theological doctrines in Christianity. The Bible states that God created the world and it was "very good" (Genesis 1). We need not concern ourselves here with debates over whether the world was created perfect or with events like meteor strikes and earthquakes before humans appeared (addressed by Fretheim 2010). Astronomical and geological events that do not impact humans are usually not categorised as disasters since definitions focus on human impact. Our reflections begin with the introduction of humans, which in the Bible starts with Adam and Eve. God gives them a few simple commands, but they quickly make a mess of things. They give in to the temptation to do things their own way. They sin and are judged by being driven from the Garden of Eden. No longer will they live in harmony with the world: childbearing will be painful, work will be toil, and instead of social harmony, conflict and violence will erupt. The claim is that sin led to death and destruction, and that even nature changed. The whole world has been groaning ever since, and bound to a path of decay (Romans 8:19–22). In this very general sense, disasters are part of God's judgment on human sin.

In the biblical account, moral evil spread quickly, and people inflicted more and more pain on one another. God saw that human wickedness became so extensive that judgment was required, resulting in Noah's Flood (Genesis 6–8). The biblical claim is that as Creator of the Universe, God is justified in upholding moral standards and punishing evil. Sometimes he does this using disasters, as declared by many Old Testament prophets. Just as human authorities are entrusted with enforcing their jurisdiction's laws, God has authority over humanity. Accepting this or not underlies the debate over God's existence and his nature, which is too extensive to review here. Human sin fractured the harmonious relationships between God and humans, among humans, and between humans and the environment. This requires a response. Ignoring sin is not compatible with God's justice. We would not tolerate a justice system that lets law-breakers go free without judgment.

However, God's justice must coexist with his love, which the Bible reveals through his extension of forgiveness. His plans culminate in Jesus's death and resurrection, and his offer of forgiveness as a free gift to all who will accept it (Ephesians 2:8–9). With this comes restoration of someone's relationship with God and spiritual healing. But people continue to live in the world as it now exists. The human body and the natural world continue according to the laws of nature, with sickness, death and disasters now part of our world. The Bible records some miracles, where God intervenes to restore physical health or counteract a law of nature. And sometimes he intervenes with a disaster to judge human sin. But for the most part, illness, death and disasters continue according to the laws of nature and the outcomes of human choices. The Bible claims that a time will come when the world will be restored after the Day of Judgment. After that, humans will live in a situation where pain and suffering will no longer exist and creation will be rid of disasters (Revelation 22). The hope of that future time is something believers can cling to as they face disasters and other forms of suffering.

3.5 Theodicy

Given the biblical claim that God has sent some disasters as judgment, many wonder if a particular disaster is a judgment from God. Even if not God's punishment, they wonder why he would not protect people from harm. The God of Christianity is said to be a loving God who cares for people, and also a powerful God who has authority over nature. Why then does he allow disasters?

Such questions have been asked throughout the Christian era and various theological responses developed. Each is called a theodicy, a term coined by Gottfried Leibniz. He published *Théodicée* in 1710 in which he argued that God had created 'the best of all possible worlds' (Leibniz, cited in Molesky 2015, 327). This belief fit well with the optimism and progress of that time, as even the climate seemed to be steadily improving (Molesky 2015). After the Great Lisbon Earthquake, Leibniz's theodicy came under considerable attack, particularly by Voltaire who argued that the disaster was incompatible with this being the best possible world. Voltaire also rejected claims that Lisbon was destroyed as part of God's judgment, sarcastically wondering if Lisbon was more evil than London or Paris. Yet, 'Lisbon is shattered, and Paris dances' (Voltaire, cited in Molesky 2015, 328).

The problem of theodicy is particularly relevant for Christianity because the Bible claims that God is all-loving and all-powerful. Not all religions hold to this view of a personal God. Reality shows that evil and suffering happen. Surely an all-powerful God would prevent bad things from happening to the people he loves. Therefore, either God is not all-loving, or he's not all-powerful, or he does not exist. The latter conclusion leads to debates between atheism and theism, while the first two conclusions raise perplexing difficulties for believers. How could the God whom Christians worship allow things like disasters?

Within such arguments lies a hidden premise. The assumption is that a loving God prevents bad things from happening to those he loves. Yet in the real world, we do not live that way. Loving parents allow their children to make age-appropriate choices, some of which have risks and sometimes negative consequences. A parent who refuses to do so, we call over-protective. Loving couples who do not allow their partners to socialise with others, we call domineering, or controlling. Within a loving relationship, people do not exercise all the power available to them to ensure everyone does the "right thing." The result is that children fall and hurt themselves, they sometimes get into trouble, and people hurt one another in their relationships. The question is whether giving people such freedom is justified. In human relationships, we believe it is.

The Free Will Defence is one theodicy that argues that God was justified in creating a world in which humans have real moral freedom. A key theological premise in Christianity (and the other Abrahamic religions, but not Eastern religions) is that God is personal and seeks loving relationships with humans. For relationships to exhibit attributes like trust, love, faith, etc., they must be entered into without compulsion (O'Mathúna 1999). Only if God was more concerned about good behaviour than personal relationships would he compel people to believe in him. Love requires freedom. A robot can be programmed to always obey its owner, but then the relationship between the two would not be personal. Freedom risks pain, and hence a child can reject his parents, a spouse can be unfaithful, or a parent can be abusive. These risks are necessary in a world where freedom, love and personal relationships exist.

If God intervened every time we could be hurt, much pain and suffering could be avoided, but our free will would be an illusion. The world as we know it would not exist. Every time someone went to punch another person, his arm would fail to work. Every time someone went to pour pollutants into the environment, the container would not open. So many "miracles" would have to happen that people 'could not entertain rational expectations, make predictions, estimate probabilities, or calculate prudence' (Reichenbach 1982, 103). A world without predictable consequences would make morality and moral responsibility impossible, or at least extremely different to what we understand by morality. Science as we know it would be impossible because God would be interfering constantly with nature and people to prevent human suffering. The result would be a world 'in which wrong actions were impossible, and in which, therefore, freedom of the will would be void; … evil thoughts would be impossible, for the cerebral matter which we use in thinking would refuse its task when we attempted to frame them' (Lewis 1940, 21). Such is clearly not the world we inhabit. Thus, our world corresponds well with the existence of an all-loving, all-powerful God who so values loving relationships that he allows free will to exist even though this risks allowing humans to experience pain and suffering.

Theodicies have tended to focus on either moral evil (suffering caused by humans) or natural evil (suffering caused by nature, such as natural disasters or genetic defects). The free will defence may seem irrelevant for natural disasters. It clearly applies to such things as sabotage leading to industrial disasters; greed that leads people to cut corners when constructing buildings so that they collapse more easily during earthquakes; hatred that leads to violence and conflict; or war that results in famine or refugee crises.

Increasingly, however, the distinction between natural disasters and manmade (or technological) disasters is becoming less tenable to hold (ten Have 2014), making the free will theodicy more relevant to disasters in general. The eighteenth century philosopher Jean-Jacques Rousseau reacted to the debate over God's role in the Great Lisbon Earthquake claiming that human decisions were more to blame for the disaster's consequences than nature or God. Responding to Voltaire, he stated 'but it was hardly Nature that had assembled there twenty thousand houses of six or seven stories. If the residents of this large city had been more evenly dispersed and less densely housed, the losses would have been fewer or perhaps none at all' (Rousseau, cited in Molesky 2015, 331).

Robert White notes that 'the deaths caused by "natural" disasters can often be attributed almost in their entirety to actions taken by people, which turned a natural process into a disaster. In that respect there is nothing "natural" about them' (2014, 19–20). As examples, he notes that many who died in the 2004 Indian Ocean Tsunami were living in areas zoned as unsuitable for houses, but they had nowhere else to live; and in the 2011 Fukushima earthquake in Japan, most fatalities were among those who ignored warnings to flee the tsunami because they assumed the sea walls would protect them. A report prepared for the Louisiana Department of Transportation and Development concluded that the deaths in New Orleans should not be blamed on Hurricane Katrina. 'This catastrophe did not result from an act of "God". It resulted from acts of "People" … because of a large number of flaws and defects that had been embedded in the system' (Team Louisiana 2006, Appendix 6).

The free will defence is applicable to such human decisions, but critics still question why an all-powerful God would not eliminate large-scale disasters that bring massive destruction and many casualties. The Natural Law Theodicy was hinted at above, which raises the necessity of an orderly universe governed by natural law. In a world where choices are to be judged as good or bad, a significant amount of predictability is required. Having a good degree of confidence in the consequences of choices is necessary to hold people accountable ethically. 'If man is to have a free and responsible choice of destiny, he needs to have a range of actions open to him, whose consequences, good and evil, he understands, and he can only have that understanding in a world which already has built into it many natural processes productive of both good and evil' (Swinburne 1987, 165).

When a boulder moves on a mountain-side, we know it will roll downhill—not uphill. When we see a natural rock-fall, we know that rolling rocks wreak havoc. We learn from nature that boulders rolling onto roads and hitting cars will probably injure or kill passengers, cause grief to their relatives and friends, and fear in other motorists. If the boulder was to stop rolling because its path could result in suffering, or if trees could be smashed but not cars because their occupants would be hurt, we would lose much of our ability to predict outcomes and this would eliminate accountability and true moral choice. Therefore, God is justified in allowing a world with potentially catastrophic events even if this can result in pain and suffering for humans.

Critics of natural law theodicy argue that God could have made a world where physical pain and suffering did not occur (e.g. a heavenly world). This raises questions about why the physical world exists, which go beyond the focus of this chapter. Given that the physical world does exist, and that we are born into it, another criticism is that the world could have different natural laws which lead to much less human suffering. However, natural laws are not abstract mathematical equations, but descriptions of how natural objects act and react under certain conditions (O'Mathúna 1999). To change these laws would require changing the very nature of those objects. For example, water would have to become something in which people could not drown. This would change many related properties that make water the material we recognise and which supports life. We have no way of predicting what "non-drowning water" would be like, and certainly no way of knowing if it would lead to a world with less suffering. In this case, the burden of proof is on the critic to provide a model of a universe with alternative natural laws. It remains reasonable to believe that God was justified in choosing the natural laws we have, even though they lead to geological events like volcanos, earthquakes, hurricanes and tornados.

The destructiveness of such events is clear and tragic, but their elimination would not be so straight-forwardly beneficial. 'But paradoxically, many of the processes that make it possible for humans to live on earth are the same as those that give rise to disasters' (White 2014, 27). Floods negatively affect more people than all other disasters combined, yet they are essential for soil fertility. For millennia, the flooding of the River Nile enabled the agricultural prosperity that allowed Egypt to flourish. In 1783, the largest volcanic eruptions in Iceland for 1000 years led to reduced rainfall in Africa (Oman et al. 2006). The following year, the Nile did not flood, and then the crops failed leading to a famine where one sixth of Egypt's population either died or left the country. In similarly paradoxical ways, earthquakes are both destructive and allow minerals and nutrients to emerge from within the Earth and allow life to thrive. We have no idea whether life on Earth would be possible without the events we call disasters (White 2014).

What can be concluded from such theological reflections is that rational justifications can be provided to address why the God of the Bible could allow disasters to occur. Whether these are found to be convincing or not is another matter. This often depends on whether someone is willing to believe that the Bible's God is trustworthy and loving, in spite of the existence of disasters and the suffering they bring. This gets at the core of what faith involves: a willingness to act on the basis of trust, in spite of the lack of certainty. As with most areas of life, evidence takes us only so far; at some point, a faith decision must be made based on trust, not certainty.

3.6 Is Someone to Blame?

Even with theodicies, people grapple with the personal dimension of suffering. Many will be more concerned about why a disaster stuck here and now, not whether God was justified. People ask, "Why didn't God protect us?" or "What have we done to deserve this?" Different religious voices add substance to these questions. The US televangelist, Pat Robertson, claimed that the 2010 earthquake in Haiti could be linked to an eighteenth century pact the Haitians made with the devil to rid themselves of their French colonisers (James 2010). Hurricane Katrina was claimed by some Christians to have been God's punishment for abortion or homosexuality (Cooperman 2005), by a Muslim official as Allah's punishment for the US's involvement in Afghanistan and Iraq (Lopez 2005), and by a former Israeli chief rabbi as punishment for President George W. Bush's support for the dismantlement of Israeli settlements in Gaza (Alush 2005). The Mayor of New Orleans during Hurricane Katrina, C. Ray Nagin, claimed, 'God is mad at America. He sent us hurricane after hurricane after hurricane' (Martel 2006). An African American, he elaborated that God 'is upset at black America also. We're not taking care of ourselves.'

Such claims can add to the pain of those already devastated by the disaster, and have been strongly criticised as theologically misguided. Each claim loses credibility when the diversity of those blamed is examined. Yet such blaming persists. After the Great Lisbon Earthquake, Roman Catholic preachers said God was judging the sins of Lisbon, Protestants said he was judging the Catholic Inquisition, and supporters of the Inquisition said God was angry because the Inquisition had not gone far enough (Lutzer 2011). Rather than explaining why any particular disaster has occurred, these attempts confirm how little people know about the divine origins of disasters, and say more about human psychology. 'Whenever tragedy strikes, we each have a tendency to interpret it in light of what we believe God is trying to say (or what we want Him to say) … We see in natural disasters exactly what we want to see' (Lutzer 2011, 9).

The Bible provides additional reasons for rejecting such speculations. Jesus was asked whether a group of Galileans killed by Pilate, and whether eighteen people killed when a tower fell on them, were worse sinners than others living in Jerusalem (Luke 13:1–5). He replied with an emphatic, No! Instead, Jesus called on his listeners to consider their own standing before God. Jesus implies that people are injured and killed in disasters because they happen to be in the wrong place at the wrong time. Another time, Jesus was asked if a man was born blind because of his own sin or that of his parents (John 9:1–3). Again, he categorically denied that the blindness was due to anyone's sin. Instead, he said that God would be revealed in this man's life. Sickness, injury or death, in a disaster or any other situation, cannot be assumed to be God's judgment on a specific sin.

Such accounts are in keeping with possibly the most extensive discussion of suffering in the Bible. The Book of Job is about a good, religious man, better than anyone else on Earth (Job 1:8). Yet God allows one disaster after another to enter his life resulting in the loss of all his livestock, wealth and even his ten children. Then he gets painful sores all over his body. Job's wife questions his integrity, and urges him to curse God and die. As he sits in grief and agony, three friends come to "comfort" him. Much like modern speculators of religious judgment, they claim Job's suffering must be due to some terrible sin, and urge him to repent. Job adamantly refuses to accept this perspective. In the end, he is vindicated by God. The disasters were not brought on by his sin. Job, like everyone, is not sinless, but God was not judging Job because of any particular sin. In an ending that many would find difficult to accept, Job was never given an explanation for why the bad things had happened in his life.

The Bible's consistent position is that in most cases, we don't know if a particular sickness, disease, or disaster has any divine involvement. We may never know why something happened. Disasters, diseases and devastation can have purely physical causes like geological upheavals, microbes, or genetic mutations, or can have a mixture of human and natural causes. Christians must also acknowledge that disasters *could* be divine judgments, since, as noted earlier, the Bible states that God has sent disasters as punishments for human sin. But these accounts note that they happened for specific actions and occurred after many warnings were ignored. Additionally, the Book of Jonah recounts the story of Nineveh, whose people listened to God's warnings, changed their behaviour, and the disaster was averted. These accounts are very different to those of today where people attempt to identify God's judging hand with retrospective speculation.

3.7 Bad Things Happen to Good People

Another related difficulty is how the Old Testament repeatedly states that God will reward those who obey his law, and punish those who do not (e.g. Deuteronomy 11:26–28). The theological context for such statements is important. These rewards and punishments were promised to ancient Israel as part of a Covenant entered willingly during a period when God's kingdom was geophysical as well as spiritual (Deuteronomy 5:27). Although God brought disaster on Israelites when they failed to live up to their side of the agreement, he repeatedly sent warnings to them through the prophets. These accounts should not be taken as the normative way God deals with all people at all times.

The Bible promises blessings for those who follow God, but also describes how followers get sick, suffer, and eventually die. The promised blessings are linked primarily to spiritual health and growth (3 John 2). Faithful followers of God are not immune from pain and suffering, nor the consequences of disasters. The psalmist observed that good things happen to bad people. 'I envied the arrogant when I saw the prosperity of the wicked. They have no struggles; their bodies are healthy and strong. They are free from the burdens common to man; they are not plagued by human ills … All day long I have been plagued; I have been punished every morning' (Psalm 73:3–5, 14). People wonder why bad things happen to good people. The Bible's response is that there has only ever been one good person, and he suffered supremely. Jesus, the son of God, was tortured to death in the most horrific way. We should not be surprised when bad things happen to us, no matter how good we believe we have been. Instead, 'there is no one who does good, not even one' (Romans 3:12). We are all on the same moral footing with God, which is why we have no basis for thinking one person is better than another or deserves to suffer more or less than another.

This returns us to the recognition that human choices are involved in many disasters. Instead of speculation about a disaster being God's judgment on someone or other, disasters should lead to reflection on the values underlying human decisions. We sense that responsibility lies somewhere, but where? Jon Sobrino is a theologian who has lived through devastating earthquakes and civil war in El Salvador. He draws a loose parallel between theodicy and anthropodicy. Sometimes God is blamed 'to excuse human beings from their responsibility for evil' (Sobrino 2004, 27). We should question God's apparent lack of involvement in disasters, but also reflect carefully about human roles. Believers can be reluctant to question God, but others are reluctant to question humanity 'so as not to diminish the power conferred by science, democracy, etc. … The challenge to God, and to human beings, is where were they *both* … in the African Great Lakes, Haiti, Bangladesh, countries that live, as we do, side by side with the scandalous profligacy of the North?' (Sobrino 2004, 27).

This may be why disasters cause such deep angst. We are confronted with the gross injustices in the world. Most people live in abject poverty while the minority consume most of the world's resources. An earthquake 'is an X-ray of the country. It is mostly the poor who get killed, the poor who are buried, the poor who have to run out with the four things they have left, the poor who sleep outdoors, the poor who live in anguish over the future, the poor who face enormous obstacles trying to rebuild their lives, the poor who cannot get financial credit' (Sobrino 2004, 3). Such injustice exists in high-income countries too. Hurricane Katrina disproportionately devastated poorer neighbourhoods in New Orleans, which years later continue to be the slowest to recover basic amenities (White 2014). The big question is why we humans regularly make choices to not provide for the poor or the oppressed, even when we have the means to do so. 'Tragedies like an earthquake have natural causes, of course, but their unequal impact is not due to nature; it stems from the things people do with each other, to each other, against each other. The tragedy is largely the work of our own hands. We shape the planet with massive, cruel, and lasting injustice' (Sobrino 2004, 3–4). This, in part, is why the Bible claims that no one is good and why judgment is justified.

In this general sense, disasters can be said to be part of God's judgment. Humans want to run the world their way, and God allows them. Disasters are a reminder that this world is not the way God wanted. Adam and Eve's sin brought judgement that resulted in disease and death, and changed the world. Now the whole of creation groans and decays. The hope of the afterlife is part of what allows Christians to hold on to the promise of a better life after this 'valley of the shadow of death' (Psalm 23:4). Even in this life, though, God allows suffering to continue, partly to permit human free will, but also to bring good out of the bad. Even though we may never know the cause of a disaster, we can work to bring good from it. This can happen if the exposure of injustice motivates people to work to restore justice, to "build back better." It can also happen if it leads people to respond to the disaster by helping those in need.

3.8 Call to Action

Throughout the Bible, believers are called to aid the poor, the sick, the oppressed, orphans, refugees—anyone who is vulnerable. In part, this is because all humans are made in the image of God, which confers everyone with both inherent dignity and moral responsibility. To live ethically is to act as an authentic image of God, doing what God would do (O'Mathúna 1995). The Bible portrays God as the defender of the weak and helpless (Psalm 68:5; Luke 6:20–22; James 1:27). This includes helping those devastated by disasters. For example, during the Roman Empire, the early spread of Christianity was influenced by how Christians responded to plagues. As healthy Romans fled their cities, Christians stayed and helped those in need, sometimes at the cost of their own lives (Stark 1996). In the sixteenth century, Martin Luther commended those Christians who felt God called them to help those afflicted with the Black Death (Luther 1527). In the nineteenth century, Henri Dunant saw first-hand the pain and suffering of wounded soldiers and committed himself to doing something about it. He gathered a small group of Swiss Christians, united in their theology and 'the moral sense of the importance of human life, the humane desire to lighten a little the torments' of those suffering (Dunant, cited in Moorhead 1998, 17). Thus was born the Red Cross, and soon led to the first Geneva Convention for the protection of wounded soldiers.

Disaster responders are motivated by many reasons, religious and nonreligious. Belief in God is not required to help others. The claim here is that followers of the Christian God *should be* motivated to help those in need. This should go beyond providing aid, as this can be a way to ease one's conscience or avoid addressing underlying injustices. Christianity calls for solidarity with others because all humans are part of one family, all equally images of God. As defined by Sobrino, 'Solidarity means *letting oneself be affected* by the suffering of other human beings, sharing their pain and tragedy' (2004, 19, emphasis original). Jesus is the example here, as he wept over his friends' grief (John 11:35), suffered on the Cross, and knows what it is like to suffer. The God of the Bible feels with humanity, and takes on the pain of their suffering.

True solidarity with those impacted by disasters should lead to internal change. Rather than looking backwards and speculating about why God allowed a disaster, believers are called to look forward to how they can learn and grow from the event. This may be in compassion towards others, taking action to help, or learning to help better. The Bible does not guarantee immunity from sickness, suffering or disasters, but offers a better way to deal with those times (Philippians 4:10–13). This involves belief and trust that a loving God has allowed something to happen and can bring good from it.

This has been called the character or soul building theodicy, where pain and suffering help us mature. As with all change, it can be painful. As noted above, injustice is deeply rooted in the world and within people. We may not be willing to change until we experience suffering, either ours or others. 'Things that contribute to a person's humbling, to his awareness of his own evil, and to his unhappiness with his present state contribute to his willing God's help' (Stump 1985, 409). Sometimes it takes a disaster to bring this to our attention.

Theological reflection about disasters must include some discussion about personal responses to disasters. Those with little time for religion may be sceptical about this, but it is key for believers. Such responses may only make sense after someone has spent time getting to know God. Joseph, well-known for his technicolour coat, is an important biblical example. His brothers beat him up and sold him into slavery. He would gain some freedom, only to suffer at the hands of someone else's evil schemes. Eventually, a disastrous famine gave Joseph the opportunity to do good for his captors, and be reunited with his brothers. Rather than seek vengeance on them, he declared that while they intended to harm him, God brought good out of their evil intentions (Genesis 50:20). God did not cause the suffering, nor encourage his brothers and others to harm Joseph, but he brought good from several bad situations. Central to that outcome was Joseph continuing to trust God in the midst of violence, betrayal and disasters. Likewise, Paul in the New Testament states that in all things, including all types of evil and disasters, God works for the good of those who love him (Romans 8:28). What is not offered is an answer to why a disaster happens, or who is to blame. Likewise, it may not be clear how, or when, or to whom, the good will come, but the promise of good is given for those who trust him. This is why waiting on God is a central theological theme.

At the same time, the Bible does not claim that pain and suffering should be accepted stoically or without protest. Psalms are the prayers of the Bible and show that lament and crying and protest in the midst of bad times are appropriate (Wilson 2002). "Why, Lord, … do you hide yourself in times of trouble?" "How long, Lord? Will you forget me forever?" "My God, my God, why have you forsaken me?" (Psalm 10, 13, 22). When situations are overwhelming, the only response left for a believer is to cling to God, "my rock, my fortress and my deliverer" (Psalm 18:2).

In the Psalms and the story of Job, answers are not provided. The same was noted above in Jesus' response to "Why?" questions. Easy explanations for the causes of disasters are not provided; guarantees that God will prevent or remove suffering are not provided. Pat answers that God will quickly make everything good do not help. Instead, faith offers confidence that God can be trusted in the midst of suffering, even if much remains unclear and uncertain. This trust is based on the nature of God's character (loving, faithful, just, etc.), and not any particular outcome, no matter how desirable. Such faith includes the hope that in the future, maybe as far away as the afterlife, things will be rectified and restored to the way God intended. In this way, religious faith, for those who believe, can contribute to personal resilience in the midst of disasters.

3.9 Conclusion

Disasters remind us that the world is not the way it should be. The world contains much beauty, and the Bible, particularly the Psalms, uses this to point towards the beauty and awe that is part of God's character. But the world also contains terrifying parts. Recently, I hiked about a kilometre from where a volcano erupted a few years earlier. Smoke still billowed forth from the crater; beside me were boulders, weighing up to 3 tonnes, which had been hurled through the sky. We are not in control of our world. The world is beautiful, but it is also dangerous. C. S. Lewis represented God as a lion in the *Chronicles of Narnia*. One character asked if the lion is safe. 'Safe?' he wrote 'Who said anything about safe? 'Course he isn't safe. But he's good. He's the King, I tell you' (Lewis 1950, 86).

The beauty of the world reminds us of God's good side, and disasters remind us of his dangerous side. He created the world with love and beauty, and humans introduced sin and ugliness. This requires a just response, which theology calls God's judgment. Injustice demands justice; ask any victim. God's judgment is how the Bible describes the bringing of justice. The Bible records that this has happened with specific events from time-to-time, but it does not claim that every disaster is the direct act of God. Various theodicies have provided justifications for why God allows disasters to continue. The Bible claims that someday this will end and the world will be restored to how it should have been. Meanwhile, living in this imperfect world, God uses suffering and disasters to call people back to himself and to act justly, love mercy, and walk humbly with him (Micah 6:8).

Such beliefs should impact someone's ethics and actions. Those who believe in a generous, loving God should express that love in practical ways. Those with the world's possessions should be moved with compassion for those in need and act in practical ways (1 John 3:16). Since God has a particular concern for the vulnerable, Christians should also (James 1:27). Given the view that all humans are made in the image of God, discrimination and injustice are unethical. At the same time, each believer is on a journey to take on more of God's character traits as his or her own character undergoes ethical transformation. And when Christians are hit by disasters, their belief that God can bring good from a bad situation should provide hope and resilience. Disasters should cause all of us to reflect deeply on what matters most in life. They remind us that we are not in control in this world, and will all ultimately face death. The Bible rejects the tendency to speculate about disasters as God's judgment on past behaviour, but instead calls on people to reflect on where we each stand with God. We don't need to be good enough to earn his acceptance; we are asked to be humble enough to accept his goodness and grace. Disasters remind us that all people deserve our help. They call on people to commit themselves to helping those in need, both through meeting their immediate needs in the disaster and working to overcome the injustices that exist in the world and contribute to the devastation of disasters.

References

Alush, Zvi. 2005. Rabbi: Hurricane punishment for pullout. http://www.ynetnews.com/articles/0,7340,L-3138779,00.html. Accessed 10 May 2018.

Behreandt, Dennis. 2005. Why does God allow calamities? *The New American* 21 (26): 31–34.

CBS. 2015. Insurance: What exactly constitutes an "Act of God"? *CBS Money Watch*. http://www.cbsnews.com/media/insurance-what-exactly-constitutes-an-act-of-god/. Accessed 10 May 2018.

Cooperman, Alan. 2005. An act of God? Where most see a weather system, some see divine retribution. *Washington Post*, September 4. http://www.washingtonpost.com/wp-dyn/content/article/2005/09/03/AR2005090301408.html. Accessed 10 May 2018.

Fretheim, Terence E. 2010. *Creation untamed: The Bible, God, and natural disasters*. Grand Rapids: Baker Academic.

James, Frank. 2010. Pat Robertson blames Haitian devil pact for earthquake. *NPR*, January 13. http://www.npr.org/sections/thetwo-way/2010/01/pat_robertson_blames_haitian_d.html. Accessed 10 May 2018.

Lewis, C.S. 1940. *The problem of pain*. London: Centenary Press.

———. 1950. *The lion, the witch and the wardrobe*. New York: HarperCollins.

Lopez, Kathryn Jean. 2005. Katrina, "Soldier of Allah." *National Review*, September 1. http://www.nationalreview.com/corner/108453/katrina-soldier-allah-kathryn-jean-lopez. Accessed 10 May 2018.

Luther, Martin. 1527/2012. Whether one may flee from a deadly plague. In *Martin Luther's basic theological writings*, 3rd edn, ed. Timothy F. Lull and William R. Russel, 475–487. Minneapolis: Augsburg Fortress.

Lutzer, Erwin W. 2011. *An act of God? Answers to tough questions about God's role in natural disasters*. Carol Stream: Tyndale House.

Martel, Brett. 2006. Storms payback from God, Nagin says. *Washington Post*, January 17. http://www.washingtonpost.com/wp-dyn/content/article/2006/01/16/AR2006011600925.html. Accessed 10 May 2018.

Molesky, Mark. 2015. *This gulf of fire: The Great Lisbon Earthquake, or Apocalypse in the Age of Science and Reason*. New York: Vintage.

Moorhead, Caroline. 1998. *Dunant's dream: War, Switzerland and the history of the Red Cross*. London: HarperCollinsPublishers.

O'Mathúna, Dónal P. 1995. The Bible and abortion: What of the 'image of God'?. Bioethics and the future of medicine: A Christian appraisal, ed. John F. Kilner, Nigel M. de S. Cameron, David L. Schiedermayer, 199–211. Carlisle: Paternoster Press.

———. 1999. Why me, God?' Understanding suffering. *Ethics & Medicine* 15 (2): 44–52.

Oman, Luke, Alan Robock, Georgiy L. Stenchikov, and Thorvaldur Thordarson. 2006. High-latitude eruptions cast shadow over the African monsoon and the flow of the Nile. *Geophysical Research Letters* 33: L18711.

Reichenbach, Bruce R. 1982. *Evil and a good God*. New York: Fordham University Press.

Sobrino, Jon. 2004. *Where is God? Earthquake, terrorism, barbarity, and hope*. Trans. Margaret Wilde. Maryknoll: Orbis.

Stark, Rodney. 1996. *The rise of Christianity: A sociologist reconsiders history*. Princeton: Princeton University Press.

Stump, Eleonore. 1985. The problem of evil. *Faith and Philosophy* 2: 392–423.

Swinburne, Richard. 1987. Knowledge from experience, and the problem of evil. In *The rationality of religious belief: Essays in honour of Basil Mitchell*, ed. William J. Abraham and Steven W. Holtzer, 41–67. Oxford: Clarendon Press.

Team Louisiana. 2006. *The failure of the New Orleans levee system during Hurricane Katrina*, Appendix 6. https://www.researchgate.net/publication/316997857_The_Failure_of_the_New_Orleans_Levee_System_During_Hurricane_Katrina. Accessed 10 May 2018.

Ten Have, Henk. 2014. Macro-triage in disaster planning. In *Disaster bioethics: Normative issues when nothing is normal*, ed. Dónal P. O'Mathúna, Bert Gordijn, and Mike Clarke, 13–32. Dordrecht: Springer.

White, Robert S. 2014. Who is to blame? Disasters, nature and acts of God, revised edn. Oxford: Monarch.

Wilson, Gerald H. 2002. *The NIV application commentary: Psalms – volume 1*. Grand Rapids: Zondervan.

Chapter 4
Disasters and Responsibility. Normative Issues for Law Following Disasters

Kristian Cedervall Lauta

Abstract Major disasters are windows to societies' deepest, darkest secrets. Moments, which allow us to sneak a peek at the categories according to which, we distribute wealth or justice and organize society as such. Law has come to play a vital role in this regard. In this chapter, I argue that (legal) conflicts after disaster are inevitable, as we have collectively changed our perception of what a disaster is. The modern disaster is anything but *natural* in its constitution; it is a deeply political, moral and cultural phenomenon. Accordingly, it is also legal. Furthermore, three overall features characterize the legal cases that arise out of disasters. They all deal with serious losses, complex causalities and tricky normative distinctions. While the first two play to the strengths of the legal order, the third is what make these cases controversial. Thus, in the process of solving the legal facts presented, courts face a number of questions of a non-legal nature. In order to perform its main function (to solve the conflict at hand) law is forced to engage with the most central questions we are confronted with in an Anthropocene world: which processes are driven by natural forces and which by culture, who is a citizen, and what belongs to sphere of scientific uncertainty or misconduct?

Keywords Disaster justice · Disaster law · L'Aquila · Disaster responsibility · Risk regulation · Law and disasters

Law has increasingly become the approach to fixing conflicts that emerge after disasters. After every major disaster in the last 30 years, legal cases on responsibility for the disastrous losses have been filed. These legal cases consider all sort of conflicts brought on by the losses of property or life. Ownership, insurance policy

---

This paper was written as part of the University of Copenhagen 2016 program for excellent interdisciplinary research: Changing Disasters.

K. C. Lauta (✉)
Center for International Law, Conflict and Crisis, Faculty of Law and Copenhagen Center for Disaster Research (COPE), University of Copenhagen, Copenhagen, Denmark
e-mail: klau@jur.ku.dk

D. P. O'Mathúna et al. (eds.), *Disasters: Core Concepts and Ethical Theories*, Advancing Global Bioethics 11, https://doi.org/10.1007/978-3-319-92722-0_4

interpretation, or damages to third-parties caused by insufficiently secured possessions are recurring themes. However, often these legal cases are forced, in the throes of solving *prima facie* trivial legal disputes, to address more fundamental normative issues.

In this chapter, I will argue that by studying the (legal) decisions in these social conflicts we get a window not only to contemporary conceptions of justice, but to the (re-)negotiation of fundamental categories on which we base our society. That is, as courts become the preferred platform to settle controversial issues in the aftermath of disasters, lawyers come to decide on things of a fundamentally non-legal nature. In other words, in order to solve conflicts, which only address a very specific sub-section of the world (e.g. what the word "flood" means in an insurance policy) – the judge has to understand, and decide upon, all the unruly complexity inherent in disasters.

The paper is structured in three overall parts. First, I will account for the way disasters are understood within law. Second, I will argue that as we increasingly interpret and approach disasters as human and social shortcomings, inevitably they become legal conflicts, and accordingly court cases. So, even though disasters are not rigidly defined or coherently approached *in* law, they play a significant role *for* law. Third, I will say something general about the legal cases courts are confronted with after disasters – about the dilemmas they pose for courts, for societies and for legislators, and how they are presently dealt with. During this exercise, I will outline which normative issues these cases bring up. That is, while they solve the concrete conflicts through traditional legal doctrine and principle, the cases simultaneously becomes a *scene* on which the (re)negotiation of basic societal and ethical categories takes place. Finally, I will offer my conclusions.

4.1 Disasters in Law

There is no uniform understanding of what a disaster is within international law. While this might seem counterintuitive to the non-lawyer, it makes sense, since there is no uniform body of international law on disasters. This is the case both at international, and to a wide extent, regional level: even the global blue print on disaster risk reduction, the Sendai framework, stands back from drawing up a clear and operable definition of "disaster".

The recently adopted International Law Commission (ILC) draft convention on the "protection of persons in the event of disasters" uses the definition "a calamitous event or series of events resulting in widespread loss of life, great human suffering and distress, mass displacement, or large-scale material or environmental damage, thereby seriously disrupting the functioning of society". While this framework offers some hope as to the development of an international law framework for disasters, an international convention not yet in force is hardly a robust starting point for the analysis of normative issues in disaster law. Today, we use a wide array of disaster definition of more less legal nature (See Kelman and Pooley 2004).

Nonetheless, we have, in the course of the last 50 years, seen a vast increase in different types of regulation either directly or indirectly addressing disasters. This legal development is driven by several factors (see more with Lauta 2015) most importantly however, a change in the common understanding of what constitutes a disaster. In the following section, I will suggest how this is so.

4.2 Law in Disasters

The epistemological genealogy of disasters can be, and has been, theoretically construed in many different ways. The traditional approach is to describe the understanding of disasters in the form of acts. In this light, the understanding of disasters have developed from acts of God over acts of an unforeseeable Nature to, now, acts of men and women (Quarantelli 2000; Lauta 2015: 11ff). Another, equally convincing approach focuses on the epistemology of the disaster. This approach takes us from God's Providence over Nature's contingency to human and social vulnerability (Ibid). In the following, I will account for these different understandings, and their role vis-à-vis law.

In pre-enlightenment Europe, disasters were the will of God. God had supreme power. Not only did God know where and whom disasters would befall – She intended it so. This meant that discussions after disasters were not on who had caused the disaster, but rather why God chose this particular disaster site or these particular victims. God was even put on trial in Leibniz' Theodicy (Leibniz 1988) to explain herself. However, beyond this fictional trial disasters were non-legal events – something to be interpreted and acted upon within religious communities and, largely seen (see e.g. Molesky 2015; O'Mathúna 2018), not in courtrooms.

With what the Israeli historian Yuval Noah Harari calls *the scientific revolution*, often associated with the enlightenment period, disasters changed meaning. Rather than Supreme knowledge, disasters became associated with lack of human knowledge. According to Harari "[m]odern science is based on the Latin injunction *ignoramus* – 'we do not know'. It assumes that we don't know everything" (Harari 2015, 250). With the introduction of ignorance as the main paradigm for science, the way we understand disasters changes accordingly. Rather than insight into God's providence, disasters become insight into how little we actually know of nature. The 1755 earthquake in Lisbon accordingly spurred an enormous interest in the natural sciences, an interest that even prompted the German philosopher Immanuel Kant to write a series of essays analysing the causes of the quake (Reinhardt and Oldroyd 1983). In this optic, disasters are no longer God's intention, but the result of an unmoral Nature's unforeseeable ways. Thus, a disaster is in this optic the confirmation of our ignorance, something to be studied further, but not something we could foresee or control. They are events beyond morality and law. In legal terms, disasters are *forces majeures* or even, somewhat ironically, *Acts of God* (Kaplan 2007; Kristl 2010; Binder 1996; Chocheles 2010; Hall 1993).

In recent years, political philosophy has adopted the theoretical idea of the *Anthropocene* (Bonneuil and Fressoz 2016; Heise 2009; Morton 2013, 2016; Nixon 2011). According to this theory, even geophysical forces or meteorological systems are today made hazardous by human activity (Crutzen 2002). This idea enables us to see that we as humans have now become a force on our own – responsible not only for our survival, but also potential demise. This turn is likewise reflected in disaster studies. Within disasters studies, the central term is today vulnerability rather than hazards – a conceptual change that seems to be endorsed by an almost unanimous global academic community.

Through this theoretical approach new causal connections come to light. Almost every "disaster pre-condition" (Oliver-Smith and Hoffman 1999, 4) exposed by a vulnerability analysis allows us to see human faults and/or neglect. This has major implications for the role of law. According to a modern conception, disasters are within human control and thereby within a moral space almost inevitably leading to legal conflict. Accordingly, when disasters are not results of a contingent, unmoral nature, but rather a defective, unjust culture – they also become subjects for legal scrutiny. In legal terms, disasters result from potential *negligence* or *omissions*.

Take the L'Aquila earthquake in 2009 as an example thereof. The shock was rated 6 rated 5.8 or 5.9 on the Richter magnitude scale and 6.3 on the moment magnitude scale, and eventually killed more than 300 local inhabitants. However, while the shock(s) that hit L'Aquila might be unpredictable and, to a certain extent, uncontrollable, the government's response, including the incorrect communication of the Major Risk Commission preceding the quake, or the enforcement of building codes in the city were not – we shall come back to this later. To be sure, the L'Aquila earthquake is, in a modern discourse, not a disaster because of the tremors of the earth, but because the effects of these tremors could have been avoided, had *someone* acted or prioritized differently (e.g. Alemanno and Lauta 2014; Alexander 2014).

This has dramatic consequences for the role of law after disasters. Today, it seems largely expected that every disaster has some kind of a legal postlude. Accordingly, we have seen legal cases after disasters all around the globe from Chile (Bonnefy 2013) to Japan (Lewis 2012), and from the United States (Lauta 2014: 110 ff) to the Philippines (Reuters 2015).

With this insight at hand, it seems we can move on to the third section of the paper, and explore what might be said in general about these legal struggles.

4.3 Disasters and Legal Responsibility

The conflicts discussed in this chapter are not only tied to the general chaos triggered by emergency: looting, random violence or family disputes. Such conflicts, though incredibly relevant and entirely crucial to the peace of the society in question, are not tied to the character of the disaster itself (See alternatively Harper and Frailing 2016).

This section addresses common features of the cases that arise from the (legal) negotiations around who is responsible for the disastrous losses of the community. In popular terms, I am not discussing crimes during disasters, but disasters *as* crimes. Furthermore, I am predominantly talking about conflicts that arise *after* disaster. Thus, it is most often after disasters that these particular cases crystalize as legal conflicts, though the recent surge of climate litigations might suggest that even this is changing (See e.g. United Nations Environment Programme 2017).

The last 30 years have provided plenty of such case law, in particular on compensation of disaster victims (Hinghofer-Szalkay 2012; Sugarman 2006; Farber and Faure 2010; Faure and Bruggeman 2007; Organisation for Economic Co-operation and Development 2004). After almost every major disaster in the last ten years, we have seen legal cases discussing the responsibility for disastrous losses. This trend cuts across continents, hazard type and size of the impact. As examples, take the cases following from Typhoon Haiyan (Reuters 2015), the 2011 Flood of Copenhagen (The City of Copenhagen 2012), the 2010 Earthquake in Chile (McClean 2012; Bonnefy 2013) or even preemptively discussing a potential volcanic eruption of Mount Vesuvius (see Viviani and Others v. Italy 2015).

Even though these disasters, their causes, and the concrete legal conflicts are very different in scale and character, as well as being embedded in different legal and cultural systems, I believe that there are some commonalities we can identify – and thereby, for the purpose of stating something general about normative issues for "law", single out what the major issues for law might be.

I will claim that three overall features characterize these court cases. Firstly, they all entail realized or potential major damage and thereby **serious losses** for the plaintiffs. That is, the plaintiffs have always suffered, or risked suffering, significant economic or personal damage. Accordingly, the cases are not driven by idiosyncrasies, moral inclination or political ideology, but rather real, and very tangible, losses.

Secondly, they almost always entail the reconstruction of a **complex *assemblage* of causalities.** As stated above, disasters are almost always multi-causal incidents with high social complexity and multiple actors. Therefore, the primary issue in most of these cases is to establish a causal link between plaintiffs' loss and the actions or omissions of the defendant.

Finally, they often necessitate courts to draw the line between law and **central political, scientific, moral or economic priorities or discretion.** That is, in order to create a legal decision, courts often have to distinguish, for example, negligent behaviour from political or economic priorities or, perhaps more directly relevant to the readership of this book, scientific uncertainty from scientific misconduct. Furthermore, in the case of *natural* disasters; courts are forced to discuss, in some detail, the limits between nature and culture. That is, which part of a given incident is attributable to naturally occurring processes ("nature"), and which are culturally/politically/socially induced? In direct continuation of this third characteristic, this chapter's main argument is presented.

In the following sub-sections, I will briefly outline the three characteristics: serious losses, complexity and the involvement of "tricky distinctions".

4.3.1 Serious Losses

Cases emerging from the dust of disaster sites often entail serious losses for the plaintiffs. Losses of lives or livelihoods are defining features of disasters (Killian 1954), and accordingly also for the legal cases arising out of disasters.

While this is a commonality for this group of cases – it is hardly something estranged from law and legal cases. Traffic accidents, inheritance cases and bankruptcies all, at least for the involved individuals, involve very serious losses. These cases are commonly accepted to be settled by courts – if anything, serious personal losses seem to strengthen the intuition that responsibility for disaster is a matter for law. Thus, law is commonly accepted to be able to deal with these questions in a just and timely manner, irrespective of the severity of the loss.

4.3.2 Complexity

Modern disasters are almost per se multi-causal and complex in origin. In New Orleans, even though it is clear that the US Army Corps of Engineers should have paid better attention to the levee-system before Hurricane Katrina, the hurricane itself was still a super-hazard, the people of New Orleans did not evacuate when asked to, and the emergency plans at municipal and state level were outdated. Disasters of a certain scope and impact always involve a multiplicity of actors, normative orders, and risks.

In disaster research, there is an increasing focus on disasters as hybrid phenomena, most often constituted of both technological and natural components, sometimes referred to as NaTech disasters (e.g. Cruz et al. 2006; Salzano et al. 2013, 470) or even technically-induced natural disasters (Ellsworth 2013). Thus, it is increasingly acknowledged that modern disasters are hybrid phenomena composed of fragments of very different orders: social, natural, and technological; and therefore phenomena with multiple causes and complex constitutions. The Fukushima incident in Japan serves as the perfect example of the mess that typifies the modern disaster. The disaster was triggered by one of most violent earthquakes ever registered, a 40.5-meter high sea wave, and a nuclear plant positioned on the Japanese east coast. The natural, technological and cultural hazards can hardly be kept apart in Fukushima; rather they constitute a destructive assemblage, causing the disaster only when combined. And yet, the main responsibility was, according to the Japanese Parliament's own assessment, not attributed to the tremendous powers of nature or even societal reliance on dangerous technology, but to particular trades in the Japanese society and culture (Commission 2012): A disaster 'made in Japan'.

In the process of attributing any form of legal responsibility, the establishment of a plausible chain of causality is entirely central. Accordingly, to attribute responsibility for a disaster, plaintiffs must demonstrate causality between the actions or omissions of the defendant and the loss(es) suffered. This is, *post* disasters, always a particularly delicate process.

Thus, returning to Japan, liability could be attributed to many actors. This field of potential causal violators includes the power plant operator, the owner of the power plant, municipal authorities, the government or the Parliament (as well as, of course, nature and/or God). This seems to lead some theorists to suggest that it makes no sense to discuss responsibility for anyone in particular, when responsibility obviously is shared by many (Reason 1990). I disagree – and so do the most courts addressing these cases. The fact that many could be responsible does not mean that no one should be. Or, in other words, the fact that an individual or organization negligently has caused disastrous losses is not exculpated by the rest of society's contributing or overlapping negligence. It is a red herring fallacy or perhaps rather a "two wrongs make a right"-line of argumentation.

More importantly, none of this is new to law. Insurance cases, custody cases, or even murder cases all deal with incredibly complex social facts with multiple causes, conflicting interests and contradictory information. Any of the true crime aficionados, who, like myself, have enjoyed Serial, the Jinx or Netflix's Making a Murderer, will know that even deciding what seems to be a straight-forward criminal case is a mind-blowingly complex exercise. Thus, even in murder cases, many often share responsibility for the wrongdoing.

The claim put forward here is not that law in general and courts in particular have always been beyond critique in this area, or do not have potential for improvement. The point here is merely that this is what courts already do. In most societies, it is indeed the very essence of law to deal effectively, and in a manner contributing to the social peace and general feeling of justice, with complex factual situations.

What makes disasters unique is that in the process of establishing these causalities a number of tricky distinctions must be made – distinctions not normally made within the realm of law, and this is the third defining feature of legal cases following disasters.

4.3.3 Tricky Distinctions

The third feature of post disaster conflict is what I believe makes these cases special. They all navigate a field where even the fundamental categories determining its function are unclear. To decide what stems from nature or culture, and who should have protection and from what, are questions entirely unsettled. Thus, the controversy in establishing causality is not, I will claim, stemming from factual complexity, but rather from the ambiguity in our understanding of even basic concepts like science, agency, and culture.

In order to illustrate this ambiguity we might return to the 2009 L'Aquila earthquake in Italy. In the aftermath of the earthquake, local, national and global attention was caught by a particular legal case (Alexander 2014; Lauta 2014). Six researchers and one public official seated on the National Risk Commission had convened in L'Aquila a week before the earthquake. They gathered to provide input to authorities on the risks of a major earthquake. The commission consisted of the leading researchers within their field as well as the top branch of the civil protection agency. In their public appearance after the meeting, the commission informed the public that there was no risk of a major earthquake, which, it turned out, was not in conformity with the commission's own findings. In other words, the representative of commission deliberately misinformed the public, and the commission members failed to clear up this misunderstanding, most likely with the intention of avoiding (unnecessary) worry for the population. A group of the relatives who lost family members in the disaster claimed that this (mis)information provided by the Commission was what convinced them to not evacuate their houses during the earthquake. The case caused global upheaval. The global controversy was not because of the incredibly complicated exercise of establishing causality between the press conference held a week before and the victims' decision to not evacuate during the earthquake. Nor was it caused by an inclination that courts should not settle cases involving the loss of life. Rather, the controversy was about the general role of scientific experts in disaster management. Accordingly, the global controversy spurred by the criminal case was not about the potential negligence of the committee – but rather the perceived adjudication of what scientific uncertainty is.

Thus, cases involving responsibility for disaster differ from most others by the fact that they often require courts to address problems, which are not commonly accepted as legal and where the delineation between orders is not clearly established. Again, they are not controversial due to the losses involved or the reconstruction of complex facts, but because they are forced to answer questions unanswered by the regimes, to which they belong: ethics, politics and science.

Law is a binary system. In spite of being constructed to work with complexity, or perhaps exactly therefore, law's purpose and *modus operandi* is to bring clarity. A legal judge is in no position to answer a question, even one of a complex character, with a complex answer. She is forced to answer any question clearly: either an action is legal or illegal; either you find for or against the claim of the plaintiffs.

The emergence of conflicts over the causes of disaster therefore drives an institutionalization of the above mentioned ambiguities: in the process of settling the legal questions, courts come to decide fundamentally non-legal issues. From the perspective of the judge(s) presiding in the case, these "decisions" are rather necessary assumptions to be able to address the legal issues. Returning to L'Aquila, the court could only start discussing causality after making a number of assumptions about the scientific findings of the committee – in a sense, assumptions only relevant in light of the bigger issue of misinformation and the legal problem of causality. However, this process looks very different from outside law – in this case, particularly from within scientific circles.

Seen in this light, the legal cases following disasters cease being greedy grabs for power or riches, and reemerge as epistemological, distributive struggles. These struggles are about who is to be considered a victim, and who might qualify as a victimizer. Thereby these legal cases seems to be the very frontier for the *Anthropocene* turn of disasters – the arena in which basic concepts are established and challenged, and the place to address and silence the ambiguity that presently haunts our thinking on climate change and disaster responsibility.

Simultaneously, as court cases are becoming the preferred vehicle to settle controversial issues, they also force courts to settle normative issues of a fundamentally non-legal nature. Thereby law, unwillingly, becomes the fix-all.

4.4 Conclusion

Major disasters are windows to societies' deepest, darkest secrets. Moments which allow us to sneak a peek at the categories according to which we distribute wealth or justice and organize society as such. Law has come to play a vital role in this regard. I have argued that (legal) conflicts after disaster are inevitable as we have collectively changed our perception of what a disaster is. The modern disaster is anything but *natural* in its constitution; it is a deeply political, moral and cultural phenomenon. Accordingly, it is also legal. I have suggested three overall features characterizing the legal cases that arise out of disasters. While the first two play to the strengths of the legal order, the third is what make these controversial. In the process of solving the problems presented, law is confronted with a number of questions of a non-legal nature. In order to perform its main function (to solve the conflict at hand) law is forced to engage with the most central questions we are confronted with in an Anthropocene world: which processes are driven by natural forces and which by culture, who is a citizen, and what belongs to sphere of scientific uncertainty or misconduct? These are all questions that must be settled before the conflict can be addressed.

Accordingly, these cases are windows to our present societal struggles on agency, responsibility (in the widest sense) and justice, and should therefore be objects for legal and moral criticism, and engagement.

References

Alemanno, Alberto, and Kristian Cedervall Lauta. 2014. The L'Aquila Seven: Re-establishing Justice after a Natural Disaster. *European Journal of Risk Regulation* 2. https://ssrn.com/abstract=2461327

Alexander, David. 2014. Communicating earthquake risk to the public: the trial of the "L'Aquila Seven". *Natural Hazards* 72: 1159. https://doi.org/10.1007/s11069-014-1062-2.

Binder, Denis. 1996. Act of god? Or act of man? A reappraisal of the act of god defense in tort law. *The Review of Litigation* 15 (1): 1–80.

Bonnefy, Pascale. 2013. Chilean judge upholds manslaughter charges linked to 2010 Tsunami, *New York Times*. May 16 2013 available at: http://www.nytimes.com/2013/05/17/world/americas/chilean-judge-upholds-manslaughter-charges-against-officials-over-tsunami-alert.html. Accessed 25 Apr 2018.

Bonneuil, Christophe, and Jean-Baptiste Fressoz. 2016. *The shock of the Anthropocene: The Earth, history, and us*. London: Verso.

Chocheles, Christopher T. 2010. No excuses: Hurricanes and the "Act of God" defence to breach of contract claims. *Louisiana Bar Journal* 57.
Commission, The Fukushima Nuclear Accident Independent Investigation. 2012. The national diet of Japan.
Crutzen, Paul J. 2002. Geology of mankind. *Nature* 415 (6867): 23.
Cruz, Ana Maria, Laura J. Steinberg, and Ana Lisa Vetere-Arellano. 2006. Emerging issues for Natech disaster risk management in Europe. *Journal of Risk Research* 9 (5): 483–501.
Ellsworth, William L. 2013. Injection-induced earthquakes. *Science* 341 (6142): 1225942. https://doi.org/10.1126/science.1225942.
Farber, Daniel, and Michael Faure (eds.). 2010. *Disaster law*. Cheltenham: Edward Elgar Publishing.
Faure, Michael G., and Bruggeman Véronique. 2007. Catastrophic risks and first-party insurance. *SSRN*.
Hall, C.G. 1993. Un unsearchable providence: The lawyer's concept of act of God. *Oxford Journal of Legal Studies* 13.
Harari, Yuval Noah. 2015. *Sapiens. A brief history of humankind*. New York: Harper.
Harper, Dee Wood, and Kelly Frailing (eds.). 2016. *Crime and criminal justice in disaster*. 3rd ed. Durham: Carolina Academic Press.
Heise, Ursula K. 2009. *Sense of place and sense of planet: the environmental imagination of the Global*. Oxford: Oxford University Press.
Hinghofer-Szalkay, Dagmar. 2012. Naturkatastrophen: Haftung des Staates für Schäden der Opfer: Rechtsvergleichende Überlegungen, USA-Österreich: Jan Sramak Publishing House.
Kaplan, Casey P. 2007. The act of God defense: Why hurricane Katrina & Noah's flood don't qualify. *The Review of Litigation* 26: 155–181.
Kelman, I., and S. Pooley (eds.). 2004. Disaster definitions. Version 2, 24 July 2004 (Version 1 was 12 July 2004). Downloaded from http://www.ilankelman.org/miscellany/DisasterDefinitions.doc.
Killian, L.M. 1954. Some accomblishments and some needs in disaster study. *Journal of Social Issues* 10: 66–72.
Kristl, Kenneth T. 2010. Diminishing the divine: Climate change and the act of God defense. *Widener Law Review* 15: 325.
Lauta, Kristian Cedervall. 2014. New fault lines? On responsiblity and disasters. *European Journal of Risk Regulation* 2: 137–145.
———. 2015. *Disaster law*. New York: Routledge.
Leibniz, G.W. 1988. *Theodicy*. Peru: Open Court Publishing.
Lewis, Ben. 2012. The legal aftershocks of Fukushima. *Law.com*. 26 January 2012, available at: https://www.theguardian.com/environment/2016/feb/29/former-tepco-bosses-charged-fukushima. Accessed 26 Apr 2018.
McClean, Denis. 2012. Chile still living with quake effects, UN-ISDR. https://www.unisdr.org/archive/25366. Accessed 25 April 2018.
Molesky, Mark. 2015. *This gulf of fire: The Great Lisbon Earthquake, or Apocalypse in the Age of Science and Reason*. Vintage Books.
Morton, Timothy. 2013. *Hyperobjects: Philosophy and ecology after the end of the world, posthumanities*. Minneapolis: University of Minnesota Press.
———. 2016. *Dark ecology: For a logic of future coexistence, Wellek Library lectures in critical theory*. New York: Columbia University Press.
Nixon, Rob. 2011. *Slow violence and the environmentalism of the poor*. Cambridge, MA: Harvard University Press.
O'Mathúna, Dónal P. 2018. Christian theology and disasters: Where is God in all this? In *Disasters: Core concepts and ethical theories*, ed. Dónal P. O'Mathúna, Vilius Dranseika, and Bert Gordijn. Dordrecht: Springer.
Oliver-Smith, Anthony, and Susannah M. Hoffman. 1999. *The angry Earth: Disaster in anthropological perspective*. New York: Routledge.

Organisation for Economic Co-operation and Development. 2004. *Large-scale disasters: Lessons learned*. Paris: Organisation for Economic Co-operation and Development.

Quarantelli, E. L. 2000. Title. Preliminary Paper.

Reason, James. 1990. Human error: Models and management. *British Medical Journal* 320 (7237): 768–770.

Reinhardt, O., and D.R. Oldroyd. 1983. Kant's theory of earthquakes and volcanic action. *Annals of Science* 40 (3): 247–272. https://doi.org/10.1080/00033798300200221.

Reuters. 2015. Philippine typhoon victims prepare lawsuit against fossil fuel companies accused of driving climate change. *South China Morning Post*. http://www.scmp.com/news/asia/south-east-asia/article/1887014/philippine-typhoon-victims-prepare-lawsuit-against-fossil. Accessed at 30 Apr 2018.

Salzano, Ernesto, Anna Basco, Valentina Busini, Valerio Cozzani, Enrico Marzo, Renato Rota, and Gigliola Spadoni. 2013. Public awareness promoting new or emerging risks: Industrial accidents triggered by natural hazards (NaTech). *Journal of Risk Research* 16 (3-4): 469–485.

Sugarman, Stephen D. 2006. Roles of government in compensating disaster victims. Issues in legal scholarship.

The City of Copenhagen, 2012. *Cloudburst Management Plan*, available on http://en.klimatilpasning.dk/media/665626/cph_-_cloudburst_management_plan.pdf. Last accessed 30 Apr 2018.

United Nations Environment Programme. 2017. *The status of climate change litigation – A global review*, available at http://columbiaclimatelaw.com/files/2017/05/Burger-Gundlach-2017-05-UN-Envt-CC-Litigation.pdf. Accessed at 30 Apr 2018.

Viviani and Others v. Italy. 2015. *European court of human rights*, application no. 9713/13.

Chapter 5
The Ethical Content of the Economic Analysis of Disasters: Price Gouging and Post-Disaster Recovery

Ilan Noy

Abstract Economics, generally, is a discipline in which relatively little attention is devoted to language and terminology. As such, economists have not really attempted to define the concept of disasters very carefully, nor have they evaluated the ethics that are behind the economic analysis of disasters. Given this absence, we believe that a better understanding of the ways in which the discipline approaches the topic of disasters and its ethics is gained not by examining the multitude of definitions in the discipline, but by examining specific examples of topics that are contested within the economic literature on disasters and their ethical content. Outlining the main arguments and methodological approaches that economists use to think about these topics will, we hope, better clarify the general approach that economists use when embarking on disciplinary research on the topic of disasters. As such, we choose to focus on two topics: price gouging, and post-disaster economic recovery. The first is a topic that is explicitly ethically challenging from an economic perspective; the second involves many implicit ethical decisions that are almost never made explicit.

Keywords Price gouging · Economic recovery · Post-disaster · Economics and ethics

5.1 Concepts and Economics

Economics, generally, is a discipline in which relatively little attention is devoted to language and terminology. When terminology is defined, it is usually within the context of a statistical or a mathematical model that requires one to very clearly specify assumptions and relationships that follow from the definition used. As such, economists have not really attempted to define the concept of disasters very

I. Noy (✉)
School of Economics and Finance, Victoria University of Wellington, Wellington, New Zealand
e-mail: ilan.noy@vuw.ac.nz

D. P. O'Mathúna et al. (eds.), *Disasters: Core Concepts and Ethical Theories*, Advancing Global Bioethics 11, https://doi.org/10.1007/978-3-319-92722-0_5

carefully, unlike sister social sciences like geography who have been defining and refining the appropriate uses of this term for decades.

Many economists are perfectly happy with a definition of disasters that just specifies an ad-hoc and arbitrary threshold of fluctuation—be it in the hazard itself, or its impact—and call this 'a disaster'. For some, a disaster is thus a significant fluctuation in weather conditions (e.g., an unusual amount of rainfall), or a disaster is defined as a significant mortality or destruction associated with a trigger of some sort (often the trigger is not defined and just the level of mortality or destruction is observed). In other cases, it is not even the destruction that is measured, but rather the reduction in the flow of goods and services that are made or consumed after the trigger event. The level that determines 'significance' is also not well determined, with, for example, the two most important global datasets collecting economic statistics on disasters (Desinventar and EMDAT) using very different thresholds; and some in economics using other thresholds as well.

In the economics literature, one can therefore find dozens of definitions of what constitutes a disaster. Maybe the most general definition is the one proposed by the United Nations International Strategy for Disaster Risk Reduction (UNISDR): It is a "serious disruption of the functioning of a community or a society at any scale due to hazardous events interacting with conditions of exposure, vulnerability and capacity, leading to one or more of the following: human, material, economic and environmental losses and impacts." But this definition is vague enough so it encompassed many different conceptions of disasters. In some ways, every paper that deals with this topic in economics has its own unique definition, depending on the specific focus of interest, the methodological approach used, and the data that is employed within this methodology. Still, even within the papers that choose similar approaches and data, one can identify large variation in the use of the terminology of disasters. However, within each paper, the definition adopted is usually very clearly specified (even if very different from other work in the same area of interest). This is in contrast with other related concepts such as vulnerability or resilience that are typically very ill-defined; with relatively little interest in the economics literature in clarifying and more precisely identifying them (an exception is Rose 2007). In some respects, most economists apply the 'duck test' to these more controversial terms (whose definition is highly contested in other disciplines). For economists, therefore, 'a bird that walks like a duck, and swims like a duck, and quacks like a duck, is called a duck' and not much is gained, in this view, by trying to carefully define what a duck is.

Given this definitional chaos, we believe that a better understanding of the ways in which the discipline approaches the topic of disasters and its ethics is gained not by examining the main definitions in the discipline, but by examining specific topics that are contested within the economic literature on disasters. Outlining the main arguments and methodological approaches that economists use to think about these topics will better clarify the general approach that economists use when embarking on disciplinary research on the topic of disasters.

Maybe the biggest ethical challenge that is central to discussions in economics is the question of the distribution of income and wealth. This topic is also present in analysis of the economics of disasters, as both the impacts of disasters and recovery from them have distributional consequences. This topic is also central to discussions of public policy interventions before or after disasters (for example, in discussions of public insurance programs—see Owen and Noy 2017). Similarly, objections to the pervasive use of utilitarianism as the primary lens through which economic analysis is being conducted have also been raised within the context of disasters.

We choose to focus in this paper on two specific topics, price gouging, and post-disaster economic recovery, as these will enable us to cover much of the general arguments within the context of this chapter. Price gouging is a topic that is explicitly challenging from an economic-and-ethics perspective; the second, involves a lot of implicit ethical decisions that are almost never made explicit.

5.2 The Problems of Price Gouging and Economic Recovery

In the wake of a natural disaster, due either to destruction of existing stocks or the difficulty of transporting goods into the disaster site, necessities such as food, water, or gasoline are often scarce. This scarcity, a basic premise in economic analysis, raises concerns that vendors of these goods (and services) will engage in what is commonly known as "price gouging:" the practice of raising the price of these goods far above the pre-disaster market price. Many economists define their discipline as the study of mechanisms to allocate scarce resources, and as such the study of "price gouging" goes directly to the heart of economic analysis.

Many non-economists find price gouging intuitively morally objectionable, as it is perceived as greedy and exploitative. This critical attitude has resulted in the implementation of a multitude of laws banning price gouging, especially in the United States (Davis 2008). The economics profession, however, is much more ambivalent or even supportive of price gouging practices, as many economists have argued that laws against price gouging are counterproductive. These laws, according to the economists' interpretations, harm those in need instead of helping them, and many have argued furthermore that there is nothing morally objectionable about the practice.

The purpose of the following two sections will be firstly to examine the economists' claim that permitting price gouging maximizes the total welfare of those in a disaster zone (a utilitarian argument), and secondly to address the vaguer ethical argument that, even if price gouging maximizes total welfare, it is morally benign and should be permissible. We will argue firstly that there is no straightforward answer as to whether price gouging is total-welfare maximizing in the way economists use these terms. Surprisingly, we could not find any empirical work by economists that attempts to examine the evidence for this. Secondly, we argue there are ethical reasons to suggest that price gouging can be morally impermissible, although our analysis suggests these reasons are not decisive.

In the last section of this chapter, we examine another ethically fraught question that has been examined by economists: the recovery from disasters. In this last section, we describe some of the ways in which recovery is being assessed, and examine the economic and ethical content of these assessments. We conclude that section by some additional observations.

5.3 Economic Analysis of Price Gouging

Economics is a discipline tightly engaged with practical distributional considerations, and there are three primary practical arguments advanced in favor of the idea that price gouging is total-welfare maximizing: (1) it discourages hoarding; (2) it ensures efficient allocation of resources to those most in need; and (3) it incentivizes producers to increase supply in the disaster-affected area. We will consider each one of these in turn. One should note, however, that a ban on price gouging should probably not be considered in isolation. Bans on price gouging may be accompanied by supplementary policies, such as a ban on hoarding (restricting the amounts of specific goods people are allowed to buy) or the provision of subsidies and assistance to producers and importers/suppliers of these goods into the affected region.

Let us firstly consider hoarding. The basic argument here is simple: if prices are low, individuals in disaster zones will buy large quantities of necessities, significantly more than they will realistically require, "just to be safe." Evidence of this sort of behavior has been observed before in the wake of natural disasters; see, for example, the discussion of the 2011 Japanese earthquake in Cavallo et al. (2014) but no general evidence for this as in Parker (2018). These excessive purchases will be greater in frequency and magnitude the more uncertainty there is about the impact of the disaster and the ability of local authorities to continually supply necessities. This uncertainty will be more pronounced the bigger the disaster, so that we should observe more hoarding when supply is more limited and authorities less able to react, compounding matters and making the post-disaster situation significantly worse. Given the inability of authorities to operate efficiently in these areas, we should doubt the efficacy of regulatory responses, and should therefore prefer market-place responses like price increases.

High prices, according to this view, cause people to think twice before buying arbitrarily large quantities, and thus prevent excessive hoarding and ensure that goods are more equally distributed across the affected populations rather than just to those that were first in the queue.

A possible response to this concern of hoarding is to implement anti-hoarding laws. Yet the potential effectiveness of these laws is unclear. The maximum amount that individuals are allowed to purchase must by necessity be set reasonably high so that individuals in genuine need of large amounts can still purchase them; but that still leaves a lot of room for other individuals to buy more than they need.

A basic premise in much of economics is that people respond to incentives. In this case, when laws and incentives clash, when the law can easily and costlessly be circumvented (for example by multiple visits to the store), and when enforcement will be non-existent (as law enforcement will have 'bigger fish to fry' in disaster zones), economists expect these laws to be largely ineffective. There is little empirical evidence either way, particularly because few places actually implement anti-hoarding laws, so the presumption among economists is that since effective implementation of anti-hoarding laws and similar quantity-mechanisms is impossible, one needs to resort to price mechanisms (price gouging) to effectively and efficiently allocate scarce resources.

There are, however, three other considerations that suggest that perhaps price gouging may not be necessary or effective as a response to hoarding. The first is simply that hoarding is already discouraged through social norms that condemn hoarders, especially in crisis situations. If social norms can lead to efficient and equitable allocation of these scarce necessities, economic (price) incentives may not be necessary. The second is that price gouging, rather than reducing the net amount of hoarding, simply means that only higher-income individuals will hoard (as even post-gouging prices will appear relatively low to high-income individuals when compared to the high stakes and risks present in a disaster zone). Hoarding, in this description, will be done just by the rich, rather than by those that are first in the queue. As such, the outcome achieved in an environment that allows price gouging is not any better than what one expects to observe when hoarding is permissible and the queue is the main allocation mechanism.

The third argument, one that has not received sufficient attention in the literature, is that gouging may in fact *increase* hoarding. Consider the impact of price gouging on a rational agent with imperfect information. High prices are a strong signal that the good is scarce, which incentivizes the individual to hoard the good. If there is no scarcity, the individual knows that if they unexpectedly run out they can simply return to purchase more; by contrast, if the good is scarce, the individual will buy a large amount of the good to hedge against the risk of running out. If, on the other hand, there is a prohibition on gouging, then low prices may signal either an inability to raise them due to the law, or an abundance of the good.

In general, and especially in post-disaster chaos, information is not easily available. Thus, consumers will not necessarily know, if prices are low, whether there is any scarcity. However, if prices are allowed to increase, and price gouging occurs, consumers will have a definite signal of scarcity, increasing their incentive to hoard. Therefore, and maybe counter-intuitively, the higher the price, the stronger the incentive to hoard more; leading to a cycle of increased prices and increased hoarding. This is of course mostly speculation, as we have no observational (empirical) research on the topic, but hopefully it serves to show that the assumption that price gouging is effective in preventing hoarding should not be taken for granted.

Of course, humans are not perfectly rational agents responding only to information and price signals, and if we introduce the possibility of irrationality, the effect may be even more extreme. There is substantial evidence to suggest that our estimation of the value of goods is formed irrationally through the confluence of a variety of factors, only one of which is price (Ariely 2008). This means that lower prices may cause individuals to irrationally believe that goods are not high-value and therefore not worth hoarding, whilst high prices may cause them to re-evaluate their behaviour, and "scare" them into hoarding, rather than away from it.

Overall, then, it is unclear whether price gouging's effect on people's propensity to hoard goods is a legitimate or significant argument in favor of allowing the practice. Yet the issue of hoarding is the most minor of the three practical arguments for price gouging. We can next consider the issue of efficient allocation.

One of the most valuable functions of a system of prices is ensuring that scarce resources are allocated efficiently; that is, they are allocated to the individuals who need them most. The more utility an individual derives from consuming a particular good, the more money that individual will be willing to pay to buy that good. In the context of price gouging, if prices are high, this will ensure that only individuals whose need for the high-priced goods is acute will purchase them. If, by contrast, prices are kept low, everyone will attempt to buy the goods, so that many of the goods will end up with individuals who do not require them as intensely. This leads to a suboptimal allocation of these goods across consumers.

There are two problems with this argument. The first is that it is contingent on the assumption that the goods being discussed are worth significantly more to some people than others: given that we are mostly discussing basic necessities like food, water, and energy, this assumption seems somewhat doubtful. One might argue that since individuals might have differing initial quantities of these goods, they may be worth much more to some individuals (who do not have large supplies of them) than to others (who do). Yet, as we will expand upon later, individuals with large existing contingency supplies of these goods are likely to be wealthy and therefore undeterred by high prices, and the individuals who most need these necessities are likely to lack easy access to large quantities of money.

The second is that although the idea of using prices to determine the extent to which people value a good is sound in most cases, it does suffer from one major flaw: money is a highly imperfect proxy for utility, because people have vastly differing incomes. This is a fairly intuitive concept, but one that may merit a digression. A basic fact about most commodities, including money, is that they are subject to diminishing marginal returns: the more you have of it, the less utility an additional unit of it provides. So, for example, $20 provides far more utility for a homeless person with no wealth than it does for a millionaire. This principle applies conversely: if a homeless person were to *lose* $20, they would lose far more utility than a millionaire would. Essentially, a certain quantity of money has a different utility value for each principal, a value that is significantly determined by that person's wealth and income.

So consider that a particular good in a disaster situation is worth 25 units of utility (henceforth 'utils') to a person of low income, and 20 utils to a person of high income. Even though the higher-income individual values the good less, they may be willing to pay significantly more for it, since money is worth less to them than it is to the lower-income individual. Thus, prices are only very roughly able to determine who values a good most across individuals.

Moreover, banning price gouging does not mean that the market entirely loses the ability to allocate the goods to those who value them most. Instead, the mechanism of prices based on monetary units is replaced by a different mechanism, one which may be distributed more equally across consumers: a mechanism of *time* prices. In a post-disaster situation where goods are scarce and cheap (due to anti-gouging laws) and everyone wants to acquire them, what often happens is that long lines form at the entrances to distributors. In such a situation, the individuals most likely to acquire the goods are those who are most willing to stand in lines for long periods of time.

Willingness to expend time may be a better proxy for an individual's valuation of a good than price, since it is immune to the distortionary effect of income differences (we all experience 24 h in any day). However, it is of course subject to a variety of other potential distortionary effects and is still imperfect. A possible objection to the use of time instead of prices is that it forces people to spend hours of precious time in a post-crisis situation queueing, when higher prices could clear out the lines and save a lot of time. Yet conversely, of course, high prices could have a crippling impact on the finances of individuals in a post-crisis situation by forcing them to expend large amounts of money on necessities. Thus, price gouging could be equally harmful in interrupting recovery.

Overall, we have hopefully cast doubt on the idea that price gouging is necessary or even appropriate for addressing the economic question of efficient allocation post-disaster. Yet efficient allocation is still not the most significant argument in favor of price gouging. That honor is reserved for the arguments surrounding supply. Essentially, high prices for particular goods in a disaster area accomplish two things: they signal to producers outside the disaster zone that there is a scarcity of these high-priced goods, and they provide the incentive to these producers to transport goods rapidly into the area. With high prices, there is plenty of profit to be made, and the profit motive may be a strong incentive to produce and import more of the scarce goods (e.g. water) into the disaster-affected region.

From an economics perspective, with its emphasis on incentives, this is a convincing argument. Banning price gouging would do little to incentivize increased supply of essential goods to the post-disaster areas. In fact, incentives may be reduced as the cost of transporting a good may rise post-disaster (e.g. when railways are damaged). However, alternative policies can be introduced to encourage suppliers to bring goods into the area: the simplest policy might be for the government to directly supply the scarce goods by buying them elsewhere and transporting them into the region; potentially distributing through regular retail supply chains. But, the government may also just provide subsidies to producers who sell necessities in the area, thus providing the same incentives to producers that high prices would whilst ensuring that the burden does not fall too harshly on consumers. This would also neatly solve another common argument against anti-gouging laws, which is that they can fail to account for increased costs or risk involved in supplying goods to a disaster zone; a generous subsidy would ameliorate that concern as well.

There are potential practical problems with the idea of using subsidies, and, as we previously observed, these practical concerns are frequently important in economic analysis. For one, their use might divert money away from other areas of government-sponsored disaster relief. Additionally, whilst they may be effective at encouraging large, established retailers who can easily access these subsidies, they may not work for other sources of supply. Informal suppliers, such as individual entrepreneurs with the ability to transport goods into disaster areas, may not find it that easy to document their actions and access government support (Zwolinski 2008). Maybe most importantly, the administrative costs of implementing such a subsidy, especially at short-notice, maybe be quite high.

The efficiency and feasibility analysis outlined above is typical for economics; most of the economics literature concerns itself with similar debates about the abilities of policies to deliver an improvement in outcomes. These outcomes are usually framed within discussions of implementability and efficiency, rather than, for example, moral considerations. Yet, before moving on to a brief discussion of the ethical issues surrounding price gouging from an economics perspective, we briefly outline two arguments *against* the idea that price gouging maximizes total welfare.

The first objection is the potential issue of monopolistic control of the available supply. In a post-disaster situation, travel is often inhibited and going long distances in search of alternative providers can become difficult and dangerous. Competition is thus curtailed. This means that the ability of different providers to compete with each other is drastically reduced, and may mean that providers become oligopolistic or even, monopolists. Under these circumstances, giving providers the flexibility to change prices as they wish may result in prices significantly *above* the market-clearing price, whereas forcing them to keep prices essentially fixed avoids allowing firms the privilege of using their newly found monopoly power to set prices above the market-clearing (and allocatively most efficient) rate.

Secondly, there are reasons to think that individuals of lower income systematically require these goods more intensely than individuals with higher income do. Higher-income individuals are more likely to be prepared for disaster situations—for example, with emergency stocks of water or food (e.g., Stats NZ n.d.; FEMA 2013—and therefore may not be in desperate need of necessities to the extent that people of lower income are. Since under price gouging, the individuals purchasing the goods are likely to be predominantly of higher incomes, even if there are more net goods supplied, this may be a worse outcome than if fewer goods were supplied, but to a more diverse mix of higher and lower income households. All of this analysis, of course, is consequentialist.

In conclusion, it is not at all clear that price gouging is an efficient tool of welfare maximization. There is no empirical evidence on the topic, and much work needs to be done before it will be possible to conclusively say whether allowing price gouging is preferable even on consequentialist terms. Next, we discuss the ethical issues pertaining to price gouging—after all, it is possible that even if it is consequentially efficient, other aspects of price gouging might incline us towards banning it.

The focus we will select here—whether it can be immoral for the state to select a particular characteristic as the basis for making distributive decisions—and is not related to the previous arguments about price gouging themselves, but to the ways economists consider them. Economists often avoid making normative ethical claims, which means they avoid large components of the discussion on policy issues.

Jeremy Snyder points out that price gouging undermines "equitable" access to necessities because individuals of lower income are priced out of the market (Snyder

2009a, b). He argues that because of this suppliers have a moral duty not to raise prices; doing so involves treating others inequitably and undermining their dignity.

This is an interesting position, but it is very difficult to link culpability for a systemic, market-wide wrong (if, indeed, it is a wrong at all) to particular individuals who are just responding to the demands of the market. It is more interesting, instead, to consider the situation from the perspective of the state, which is making a simple decision: on which basis will resources be distributed? Will they be distributed randomly (to whomever turns up to the shops first) or on the basis of a similarly random characteristic, which is difficult to pin down to a particular group (e.g. willingness to wait in line)? Or, alternatively, will they be distributed systematically to individuals of higher income?

Zwolinski responds to this objection by noting that random chance is a morally irrelevant basis for decision-making in the same way as income is a morally irrelevant characteristic (Zwolinski 2009). Yet we think that most economists (and others) will intuitively believe random chance to be a morally superior mechanism of allocation when compared to making decisions based on certain pre-existing differences between individuals (such as wealth). Why is this?

It is clear, firstly, that our intuitive repulsion to the idea of using income or wealth as a basis for allocation is not due simply to the fact that *some* characteristic is chosen in the place of random chance. If, instead, the decision had been based on whoever happens to be wearing orange shirts, few would find it to be intuitively morally objectionable. So, it is clear that our indignation is contingent on the fact that the differentiating characteristics—e.g. wealth—are salient features that are significant in our society. So, in order to fully deal with this argument, we need a theory to explain why making allocative decisions on the basis of significant observable characteristics is immoral.

It is possible that our repulsion is not due to the fact that the decision itself is objectionable, but that it instead reveals something objectionable or bigoted about the character of the individual making it. In the case of price gouging, then, because the decision to allow it is motivated not by any bigotry or preference but simply by a desire for an efficient market, permitting price gouging should be perfectly acceptable. Yet we will argue that there may be a rational basis for our repulsion, even if the motives behind the action are innocent.

The first reason for this is that it is impossible for the sellers in this case to be making a decision that is truly objective. They will inevitably share some characteristics with certain groups of people in the crisis situation and will undoubtedly have their own opinions and biases. In this context, it is impossible for any decision that selects a particular group of people (the buyers) to have entirely pure motives—even the decision to privilege market efficiency. The only way for the agent to avoid the potentially corrupting influence of their context is to select a method of allocation that is not premised on any of the facts of the situation or characteristics of the people involved, and is therefore context-free: specifically, random allocation.

Secondly, if we take the use of random chance as a natural baseline, then the choice to make an allocative decision on any other basis implicitly involves elevating that characteristic into a status of moral relevance. If that characteristic is one that is integral to people's identities and the way they interact with the world, then the decision to privilege one such characteristic over the others involves degrading the dignity and identity of everyone whose characteristics are being used as a way to deny them resources.

These principled arguments are not decisive, but importantly in the context of our chapter, ones that are rarely engaged on by economists. Economics, in general, prefers to use what it inaccurately views as 'morally neutral'—the criterion of efficient allocation, and rarely examines the implicit moral content of that choice. Economists are either consequentialists—for whom the process of allocation is less important and the efficiency criterion is very important, or libertarians—for whom any government intervention in prohibiting the operations of the market has to pass a very high threshold of justification (usually some significant market imperfection). However, as we observed, there are reasons to cast some doubts about the consequentialist benefits of price gouging, and equally about the libertarian argument against banning it; see also Rapp (2005) and Brewer (2007) for additional discussion of these arguments.

5.4 Long-Term Recovery

Disasters lead to significant direct damage to infrastructure, to raw materials, crops, extractable natural resources, the natural environment and, most tragically, to people. Disasters, however, also cause more indirect impacts—often termed "losses" by economists—though the terminology, as we pointed out earlier, is not universally discussed nor agreed upon. Economic losses refer to the flow of economic activity, in particular the production of goods and services, which will not take place as a consequence of the disaster, both in the short and possibly in the long term. These economic losses have as much impact on society's long-term prosperity and well-being as the immediate damages to physical infrastructure and people. One can even contemplate long-term losses on experienced well-being, and even indirect mortality (Noy 2016b).

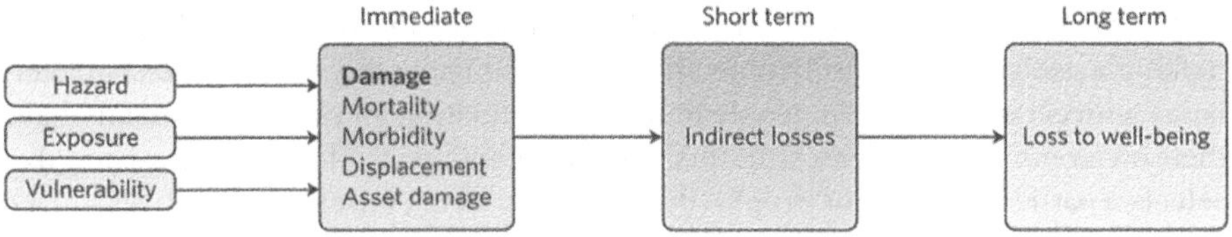

Source: Noy (2016a)

The standard approach in economics to deciphering the long-term recovery prospects of postdisaster economies starts with the assumption that the recovery from the destruction will be complete: that is to say, an economy will experience accelerated growth postdisaster until it returns to its previous trajectory (or status quo). From Adam Smith and John Stewart Mill—founding fathers of modern economics—to Gary Becker—a more recent Nobel prize winner in Economics—much of the profession assumes that indeed this is what typically happens after large shocks (be they triggered by natural hazards or by man-made triggers such as wars or large accidents).

Over the past 30 years, there have been several challenges to this idea of inevitable full recovery within the profession. If, for example, a disaster changes the competitive advantage of production in a specific region, even temporarily, businesses and customers may end up going elsewhere, leading to long-term decline. This scenario describes fairly well the fate of the Japanese Port of Kobe after a destructive earthquake hit the city in 1995. Despite the fact that the port was reconstructed in less than two years after suffering severe damage, the container traffic that used to flow through it—it was previously one of the busiest ports in the world—never returned to its pre-disaster level (Chang 2000; duPont et al. 2015).

An alternative theory is that the long-term trajectory may even turn out to be beneficial. This is usually termed 'creative destruction.' This interpretation of creative destruction revolves around the idea that buildings and infrastructure destroyed by disasters are replaced by newer and more productive alternatives, which allows more productive use of available resources—better public transportation networks, smarter electricity or telecommunication grids, or more energy-efficient factories, for example. This improved infrastructure leads to additional prosperity. In theory, positive long-term impact can occur not only from technological innovation, but also from "build-back-better" policies that allow for improved reconstruction (perhaps through better zoning).

Most examinations of moderately prosperous countries, at least at the national level, find that there are no significant long-run national impacts associated with natural disasters, even when these are catastrophic (Cavallo et al. 2013). Researchers who disagree, however, always find evidence that disasters hinder and delay (possibly permanently) development and creation of prosperity. Indeed, for small and poor countries that have trouble accessing resources for reconstruction, for example Haiti, it is unfortunately plausible to expect a long-term decline in well-being as a result of the 2010 earthquake (Katz 2013).

In countries with fewer resources, natural disasters can also have more long-lasting, negative effects through their impact on education and health. The damage to the educational infrastructure and transportation networks, for example, can lead to a decline in educational achievements, which in turn has implications for the long-term prospects of affected individuals. Most troubling is research that shows a decrease in years-of-schooling for children who were in utero during the destructive 1970 Peruvian earthquake (Caruso and Miller 2015). In the Peruvian case, this negative impact on educational attainments persisted even into the next generation, so that the children of mothers affected by the natural disaster while the mothers were still in utero also experience lower educational achievement.

New Orleans in the aftermath of Hurricane Katrina is a particularly well-studied case. The hurricane has had a particularly profound and enduring impact on the local population of New Orleans. Many of the households displaced by the hurricane have remained dispersed in neighboring states and cities. Income prospects elsewhere played a significant role in a household's decision whether to return or not. In this case, lower-income households found it particularly difficult to return as the neighborhoods least likely to get rebuilt were populated more densely by the (mostly African-American) poor. These households also found that their prospects had improved "in exile," further reducing their incentive to return (Deryugina et al. 2018). A decade after the hurricane, the population of the city is almost 20% lower than it was the week before Katrina hit the Gulf Coast. But this net decline hides a bigger churning of people and more fraying of the city's original social fabric.

In cases where the politics and power relations are skewed, a disaster may also serve as a catalyst for changes that can be either positive or negative. In Haiti, for instance, there was much hope that its under-performing economy and dysfunctional government would be improved in the disaster's aftermath with the large inflow of foreign assistance. Tragically, this was not the case, and the government today is perceived as dysfunctional as before the quake (Katz 2013). Similar hopes were expressed, for example, with respect to New Orleans pre-hurricane under-performing public education system.

However, as Naomi Klein documents in her book, the *Shock Doctrine* (2010), there are also many instances in which entrenched powers use the 'opportunity' of disasters to further solidify their control and push through changes that they favour. These changes would have otherwise faced fiercer resistance. This resistance either dissipates or is easier to ignore because of the 'fog of war' during the disaster's aftermath.

More optimistic scenarios can also be found. A build-back-better economy may be an unintended consequence of the changes wrought by the disaster. The Mississippi Flood of 1927, for example, led to the modernization of agriculture in the flooded areas, inevitably because the day laborers (mostly African-American) left. This outmigration forced farmers to adopt new technologies. In contrast, where labour shortages were not acute, modernization did not take place (Hornbeck and Naidu 2014).

All of this analysis, however, is purely an examination of ultimate consequences, and ignores the process that led to the examined outcomes. But, even from a consequentialist perspective, it is often incomplete. The standard framework in the social sciences identifies disaster risk as a confluence of the hazard, exposure to the hazard, and the vulnerability of the exposed populations (and assets). As such, an analysis of recovery should also examine the impact of the process on these three components (though the hazard risk is usually assumed constant in the time spans implicitly examined). What happens to this risk triangle (hazard, exposure, and vulnerability) is clearly important, but is often ignored in the economic analysis. For example, one can imagine a trade-off between reducing exposure and reducing vulnerability in post-disaster recovery. Such a trade-off is identified in the case of Sri Lanka's coastal reconstruction policy in the aftermath of the 2004 Aceh tsunami. Ingram et al. (2006) argue that the initial post-disaster law prohibiting any reconstruction within 100 or 200 m of the high tide mark emphasized reducing exposure at the (significant) cost of increasing vulnerability of the impacted populations.

Those previously living along the coast were economically dependent on access to that coast (mostly as their income was either from tourism or from fishing). Thus, the enforced distance from the ocean was diminishing their livelihoods and increasing their vulnerability. Later, the government backed away from this law, exactly because it realized the increased vulnerability it was creating.

Currently, economists lack satisfactory tools to sufficiently consider these trade-offs. While modeling well-being and measuring social welfare has been developing within the profession, the frameworks that will allow one to considerately evaluate the various consequentialist trade-offs inherent in a post-recovery process are still in their infancy. And, if one were to eschew consequentialist analysis, economics as a methodological approach does not have much to add to the conversation.

From a more practical, policy-oriented perspective, the main message of this chapter is that economists need to be more explicit about the ethical content of their analysis and evaluate it more thoroughly in those terms. Consequentialism, in and of itself, is an ethical choice, but even within this framework, the reigning one in Economics, there are many ethical choices that are made, often implicitly. These ethical choices are important in determining policy recommendations, and economists ignore them at their peril.

References

Ariely, Dan. 2008. *Predictably irrational: The hidden forces that shape our decisions*. New York: Harper.

Brewer, Michael. 2007. Planning disaster: Price gouging statutes and the shortages they create. *Brooklyn Law Review* 72: 1101.

Caruso, German, and Sebastian Miller. 2015. Long run effects and intergenerational transmission of natural disasters: A case study on the 1970 Ancash Earthquake. *Journal of Development Economics* 117: 134–150.

Cavallo, Eduardo, Sebastian Galiani, Ilan Noy, and Juan Pantano. 2013. Catastrophic natural disasters and economic growth. *The Review of Economics and Statistics* 95 (5): 1549–1561.

Cavallo, Eduardo, Alberto Cavallo, and Roberto Rigobon. 2014. Prices and supply disruptions during natural disasters. *The Review of Income and Wealth* 60 (S2): 449–471.

Chang, Stephanie. 2000. Disasters and transport systems: Loss, recovery, and competition at the Port of Kobe after the 1995 earthquake. *Journal of Transport Geography* 8 (1): 53–65.

Davis, C.W. 2008. *An analysis of the enactment of anti-price gouging laws*. Unpublished master's thesis, Montana State University, USA. http://scholarworks.montana.edu/xmlui/bitstream/handle/1/1145/DavisC0508.pdf?sequence=1. Accessed 21/04/2018.

Deryugina, Tatyana, Laura Kawano, and Stephen Levitt. 2018. The economic impact of hurricane Katrina on its victims: Evidence from individual tax returns. *American Economic Journal: Applied Economics* 10 (2): 202–233.

duPont, William, Ilan Noy, Yoko Okuyama, and Yasuhide Sawada. 2015. The long-run socio-economic consequences of a large disaster: The 1995 earthquake in Kobe. *PLoS One* 10 (10): e0138714.

FEMA. 2013. *Personal preparedness in America: Findings from the 2012 FEMA national survey*. Washington, DC: Federal Emergency Management Agency. Web. 15 Nov. 2016.

Hornbeck, Richard, and Suresh Naidu. 2014. When the levee breaks: Black migration and economic development in the American South. *American Economic Review* 104 (3): 963–990.

Ingram, Jane C., Guillermo Franco, Cristina Rumbaitis-del Rio, and Bjian Khazai. 2006. Post-disaster recovery dilemmas: Challenges in balancing short-term and long-term needs for vulnerability reduction. *Environmental Science & Policy* 9 (7): 607–613.

Katz, Jonathan. 2013. *The big truck that went by: How the world came to save Haiti and left behind a disaster*. New York: St. Martin's Press.

Klein, Naomi. 2010. *The shock doctrine: The rise of disaster capitalism*. New York: Metropolitan Books.

Noy, Ilan. 2016a. Tropical storms: The socio-economics of cyclones. *Nature Climate Change* 6: 343–345.

———. 2016b. New ways of defining success in post-disaster recovery. *World Politics Review* 5/7/16.

Owen, Sally, and Ilan Noy. 2017. The unfortunate regressivity of public disaster insurance: A quantitative analysis of a New Zealand case. CESifo Discussion Paper #6540.

Parker, Miles. 2018. The impact of disasters on inflation. *Economics of Disasters and Climate Change* 2 (1): 21–48.

Rapp, Geoffrey. 2005. Gouging: Terrorist attacks, hurricanes, and the legal and economic aspects of post-disaster price regulation. *Kentucky Law Journal* 94: 535.

Rose, Adam. 2007. Economic resilience to natural and man-made disasters: Multidisciplinary origins and contextual dimensions. *Environmental Hazards* 7 (4): 383–398.

Snyder, Jeremy. 2009a. What's the matter with price gouging? *Business Ethics Quarterly* 19 (2): 275–293.

———. 2009b. Efficiency, equity, and price gouging. *Business Ethics Quarterly* 19 (2): 303–306.

Stats NZ (n.d.). How prepared are New Zealanders for a natural disaster? http://www.stats.govt.nz/browse_for_stats/people_and_communities/Households/natural-disaster-how-prepared-nzers.aspx. Accessed 21/04/2018.

Zwolinski, Matt. 2008. The ethics of price gouging. *Business Ethics Quarterly* 18 (3): 347–378.

———. 2009. Dialogue on price gouging. *Business Ethics Quarterly* 19 (2): 295–303.

Chapter 6
Political Science Perspectives

Rob A. DeLeo

Abstract Government institutions play an important role in guiding disaster preparedness, mitigation, and recovery. In turn, political scientists have devoted considerable attention to the study of hazards and disasters, including the impact of disasters on election outcomes, the capacity of disasters to help set the crowded government agenda, the various organizational strategies used by emergency management agencies, as well as scores of other related topics. The following chapter considers three areas of political science research examining the intersection of politics, policy, and disaster. It specifically considers the literatures on policy change, myopic voting and reactive decision making, and organizational behavior. This review also considers the literature on disaster resilience, a topic that overlaps various subfields within the discipline. In addition to assessing the strengths and weaknesses of each area of research, this chapter highlights a number of potentially fruitful areas of future research.

Keywords Political science · Public policy · Resilience · Agenda setting · Myopic voting · Focusing events · Policy change

Scholars, public officials, the general public, and the media have long recognized the link between government and the damage suffered in the aftermath of disaster. From the famed flood mitigation programs of Egyptian Pharaoh Amenemhet III to the mass evacuations of Pompeii to the Biblical tale of Noah's Ark, history is littered with stories illustrating the importance of leadership during disaster (Cimellaro 2016). For centuries, humankind has looked to its leaders in times of crisis. Political leaders are uniquely positioned to leverage our collective social resources to help mitigate and, ideally, prevent the destruction caused by disaster. Disasters are often watershed moment in a politician's career, forcing them to make tough choices in the face of extreme uncertainty, panic, and stress.

R. A. DeLeo (✉)
Department of Global Studies, Bentley University, Waltham, MA, USA
e-mail: rdeleo@bentley.edu

D. P. O'Mathúna et al. (eds.), *Disasters: Core Concepts and Ethical Theories*, Advancing Global Bioethics 11, https://doi.org/10.1007/978-3-319-92722-0_6

Not surprisingly, then, scholars interested in the political process have devoted considerable attention to the study of disaster, a tradition that can be traced to at least the late eighteenth century when political philosopher Jean Jacques Rousseau penned his account of the 1775 Lisbon, Portugal earthquake. Commenting on the disaster, Rousseau writes: "nature did not construct twenty thousand houses of six or seven stories there, and if the inhabitants of this great city had been more equally spread equally spread out and more lightly lodged, the damage would have been much less and perhaps of no account" (Dynes 2000, p. 106). Rousseau's work, which is considered the first social scientific account of the politics of disaster, concluded that better urban planning on the part of elected officials could have prevented the enormous loss of life suffered in the wake of the earthquake.

If Rousseau's study represents one the first social scientific accounts of disaster, then Samuel Prince's study of the 1917 Halifax maritime explosion is the first systematic analysis of the political dynamics of hazard and disaster policymaking. A sociologist by training, Prince meticulously documents the Canadian government's response to the disaster, which saw nearly 2000 people perish after a cargo ship filled with explosives and other incendiary devices exploded in Halifax harbor. Analyzing the various laws and rules enacted by the Canadian government in the months following the event, Prince shows disaster can provide an important catalyst for policy and social change (Scanlon 1988). His work remains influential to this day. Scores of researchers have set out to explain the relationship between disaster and policy, a theme discussed in greater detail below.

Disasters are an important area of inquiry for political scientists. Because the study of disasters has always been an interdisciplinary enterprise, political science research on disasters overlaps with many of the other fields surveyed in this book, including sociology, economics, anthropology, geography, and others. Nor is there a singular theory of disaster politics. Instead, considerable variance exists across various the discipline's various subfields, each of which differs with respect to its unit of analysis and conceptual foci.

There is, however, general consensus that disasters are social constructs. Whether or not a particular hazard (a potential source of harm) becomes a disaster (an event that strains the response capacity of a social system or organization) is dictated not only by the size and scope of the hazard, but also by existing vulnerabilities as well as a particular community's capacity to prepare for, respond to and recover from disaster (Comfort 2005; Lindell et al. 2006; Islam and Ryan 2016). Because government institutions play a critical role in determining how resources are distributed before, during, and after disaster, politics often determines if a hazard becomes a disaster or, worse yet, a catastrophe (Gerber 2007). Communities look to their political leaders to help decipher between those hazards that are dismissed as little more than a tragic, but unavoidable, confluence of events and those that are somehow the byproduct of human error (e.g., poor planning, a slow response, inadequate resources) and thus can be avoided in the future (Birkland 1997, 2004, 2006, 2010; Jasanoff 2010; Roberts 2010).

The following chapter considers three areas of political science research examining the intersection of politics, policy, and disaster. First, it considers the ways in which disasters lead to policy change. Policy change is the process through which new policies are created and old ones are amended and altered across time (Cobb and Ross 1997; Parsons 1995). By aggregating death, destruction, and economic loss, disasters play an integral role in drawing policymaker, media, and public attention to certain issues thereby helping them access the crowded government agenda, an important precursor to policy change (Birkland 1997).

Second, it considers the literature on myopic voting and reactive decision making. Legislators are often characterized as being reactive, meaning they only attend to those issues that have an immediate impact on their constituency as opposed to those that threaten future harms. A thriving body of research has consider the social and political determinants of myopic voting, in larger part because they provides useful insights into the ways in which elected officials cater to the desires of their constituents. Disaster policy offers an excellent context for investigating this topic since it allows for an assessment of policy rendered *before* an event (e.g., disaster preparedness policy) as well as policy created *after* and in response to an event (e.g., disaster recovery and relief policy) (Fiorina 1974, 1981; Healy and Malhotra 2009, 2010, 2013; Anderson 2000). Put differently, it creates a rather distinctive natural experiment for contrasting proactive versus reactive policymaking.

Finally, this chapter briefly reviews the research examining the administration and management of disaster situations. Unlike the sections on policy change and myopic voting, which focus on fairly well-specified areas inquiry, this section is not necessarily organized around a single research question—or even set of questions for that matter. Instead, it aims to sample some of the political science research that has set out to address both conceptual and, often times, applied questions regarding the ways in which politics impacts different phases in the disaster management cycle, namely disaster response and recovery.

The chapter closes by briefly highlighting a number of gaps in the political science literature and suggesting future research directions. Note that this chapter is intended to serve as a useful entry point into the literature on politics, policymaking, and disaster. It is by no means exhaustive and focuses primarily on U.S. domestic policy, which is, in large part, a testament to the author's own area expertise. However, scholars studying comparative politics and international relations have also made important contributions to our understanding of disasters, despite the fact that their work is not accounted for in the text ahead.

6.1 Policy Change and Disaster

Few subfields have devoted more sustained attention to the study of disasters than the policy sciences, as evidenced in the Policy Studies Organization's 2010 creation of *Risk, Hazards & Crisis in Public Policy*, a peer-reviewed journal devoted entirely to disseminating research on the policy and political dynamics of hazards and disasters. Disasters factor prominently into virtually every major theory of policy change. Abrupt shocks are said to draw policymaker, media, and public attention to once ignored issues, providing new opportunities for policy change (Kingdon 2003; Baumgartner and Jones 1993; Sabatier 1988; Sabatier and Weible 2007; Sabatier and Jenkins-Smith 1999).

Public policy encompasses a broad intellectual universe. Textbook accounts present the policy process as including a series of distinct but overlapping stages, including the identification and definition of social issues (problem definition); the selection of issues for explicit government attention (agenda setting); the development and adoption of policy alternatives (policy formulation and adoption); the execution and administration of laws, rules, and regulations (policy implementation); and the assessment and appraisal of new and existing programs (program evaluation) (Anderson 2010). Moreover, the term "public policy" refers to an eclectic array of decisions or governmental outputs, including statutes and laws, court decisions, agency regulations and rules, and orders issued by executive officials (Parsons 1995). Some scholars suggest agreements between various non-governmental or transnational institutions also constitute policy, particularly when these agreements result in the provision of some sort of public good (Stone 2008).

A great deal of policy research has focused on the distinct but interrelated processes of agenda setting, which describes the process through which issues are selected for consideration by a decision making body, and policy change, which broadly describes the creation of new policies or the revision of existing ones (Anderson 2010). Agenda setting is a precursor to policy change in that policy cannot be reformed unless an issue first accesses the agenda of a decision-making body or policy venue. Just as there are a myriad of different types of policy, so too are there different venues. Examples include specific committees within a legislature, government agencies, and state and local governments. Groups seeking policy change need to be careful to select a venue with jurisdiction over the issue in question and, more importantly, one that is receptive to their calls for change. Venues therefore serve as gatekeepers within the political system (Pralle 2006).

Various theories of agenda setting and policy change recognize the importance of disasters. Consider Kingdon's multiple streams framework (MSF hereafter), which is one of the three most widely cited theories of policy change (Zahariadis 2014). Kingdon's (2003) theory uses a metaphor depicting multiple streams of policymaking activity to conceptualize the agenda setting process. The *politics stream* denotes the various constellations of interest groups and policymakers petitioning for change. The politics stream also includes macro-political forces, like public opinion and the national mood. The *problem stream* describes the various ways in which problems are revealed to policymakers, the general public, and the media. As noted below, disasters are one of a number of mechanisms that help bring issues in the problem stream to the attention of policymakers. Finally, the *policy stream* describes the various policy proposals and ideas circulating a particular policy community. Put differently, it includes the various options and ideas for addressing problems in the problem stream. Policy change occurs when a committed and politically savvy individual, a so-called policy entrepreneur, draws together or couples elements from the various streams thereby coupling the streams. Coupling in turn opens a policy window or an opportunity for organized interests to push their preferred policy onto the government agenda and, ideally, induce policy change.

According to Kingdon (2003), disasters are an important element of the problem stream. Other elements of the problem stream include indicators, which describe the various statistics and numeric measures used to quantify a problem, as well as feedback, which describes information generated during the implementation of program. Disasters are said to represent focusing events or attention grabbing incidents that rapidly aggregate death and destruction. Kingdon notes that certain events, particularly those that are seen as being emblematic of government failure, have the ability to "bowl over everything standing in the way of prominence on the agenda" (p. 96).

MSF is hardly the only theory of policy change to highlight the importance of disasters. The punctuated equilibrium model argues disasters can disrupt existing policy monopolies—areas of policymaking dominated by a select group of individuals and institutions—by drawing attention to a once ignored issue that challenges the status quo (Baumgartner and Jones 1993). What is more, the advocacy coalition framework (ACF), which argues policy change results from changes in the belief systems of organized interests or advocacy coalitions, argues crisis provides a powerful opportunity for coalitions to learn and, in some cases, alter the ways in which they perceive a particular problem (Sabatier and Jenkins-Smith 1999; Nohrstedt 2005, 2008). Alas, from a policy perspective, disasters can, in some cases, provide an impetus for policy change.

However, rarely is policy change a forgone conclusion. Birkland's (1997) seminal work on disasters and agenda setting stresses that disasters represent *potential* focusing events, meaning a number of variables, many of which are seemingly unrelated to the event itself, determine the outcome of a post-event policy debate. Problem definition is particularly important. Problem definition assigns meaning to disaster. It communicates the scale and scope of a disaster, describes the population impacted by the event, identifies one or a handful of causal factors that led to the event, and even presents various solutions that can be used to help prevent a similar event from occurring in the future (Rochefort and Cobb 1994; Stone 2002; McBeth et al. 2007). Disasters, in other words, are socially constructed. Roberts (2013) summarized this process writing:

> Congress, disaster managers, presidents, and the media inadvertently shape what counts as a disaster and how much responsibility the federal government has in addressing it. This process of social construction occurs while various actors pursue their own interest, whether winning reelections, making promises to voters, managing organizations, reporting the news, or preparing for disasters. (p. 176)

Proponents of policy change need to use the problem definition process to, first, demonstrate that government was somehow negligent in its responsibility to protect against a particular hazard and, second, convince others that policy change is needed (Birkland 1997; Nohrstedt 2005).

Problem definition helps mobilize organized interests to support policy change. Proponents of change use these narratives to recruit previously disinterested groups who may not have been impacted by the disaster, but who could come to see the event as pertinent to their work and lives (Schattschneider 1960; Pralle 2006). Widespread mobilization is especially important in disaster domains. Unlike many other areas of policymaking, public risk domains, which encompass an array of man-made (e.g., technological accidents, terrorism) and naturally occurring (e.g., earthquakes, hurricanes, aviation disasters, oil spills) disasters, are said to lack an organized public (Huber 1986; May and Koski 2013). Very few interest groups actively lobby for things like earthquake preparedness programs or flood mitigation policies. Instead, disaster policy tends to be dominated by experts and technocrats whose primary source of influence is information and knowledge, as opposed to money and campaign donations. Disaster policy therefore lacks the salience of other, more contested areas of policymaking, like health care, education, or economic policy (May 1991; May and Birkland 1994; May and Koski 2013). In turn, proponents of widespread change need to capitalize on the fear and anger engendered by disaster and cobble together a coalition capable of upending the status quo and creating substantive policy change. When it comes to post-disaster mobilization, time is obviously of the essence, as this uptick in salience will begin to wane once the media stops covering the event (Birkland 1997).

Meanwhile, opposing groups work to communicate narratives that counter these pro-policy change definitions in hopes that they can block their competitors from accessing the government agenda (Cobb and Ross 1997). Those seeking to prevent policy change often have the distinct advantage of representing status quo, meaning they somehow benefit from existing policy arrangements (Baumgartner and Jones 1993). In turn, they usually have preexisting and longstanding connections to policy venues with jurisdiction over the issue. In fact, groups seeking policy change often need to shift the issue to an entirely new venue, as existing venues are rarely receptive to narratives challenging the status quo (Pralle 2006).

Disasters are heavily politicized but this does not mean the objective features (e.g. number of deaths, economic impact, etc.) of an event are totally irrelevant. In fact, some events are so dramatic that change is almost unavoidable. The September 11, 2001 terrorist attacks are one of the best examples of this phenomenon. September 11 opened policy windows across a variety of policy domains, including transportation, public health, national security, law enforcement, and others (May et al. 2011; Avery 2004; Birkland 2004). There was ample opportunity to capitalize on this particular event and promote policy change across a variety of different policy areas, including those that, at least at first glance, were only loosely related to the incident itself. However, these types of events are rare and few disasters trigger such widespread mobilization. Indeed, most disasters evoke little more than "thoughts and prayers" from government officials, let alone a comprehensive policy response.

Finally, it is important to note that policy change does not always reduce risk. Policymakers are susceptible to deriving the wrong types of lessons from disaster and adopting laws that fail to mitigate existing vulnerabilities. What is more, many of the lessons learned after disaster are not entirely novel, but are instead ideas that have been circulating policy communities for years (Birkland 2004). Disaster provides an opportunity for organized interests to attach their pet projects to a pressing problem. Success, it seems, can only occur if and when policymakers are ready to explicitly consider the viability of existing policies and programs, as opposed to exploiting a disaster as an opportunity to score political points (Birkland 2006).

6.2 Myopic Voting and Disaster Preparedness

When it comes to emergency management, legislators are said to be reactive, meaning they tend to overinvest in policies that help communities recover from disaster but devote far fewer resources toward programs that aim to prepare for, mitigate, and, in some instances, prevent disaster. Various studies have demonstrated an enormous gap between disaster relief and preparedness spending (Mileti 1999; Healy and Malhotra 2009; Sainz-Santamaria and Anderson 2013). One of the more recent studies estimates that between 1985 and 2008 the U.S. government spent nearly $82 billion on relief but a mere $7.5 billion on preparedness (Sainz-Santamaria and Anderson 2013).

This spending pattern is perplexing given that preparedness has been shown to save both lives and money. Rose et al. (2007) estimate that every $1 in preparedness spending offsets roughly $4 in relief spending. Healy and Malhotra (2009) indicate that every $1 spent on preparedness results in upwards of $7 in immediate savings but close to $15 in future damage reductions. Aside from saving money, preparedness also saves lives. Preparedness programs, such as revising building codes, prohibiting construction in high-risk areas, and reinforcing vulnerable structures, have been shown to protect citizens by helping to shield them from harm's way (Godschalk et al. 2009).

Disparities in relief versus preparedness spending have been attributed to a number of factors. The emphasis on recovery is partially an outgrowth of the way in which individuals conceptualize risk. Faced with an innumerable number of pressing agenda items, policymakers rarely concern themselves with protecting against low probability, high consequence events, many of which may or may not occur until months if not years in the future (Burby and May 1998; May and Koski 2013). This finding echoes a rich body of psychology literature documenting the propensity of individuals to disregard future benefits in lieu of immediate gratification (Quoidbach et al. 2013). Many individuals are too busy to concern themselves with temporally remote problems that may or may not occur at some yet-to-be-determined point in the future.

The literature on myopic voting provides yet another explanation of this spending paradox: Electoral politics. It builds from the assumption that, although legislators need to account consider a myriad of factors (e.g., party affiliation, personal values and goals, the priorities of their party) when deciding how to vote, constituency concerns are often weighted above all else (Kousser et al. 2007). Specifically, unless an elected official maintains a healthy relationship with the voters in their district, they risk losing their job.

Voters are said to keep a running tally of incumbent performance. Over the course of an incumbent's term, voters closely monitor the issues that most directly impact their lives and, when it comes time to vote, make a determination as to whether their lives have improved over the last 2–6 years. In this respect, voters are myopic. One of the clearest illustrations of myopic voting is the relationship between election results and economic performance. A poor economy has been shown to raise the specter of voter backlash. Citizens are, for obvious reasons, quite sensitive to their financial well-being and look to punish elected officials for failing to ensure a healthy economy (Lewis-Beck 1990).

Disaster provides an even more interesting context for studying myopic voting. First, unlike the economy, natural hazards and disasters are generally assumed to fall outside the boundaries of policymaker control. While government plays an important role in guiding preparedness and response activities, elected officials can do little to prevent tragedy. This stands in stark contrast to economic health, which many voters believe is directly tied to policy decisions. Second, and as noted above, disaster policymaking sets up a rather convenient natural experiment. It allows scholars to assess voter and legislator behavior both before and after disaster. Taken further, they can assess the electoral benefits of investing in preparedness versus relief programs.

Not surprisingly, then, a great deal of the literature on myopic voting has focused on emergency management policy. Much like a poor economy, hazards and disasters, including droughts, bad weather, and even shark attacks, can be deleterious to an incumbent's reelection prospects (Achen and Bartels 2004, 2012, 2016; Gasper and Reeves 2011). Voters perceive themselves as being worse off in the aftermath of disaster and—rightfully or wrongfully—blame elected officials. This does not mean politicians sit idly and allow themselves to take the brunt of voter criticism. The policy change literature stresses that elected officials and other actors (e.g., interest groups, the media, experts) work diligently to frame and define disasters in ways that advance their political goals (Birkland 1997).

Elected officials risk punishment in the next election if they fail to attend to the concerns of their constituents (Achen and Bartles 2004, 2016; Gasper and Reeves 2011; Arceneux and Stein 2006). But disaster need not be a death knell for the incumbent politician. On the contrary, disaster can represent an opportunity, as voters often reward incumbents who secure ample relief money (Gasper and Reeves 2011). In fact, something as simple as a disaster declaration has been shown to result in a vote share twenty-times greater than the share lost after disaster (Reeves 2011). In this respect, the ability to distribute disaster relief money positions incumbents to benefit from disaster (Chen 2013; Healy and Malhotra 2010).

Because it allows elected officials to distribute resources back to their district, recovery policy is obviously a highly salient policy type (Berke and Beatley 1992; May and Birkland 1994; Burby and May 1998). From a voter perspective, this salience is magnified by the fact that recovery programs relieve the suffering caused by disaster, be it through repairing homes or rebuilding critical infrastructure. Preparedness, on the other hand, is far less salient, despite the above described benefits of investing in pre-event activities. Relative to relief policy, candidates who support preparedness policy enjoy a much smaller vote share in the next election (Healy and Malhotra 2009). And because it lacks the obvious observability of relief policy, voters are generally disinterested in preparedness.

Electoral politics thus creates a perverse incentive structure wherein elected officials are rewarded for responding to, as opposed to mitigating and preparing for, disaster. Regrettably, the literature on myopic voting provides few insights into how policymakers can overcome voter apathy toward preparedness. Gerber and Neely (2005) found that individuals will, on occasion, support preparedness programs when they are presented with adequate information on a particular risk. What is more, Healy and Malhotra (2009) suggest targeted investments in preparedness at a community or even household level can increase voter interest in preparedness policy, but they concede that this research is underdeveloped. Future work should revisit the viability of these and other strategies.

6.3 Disaster Management, Leadership, and Resilience

Political scientists have also contributed to the larger, interdisciplinary field of disaster management. This work encompasses virtually every step in the disaster management cycle, although this section emphasizes research on the management of public sector agencies during times of crisis (Boin et al. 2006; Wise 2006) as well as research on the various strategies for improving disaster recovery and resilience (Aldrich 2012; Ross 2015; Kapuco et al. 2014).

Government capacity, which is broadly defined as "the ability of government to respond effectively to change, make decisions efficiently and responsibly, and manage conflict" (Bowman and Kearney 2014, p. 3), is an important determinant of how well a community will navigate an unexpected event, including disaster. Other factors, such as the size of the disaster, health of the economy, and even sociodemographics, have also been shown to influence emergency management, although political scientists have, for obvious reasons, tended to emphasize role of government (Aldrich 2012).

The twenty-first century ushered in an important shift in the organization and administration of emergency management agencies. Many industrialized nations, and especially the U.S., have expanded the national government's role in disaster management. Emergency management was once seen as squarely the province of subnational governments, which were assumed to be better equipped to rapidly respond to crisis. While subnational units remain important drivers of emergency management policy, the attacks of September 11, 2001 prompted policymakers in the U.S. (and later throughout Europe) to revisit this arrangement (Gerber 2007; Roberts 2013). In the wake of September 11, the U.S. adopted an "all hazards" approach to disaster management, which mandated federal agencies protect against an array of naturally occurring and man-made hazards, including terrorism, hurricanes, disease outbreaks, earthquakes, and others (May et al. 2011). This change codified a much larger role for the national government in emergency response. More importantly, it permeated the collective consciousness of the general public. More than ever before, citizens expect national agencies, including the Federal Emergency Management Agency (FEMA), to take the lead during times of crisis (Roberts 2013).

Many European countries have adopted a similar approach to hazard management (Djalali et al. 2014). France, for example, moved away from a disaster-specific system and adopted a complex risk approach, which aims to prepare the country for an array of multifaceted and often cascading hazards (Renda-Tenali and Mancebo 2009). Germany adopted a similar approach in 2004, consolidating all of its emergency management offices under a single agency, the Federal Office of Civil Protection and Disaster Assistance (Connolly 2009).

Of course, agency structure alone does not determine how well a government will respond to disaster. Individual behavior—within emergency management organizations, government, and even at a community level—is equally important. Political scientists have long emphasized the importance of leadership. Boin et al.'s (2006) *The Politics of Crisis Management: Public Leadership Under Pressure* underscores five common difficulties leaders face during times of crisis: (1) *sense making*, which describes the ability of policymakers to identify and interpret signs implying the possibility of an emerging crisis; (2) *decision making and coordinating implementation*, which refers to the overseeing and coordination of crisis response activities; (3) *meaning making*, which describes the shaping of public understanding of crisis; (4) *accounting and ending*, which describes actions taken to achieve closure and allow society to move on; and (5) *learning*, which describes the process through which lessons are drawn from a crisis. Suffice it to say, the modern crisis manager has to juggle a variety of distinctive responsibilities, each of which is complicated by the enormous complexity and uncertainty associated with contemporary crises.

The last two decades have also seen a marked uptick in interest in resilience, which describes "the capacity of a social system (e.g., an organization, city, or society) to proactively adapt to and recover from disturbances that are perceived within the system to fall outside the range of normal and expected disturbances" (Boin et al. 2010, p. 9). Political scientists trace to term to Wildavsky's (1988) seminal book, *Searching for Safety*, which introduces two competing patterns for managing uncertainty. The first pattern, the anticipatory approach, sees policymakers try to anticipate threats before they emerge in order to prepare for and, ideally, prevent them. The second pattern, the resilience approach, works to ensure adaptability and flexibility in the face of extreme events, allowing society to quickly "bounce back" from disaster (p. 77). Wildavsky ultimately argues that while anticipation may seem desirable, it is impossible to predict each and every crisis. As such, resilience represents the most logical approach to dealing with low probability, high consequence events.

It goes without saying that organizations and institutions play an important role in determining how quickly a community will bounce back from disaster. How government chooses to organize its resources is inextricably linked to resilience and sound disaster management (Mileti 1999). But perhaps the most important (and admittedly surprising) contribution of the thriving body of literature on resilience is the fact that it often *deemphasizes* the importance of government. Resilience is thought to transcend the state. Instead it involves factors that seemingly fall outside the immediate purview of government control. (Tierney 2014; Aldrich 2012).

Aldrich (2012), for example, suggests social capital is the single most important determinant of resilience. His analysis of disaster response in Tokyo after the 1923 earthquake, Kobe following the 1995 earthquake, Tamil Nadu after the 2004 Indian Ocean Tsunami, and New Orleans after Hurricane Katrina shows social networks and interpersonal connections (linking social capital) are best suited to distribute precious resources and guide recovery efforts in the wake of disaster. Aldrich's model obviously stands in stark contrast to the typical disaster management process utilized by the U.S. government, which has increasingly relied on top-down measures emanating from the national government (Roberts 2013). Large-scale infrastructure projects and national guard deployments fail to address the important community level factors that often determine local resiliency. Instead, Aldrich (2012) advocates for hyper-localized programs that build social ties among residents. Investments in things like community centers or block parties can go a long way toward cultivating neighborhood partnerships that can be activated during times of crisis. Far more than a buzzword, the concept of resilience thus raises important questions about the efficacy of top-down and hierarchical emergency management programs.

6.4 Future Directions

The three literatures surveyed in this chapter provide an admirably comprehensive depiction of the political dynamics of emergency management. Disaster creates an opportunity for policy change, assuming interest groups and politicians are able to stoke public concern and convince voters that the event is symbolic of government failure. Policy change, even after disaster, is never guaranteed, although elected officials routinely find ways to capitalize on these events and distribute resources back to their district. The same cannot be said about preparedness policy, which is often overlooked by politicians and voters alike. Moreover, government spending is not the only determinant of how quickly a community will bounce-back from disaster. Connections forged at the local level are equally if not more important to ensuring resilience, a finding that no doubt calls into question the recent movement to centralize important emergency management functions within the national government.

Despite these important contributions, there are a number of obvious gaps in the political science literature on hazards and disasters. Most glaringly, all three literatures—and especially the literatures on policy change and myopic voting—say relatively little about disaster preparedness, save underscoring the fact that elected officials are reluctant to invest in these types of programs. For example, the policy change literature has focused almost exclusively on policymaking after disaster. This relatively narrow conceptualization of disaster policy overlooks those cases, however rare they may be, when policy is created in anticipation of an emergent hazard, such as pandemic influenza or even coastal flooding. Policy scholars have begun to address this shortcoming (DeLeo 2010, 2015, 2018), but the subfield's understanding of preparedness policymaking remains noticeably underdeveloped.

To this end, policy scholars should consider the possibility that focusing events are not the only mechanism through which hazards and disasters reveal themselves to policymakers. Kingdon (2003) notes indicators, which, as noted above, refer to numeric measures and statistics, constitute yet another element of the problem stream. Research has already established that many public health problems, including Ebola and pandemic influenza, reveal themselves gradually and across time through a slow accumulation of indicators, namely disease cases and deaths (Birkland 2006; DeLeo 2018). The gradual accumulation of indicators implies that a much larger disease outbreak is on the horizon, thus allowing policymakers to fashion legislation and allocate resources to prepare for a looming event. This pattern obviously differs from policy sequence evidenced in the aftermath of a focusing event, but is no less important to emergency management and preparedness.

In additional to emerging diseases, a host of other "slow onset" disasters are likely revealed through indicators, including droughts, wildfires, and the various hazards associated with climate change. To what extent does the policymaking pattern evidenced in these cases differ from post-event policymaking? What types of narrative strategies do policymakers use to define problems that have yet to occur? How do policymakers fashion legislation in anticipation of disaster? Again, while research has begun to address some of these and other questions, policy scholars have largely overlooked the political dynamics of pre-event and preparedness policymaking.

The literature on myopic voting is marked by similar deficiencies. While it is well established that voters tend to reward politicians for supporting disaster relief, relatively little research has considered potential strategies for overcoming myopic voting. This shortcoming is partially an outgrowth of the methodologies used in these studies, which focus primarily on measuring election results relative to district-level spending. Healy and Malhotra (2009) suggest a different approach, writing: "Future scholarship could use surveys, as well as lab and field experiments, to determine the extent to which voter decisions can be influenced by government efforts at increasing the salience of issues and policies in areas such as disaster preparedness" (p. 403).

Surveys or even qualitative research designs could provide important insights into the decision nexus of elected officials. Voters are surely not the only factor influencing legislator decision making. For example, to what extent are legislator decisions influenced by expert opinion? To what extent do voter and policymaker preferences for preparedness vary geographically? For example, are individuals from coastal states, many of which now suffer from chronic flooding, more likely to support preparedness projects? And, what, if anything, can be done to help overcome myopic voting and reactive decision making? Are there any messaging strategies, for example, that organized interests can use to increase policymaker interest in preparedness? Is there an uptick in voter interest in preparedness in the weeks and months following disaster?

Developing a more comprehensive understanding of when and under what conditions government prepares for disaster will help advance extant political science theory by allowing scholars to investigate important concepts (e.g., policy change and voter behavior) in a distinctive temporal context, namely the months or weeks leading up to disaster. Equally important, these findings promise to inform the advocacy strategies of interest groups and experts working in a variety of policy domains. For example, the last decade has seen an uptick in interest in climate change adaptation, particularly in coastal communities. Adaptation will that require politicians grapple with a slew of temporally remote problems, even in the face of voter confusion and, at times, disinterest. Understanding how these types of threats can be better communicated to policymakers will be critical to ensuring our collective security.

The global proliferation of all hazards preparedness also deserves closer examination. Curiously, scholars have said relatively little about the various factors that helped facilitate the international diffusion of this distinctive approach to emergency management, save acknowledging the domestic and global significance of September 11. To what extent are the all hazards regimes in Europe similar to the model used in the U.S.? How are they different? More broadly, does the proliferation of an all hazards approach suggest a convergence of global emergency management systems or does it remain a highly localized process? In short, the spread of all hazards management raise a number of fascinating applied and conceptual questions, particularly in light of recent backlash against globalization and the uptick of nationalist sentiments in many industrialized democracies.

6.5 Conclusion

There exists a thriving body of political science literature dedicated to the study of risk, hazards, disasters, and crises. This chapter specifically examined three distinct sub-streams of research (the literatures on policy change, myopic voting, and disaster management) but, as noted above, this is only a sampling of the political science research on risk, hazards, and disasters. Political scientists have proven instrumental in highlighting both the strengths and, perhaps more importantly, the limitations of government in disaster situations. Electoral concerns, interest group competition, and discursive conflict can derail even the most well-intentioned disaster mitigation programs. By highlighting these pitfalls and, at times, suggesting potential strategies for overcoming them, political scientists have helped to inform our shared understanding of hazard and disaster management. Disaster have been and always will be political events. As such, it is safe to say political scientists will continue to weigh-in on these debates for many years to come.

References

Achen, Christopher H., and Larry M. Bartels. 2004. Blind retrospection: Electoral responses to drought, flu, and shark attacks. https://www.ethz.ch/content/dam/ethz/special-interest/gess/cis/international-relationsdam/Teaching/pwgrundlagenopenaccess/Weitere/AchenBartels.pdf. Accessed 5 May 2018.

———. 2012. Blind retrospection: Why shark attacks are bad for democracy. Center for the Study of Democratic Institutions, Vanderbilt University. https://www.vanderbilt.edu/csdi/research/CSDI_WP_05-2013.pdf.

———. 2016. *Democracy for realists: Why elections do not produce responsive government*. Princeton: Princeton University Press.

Aldrich, Daniel P. 2012. *Building resilience: Social capital in post-disaster recovery*. Chicago: University of Chicago Press.

Anderson, Christopher J. 2000. Economic voting and political context: A comparative perspective. *Electoral Studies* 19: 151–170.

Anderson, James. 2010. *Public policymaking*. 7th ed. Boston: Cengage.

Arceneux, Kevin, and Robert M. Stein. 2006. Who is held responsible when disaster strikes? The attribution of responsibility for a natural disaster in an urban election. *Journal of Urban Affairs* 28: 43–53.

Avery, George. 2004. Bioterrorism, fear, and public health reform: Matching a policy solution to the wrong window. *Public Administration Review* 64: 275–288.

Baumgartner, Frank R., and Brian D. Jones. 1993. *Agendas and instability in American politics*. Chicago: University of Chicago Press.

Berke, Philip R., and Timothy Beatley. 1992. *Planning for earthquakes: Risks, politics, and policy*. Baltimore: The Johns Hopkins University Press.

Birkland, Thomas A. 1997. *After disaster: Agenda setting, public policy, and focusing events*. Washington, DC: Georgetown University Press.

———. 2004. The world changed today: Agenda-setting and policy change in the wake of the September 11 terrorist attacks. *Review of Policy Research* 21: 179–200.

———. 2006. *Lessons of disaster: Policy change after catastrophic events*. Washington, DC: Georgetown University Press.

———. 2010. Federal disaster policy: Learning, priorities, and prospects for resilience. In *Designing resilience: Preparing for extreme events*, ed. Louise K. Comfort, Arjen Boin, and Chris C. Demchak, 106–128. Pittsburgh: University of Pittsburgh Press.

Boin, Arjen, Paul t'Hart, Eric Stern, and Sundelius Bengt. 2006. *The politics of crisis management: Public leadership under pressure*. Cambridge: Cambridge University Press.

Boin, Arjen, Louise K. Comfort, and Chris C. Demchak. 2010. The rise of resilience. In *Designing resilience: Preparing for extreme events*, ed. Louise K. Comfort, Arjen Boin, and Chris C. Demchak, 1–12. Pittsburgh: University of Pittsburgh Press.

Bowman, Ann O'.M., and Richard C. Kearney. 2014. *State and local government: The essentials*. 6th ed. Boston: Cengage.

Burby, Raymond, and Peter J. May. 1998. Intergovernmental environmental planning: Addressing the commitment conundrum. *Journal of Environmental Planning and Management* 41: 95–110.

Chen, Jowei. 2013. Voter partisanship and the effect of distributive spending on political participation. *American Journal of Political Science* 57: 200–217.

Cimellaro, Gian Paolo. 2016. *Urban resilience for emergency response and recovery: Fundamental concepts and applications*. Cham: Springer.
Cobb, Roger W., and Mark H. Ross. 1997. *Cultural strategies of agenda denial: Avoidance, attack, and redefinition*. Lawrence: University of Kansas Press.
Comfort, Louise K. 2005. Risk, security, and disaster management. *Annual Review of Political Science* 8: 335–356.
Connolly, Maureen. 2009. Emergency management in the federal republic of Germany: Preserving its critical Infrastructures from hazardous natural events and terrorist acts. FEMA Emergency Management Institute. Comparative Emergency Management. Chapter 10. Available at: https://training.fema.gov/hiedu/aemrc/booksdownload/compemmgmtbookproject/.
DeLeo, Rob A. 2010. Anticipatory-conjectural policy problems: A case study of avian influenza. *Risk, Hazards, & Crisis in Public Policy* 1: 147–184.
———. 2015. *Anticipatory policymaking: When government acts to prevent problems and why it is so difficult*. New York: Routledge.
———. 2018. Indicators, agendas, and streams: Analysing the politics of preparedness. *Policy & Politics* 46: 27–45.
Djalali, Ahmadreza, Francesco Della Corte, Marco Foletti, Luca Ragazzoni, Alba Ripoll Gallardo, Olivera Lupescu, Chris Arculeo, Götz von Arnim, Tom Friedl, Michael Ashkenazi, Philipp Fischer, Boris Hreckovski, Amir Khorram-Manesh, Radko Komadina, Konstanze Lechner, Cristina Patru, Frederick M. Burkle Jr, and Pier Luigi Ingrassia. 2014. Art of disaster preparedness in European Union: A survey on the health systems. *PLOS Currents Disasters* Dec. 17.
Dynes, Russell R. 2000. The dialogue between Voltaire and Rousseau on the Lisbon earthquake: The emergence of a social science view. *International Journal of Mass Emergencies and Disasters* 18: 97–115.
Fiorina, Morris P. 1974. *Representatives, roll calls, and constituencies*. Lexington: Lexington Books.
Fiorina, Morris P. 1981. *Retrospective voting in American national elections*. New Haven, Connecticut: Yale University Press.
Gasper, John T., and Andrew Reeves. 2011. Make it rain? Retrospection and the attentive electorate in the context of natural disasters. *American Journal of Political Science* 55: 340–355.
Gerber, Brian J. 2007. Disaster management in the United States: Examining key political and policy challenges. *The Policy Studies Journal* 35: 227–238.
Gerber, Brian J., and Grant W. Neeley. 2005. Perceived risk and citizen preferences for governmental management of routine hazards. *Policy Studies Journal* 33: 395–418.
Godschalk, David, Adam Rose, Elliot Mittler, Keith Porter, and Carol Taylor West. 2009. Estimating the value of foresight: Aggregate analysis of natural hazard mitigation benefits and costs. *Journal of Environmental Planning and Management* 52: 739–756.
Healy, Andrew, and Neil Malhotra. 2009. Myopic voters and natural disaster policy. *American Political Science Review* 103: 387–406.
———. 2010. Random events, economic losses, and retrospective voting: Implications for democratic competence. *Quarterly Journal of Political Science* 5: 193–208.
———. 2013. Retrospective voting reconsidered. *Annual Review of Political Science* 16: 285–306.
Huber, Peter W. 1986. *The Bhopalization of American tort law*, Hazards: Technology and Fairness, 89–110. Washington, DC: National Academy Press.
Islam, Tanveer, and Jeffrey Ryan. 2016. *Hazard mitigation in emergency management*. Waltham: Elsevier.
Jasanoff, Sheila. 2010. Beyond calculation: A democratic response to risk. In *Disaster and the politics of intervention*, ed. Andrew Lakoff, 14–41. New York: Columbia University Press.
Kapuco, Naim, Christopher V. Hawkins, and Fernando I. Rivera. 2014. *Disaster resiliency: Interdisciplinary perspectives*. London: Routledge.
Kingdon, John W. 2003. *Agendas, alternatives, and public policies*. 2nd ed. New York: Addison-Wesley Educational Publishers.
Kousser, Thad, Jeffrey B. Lewis, and Seth E. Masket. 2007. Ideological adaptation? The survival instinct of threatened legislators. *The Journal of Politics* 69: 828–843.

Lewis-Beck, Michael S. 1990. *Economics and elections: The major Western democracies*. Michigan: Michigan University Press.
Lindell, Michael K., Carla Prater, and Ronald W. Perry. 2006. *Introduction to emergency management*. New York: Wiley.
May, Peter J. 1991. Addressing public risks: Federal earthquake policy design. *Journal of Policy Analysis and Management* 10: 263–285.
May, Peter J., and Thomas A. Birkland. 1994. Earthquake risk reduction: An examination of local regulatory efforts. *Environmental Management* 18: 923–937.
May, Peter J., and Chris Koski. 2013. Addressing public risks: Extreme events and critical infrastructures. *Review of Policy Research* 30: 139–159.
May, Peter J., Ashley E. Jochim, and Joshua Sapotichne. 2011. Constructing homeland security: An anemic regime. *Policy Studies Journal* 39: 285–307.
McBeth, Mark K., Elizabeth A. Shanahan, Ruth J. Arnell, and Paul L. Hathaway. 2007. The intersection of narrative policy analysis and policy change theory. *Policy Studies Journal* 35: 87–108.
Mileti, Dennis. 1999. *Disasters by design: A reassessment of natural hazards in the United States*. Washington, DC: Joseph Henry Press.
Nohrstedt, Daniel. 2005. External shocks and policy change: Three-Mile Island and Swedish nuclear energy policy. *Journal of European Public Policy* 12: 1041–1059.
———. 2008. The politics of crisis policymaking: Chernobyl and Swedish nuclear energy policy. *Policy Studies Journal* 36: 257–278.
Parsons, Wayne. 1995. *Public policy: An introduction to the theory and practice of policy analysis*. Cheltenham: Edward Elgar.
Pralle, Sarah B. 2006. *Branching out, digging in: environmental advocacy and agenda setting*. Washington, DC: Georgetown University Press.
Quoidbach, Jordi, Daniel T. Gilbert, and Timothy D. Wilson. 2013. The end of history illusion. *Science* 339: 96–98.
Reeves, Andrew. 2011. Political disaster: Unilateral powers, electoral incentives, and presidential disaster declarations. *The Journal of Politics* 73: 1142–1151.
Renda-Tenali, Irmak, and François Mancebo. 2009. French emergency management system: Moving toward an integrated risk management policy. Comparative Emergency Management. https://training.fema.gov/hiedu/aemrc/booksdownload/compemmgmtbookproject/. Accessed 5 May 2018.
Roberts, Patrick S. 2010. Private choices, public harms: The evolutions of national disaster organizations in the United States. In *Disaster and the politics of intervention*, ed. Andrew Lakoff, 42–69. New York: Columbia University Press.
———. 2013. *Disasters and the American state: How politicians, bureaucrats, and the public prepare for the unexpected*. Cambridge: Cambridge University Press.
Rochefort, David A., and Roger W. Cobb. 1994. Problem definition: An emerging perspective. In *The politics of problem definition: Shaping the policy agenda*, ed. David Rochefort and Roger W. Cobb, 1–31. Kansas: University of Kansas Press.
Rose, Adam, Keith Porter, Nicole Dash, Jawhar Bouabid, Charles Huyck, John Whitehead, Douglass Shaw, Ronald Eguchi, Craig Taylor, McLane Thomas, L. Thomas Tobin, Philip T. Ganderton, David Godschalk, Anna S. Kiremidijian, Kathleen Tierney, and Carol Taylor West. 2007. Benefit-cost analysis of FEMA hazard mitigation grants. *Natural Hazards Review* 8: 97–111.
Ross, Ashley D. 2015. *Local disaster resilience: Administrative and political perspectives*. New York: Routledge.
Sabatier, Paul A. 1988. An advocacy coalition framework of policy change and the role of policy-oriented learning therein. *Policy Sciences* 21: 129–168.
Sabatier, Paul, Hank Jenkins-Smith. 1999. The advocacy coalition framework: An assessment. Theories of the policy process. Paul Sabatier 117–166. Boulder: Westview Press.

Sabatier, Paul A., and Christopher C. Weible. 2007. The advocacy coalition framework: Innovations and clarifications. In *Theories of the policy process*, ed. Paul Sabatier, 189–122. Boulder: Westview Press.
Sainz-Santamaria, Jamie, and Sarah E. Anderson. 2013. The electoral politics of disaster preparedness. *Risks, Hazards & Crisis in Public Policy* 4: 234–249.
Scanlon, T. Joseph. 1988. Disaster's little known pioneer: Canada's Samuel Henry Prince. *International Journal of Mass Emergencies and Disasters* 6: 213–232.
Schattschneider, Elmer E. 1960. *The semisovereign people: A realist's view of Democracy in America*. Hinsdale: Dryden Press.
Stone, Deborah. 2002. *Policy paradox: The art of political decision making*. New York: W.W. Norton.
Stone, Diane A. 2008. Global public policy, transnational policy communities, and their networks. *Policy Studies Journal* 36: 19–38.
Tierney, Kathleen. 2014. *The social roots of risk: Producing disasters, promoting resilience*. Stanford: Stanford Business Books.
Wildavsky, Aaron. 1988. *Searching for safety*. New Brunswick: Transaction Books.
Wise, Charles E. 2006. Organizing for homeland security after Katrina: Is adaptive management what's missing? *Public Administration Review* 66: 302–318.
Zahariadis, Nikos. 2014. Ambiguity and multiple streams. In *Theories of the policy process*, ed. Paul Sabatier and Chris Weible, 3rd ed., 25–58. Boulder: Westview Press.

Chapter 7
You Can't go Home Again: On the Conceptualization of Disasters in Ancient Greek Tragedy

Jan Helge Solbakk

Tragedies don't mean anything.
They do something.

(Bryan Doerries 2015)

Victory over an enemy force can be interpreted as a licence to rape, with women's bodies seen as the spoils of war.

(Amnesty International 2004)

Abstract The ancient Greek tragedy represents one of the earliest and most dramatic ways of dealing with the phenomenon of disaster in literature. This ancient literary form will be used as a kind of template in the search for recurrent forms of moral attitudes and behaviour that seem to follow almost universally in the wake of war and armed conflicts. First, the focus will be on war veterans' experiences and narratives of going home again, i.e. of returning from combat back to a life called 'normal'. These are experiences that render both the victorious and the defeated representatives of such conflicts extremely vulnerable and susceptible to harm, as dramatically displayed in Sophocles' tragedy *Ajax*. Second, Euripides' plays *Andromache*, *Hecuba and The Trojan women* will be made use of. In these plays, unvarnished versions of the horrors women and children are subjected to as a consequence of war are dramatically displayed. To demonstrate the moral timelessness and didactic potentials of these ancient representations, the fate of war veterans, women and children in the wake of modern wars and armed conflicts will then be displayed through Bryan Doerries' narrative, *Theater of war*, of exposing US war veterans to Sophocles play *Ajax*, and through the narratives of 50 Syrian women, all refugees living in Aman, Jordan because of the civil war in Syria, of staging Euripides' play *The Trojan women*.

J. H. Solbakk (✉)
Centre for Medical Ethics, Institute of Health and Society, Faculty of Medicine, University of Oslo, Oslo, Norway
e-mail: j.h.solbakk@medisin.uio.no

D. P. O'Mathúna et al. (eds.), *Disasters: Core Concepts and Ethical Theories*, Advancing Global Bioethics 11, https://doi.org/10.1007/978-3-319-92722-0_7

Keywords Catharsis · Error · Fate · Guilt · Honour · Hamartia · Misery · Mistake · Revenge · Tragic conflicts

7.1 Introduction

From the very start of drafting this chapter two lines in Thomas Wolfe's magnificent novel, *You can't go home again*, have been resounding in my mind. The lines occur in the last chapter of Book Six of the novel, a chapter entitled 'The Way of No Return', and they run like this: "He was 'out'. And, being 'out', he began to see another way, the way that lay before him. He saw now that you can't go home again – not ever" (Wolfe 1934, 600). This quotation may serve as an epitaph to one of the earliest and most dramatic ways of dealing with the phenomenon of disaster in literature; i.e. the ancient Greek tragedy. There are two reasons for making use of the literary form of the ancient Greek tragedy with disasters. The first reason is that in ancient Greek tragedy the ethical dimensions of disaster are at the centre of the playwright's attention. Second, in the ancient Greek tragedy a word often used as a synonym for disaster, i.e. *catastrophe* (Gr: **καταστροφή**), plays a lead role. The word *καταστροφή* means 'an overturning; a sudden end' and derives from *katastrephein* – 'to overturn, turn down, trample on; to come to an end'-, *katá* means 'down, against' and *strephein* means 'turn'. It was used to denote the final part of the play, i.e. the part where the final destiny of the main characters are unraveled, and notably very often – although not always – in the form of an unexpected fatal turn from bliss to misery. Extension of the word catastrophe to mean 'sudden disaster' is first recorded in 1748.[1]

In this chapter I aim at addressing the ethical dimensions of disaster using this ancient literary form as a kind of template or paradigm in the search for recurrent patterns of attitudes and behavior that come to life in the wake of disasters caused by humans (and gods). This implies that the handling of *natural* disasters in literature will fall outside the scope of this chapter. It should be noted here, however, that the distinction between man-made and natural disasters is a modern one, in the sense that such a differentiation was not reflected in the word from the very start of its use. This is evident already from the etymology of the word 'disaster'. The English word *disaster* derives from the Middle French *désastre* and that word from Old Italian *disastro* (ill-starred), which again comes from the Greek pejorative prefix *dys*– (bad; Gr: δυσ-) + *astēr* (star; Gr: ἀστήρ). So literally speaking disaster means "bad star" and indicates the understanding of such calamities all being caused by an unfavorable position of a planet.[2] Another possible limitation follows from the selection of the ancient Greek tragedy as the literary point of departure, since this favors a *narrative* approach instead of a focus on conceptual issues. So in short, what this chapter aims at is an account of human disasters in literature using the

[1] http://www.etymonline.com/index.php?term=catastrophe.

[2] http://www.etymonline.com/index.php?term=disaster.

literary form of ancient Greek tragedy as a template to identify recurrent forms of moral injury and transgression following in the wake of such upheavals.

7.2 On the Literary Form and Morality of the Ancient Greek Tragedy

Tragedies are not easily amenable to *theoretical* and *methodological* systematisation and categorisation (Gellrich 1988, 10). This is already evidenced in Aristotle's famous account of this literary form in the *Poetics*, where emphasis is on representation, action and plot, not on conceptualization:

> Tragedy is a representation of a serious, complete action which has magnitude, in embellished speech, with each of its elements [used] separately in the [various] parts [of the play]; [represented] by people acting and not by narration; accomplishing by means of pity [*eleos*] and terror [*fobos*] the catharsis of such emotions.
> By 'embellished speech', I mean that which has rhythm and melody, i.e. song; by 'with its elements separately', I mean that some [parts of] are accomplished only by means of spoken verses, and others again by means of song. (Aristotle 1984, 49b23–31)

In order to get a grasp on what constitutes a tragedy Burian suggests to look for "story patterns" characteristic of tragedy, while at the same time renouncing the idea of *the paradigmatic story*. This brings him to what he calls the «starting-point of all story-telling», the notion of conflict:

> Tragic narrative patterns can usefully be classified by their characteristic conflicts, and something can be said in general about the kinds of conflicts that tragic plots seem to require. (Burian 1997, 181)

Burian operates with three qualifications of tragic conflicts, of which the first – *extremity* – is of particular relevance here. A characteristic feature of such conflicts, he says, is that possibilities of resolution in terms of "compromise" or "mediation" are *de facto* non-existing options. Whatever choice is made, it will by necessity lead to an extreme degree of misery and suffering (Burian 1997, 181). Kuhn in his account adds a moral dimension to the qualification of extremity, by introducing the notion of *guilt*: tragic suffering conceived of as the result of an inexplicable disproportion of guilt and misery (Kuhn 1941, 12). Also Nussbaum attributes importance to this dimension. According to her reading, in situations of tragic conflict, choice is under a *double* constraint: the absence of a "guilt-free course" amidst the necessity to choose (Nussbaum 1986, 34). In other words, the possibility of *abstaining* from making a choice is non-existent as is the possibility of making a choice not contaminated with guilt.[3] So whatever is the answer to the haunting question "What shall I do?" (Lattimore 1964, p. 29), the moral agent cannot escape making «une decision capitale, souvent mortelle, toujours irrevocable» (Rivier 1944, 33). Guilt in

[3] For such situations, see for example Aeschylus' play, *Libation-Bearers*, 924–927, Sophocles', *Oedipus at Colonos*, 988–994 and Euripides', *Electra*, 966–987.

situations of tragic conflict, however, cannot be fully understood without taking into account the role played by 'error' or 'mistake' – of *hamartia* – in conflicts of this kind. The word *hamartia* has a wide variety of meanings ranging from the purely epistemological 'mistake of fact', 'ignorance of fact', 'error of judgement', 'error due to inadequate knowledge of particular circumstances' and 'tragic error' to moralised forms of interpretation such as 'moral error', 'moral defect', 'moral flaw', 'moral mistake', 'defect of character', 'tragic error' and 'tragic flaw' (Stinton 1975; Østerud 1976; Sorabji 1980; Schütrumpf 1989; Solbakk 2004). It is important to keep in mind the plurality of meanings attributed to *hamartia* in tragedy since this implies that guilt in this context has to be interpreted within a context with both moral and epistemological connotations.

What is more important for our purposes is Aristotle's differentiation in *Poetics* 51a37-b33 of tragedy from history. The first of their distinguishing traits is that history narrates things that *have* happened, while tragedy relates to events or incidents that *may* happen. This, he says, is the reason why poetry, in particular tragic poetry, is more *philosophical* than history; it speaks of universals, while history is an account of particulars. "A universal", says Aristotle, "is the sort of thing that a certain kind of person may well say or do in accordance with probability or necessity – this is what poetry aims at, although it assigns names [to people]. A particular is what Alcibiades did or what he suffered" (Aristotle 1984, 51b8–12). This remark about the use of *historical* names in tragedies, and thereby about the representation of events that have actually taken place, is important, because it informs us that not everything in a tragedy is fictional. More important, however, is the explanation Aristotle gives for the poet's use of historical material. For tragic accounts to be trustworthy, they must be *possible*, and things which have happened, says Aristotle, are obviously possible. Consequently, by using events, names or things that have actually existed or taken place, as templates for giving shape to a tragic plot, the poet is free to invent for himself a whole that *may* have taken place (Aristotle, 53b23–27). Thereby, out of the creative reconfiguration of the historical and particular, emerge neither *imaginary* accounts nor wild *thought experiments* but accounts that are possible and at the same time of universal moral relevance and value (Solbakk 2006). The playwright Edward Albee has formulated this insight in a way I find particularly illuminating: "A play is fiction – and fiction is fact distilled into truth" (*New York Times* 18.09 1966).

7.3 On the Ancient Greek Tragedy as a Paradigmatic Case of Human Disaster

The kind of distilled truths that will be the subject of attention in the rest of this chapter originate from a group of ancient Greek tragedies that dramatize the aftermaths of war, i.e. the kind of conflict Heraclitus considers the starting point of everything: "War is the father and king of all, and has produced some as gods and some as men, and has made some slaves and some free" (Πόλεμος πάντων μὲν πατήρ ἐστι πάντων δὲ βασιλεύς, καὶ τοὺς μὲν θεοὺς ἔδειξε τοὺς δὲ ἀνθρώπους, τοὺς μὲν δούλους ἐποίησε τοὺς δὲ ἐλευθέρους).[4] More precisely the focus of attention will be on recurrent forms of moral attitudes and behavior that seem to follow almost universally in the wake of wars and armed conflicts. First, the focus will be on war veterans' experiences and narratives of going home again, i.e. of returning from combat back to a life called 'normal'. These are experiences that render both the victorious and the defeated representatives of such conflicts extremely vulnerable and susceptible to harm, as dramatically displayed in Sophocles' tragedies *Ajax* and *Philoctetes*, as well as in Euripides' play *The madness of Hercules*. Second, while turning our attention to the first victim of war, i.e. the truth, could have been an interesting exercise in itself, I suggest instead to listen to eye-witness experiences of the second and third victims of such disasters, i.e. women and children trapped in such conflicts. This is the kind of material from which Sophocles' tragedies *Antigone* and *The women of Trachis,* as well as Euripides' plays *Andromache*, *Hecuba,* and *The Trojan women,* have been woven.

7.4 Patterns of Behavior in the Wake of War: A Typology from Ancient Greek Tragedy

What are the recurrent patterns of human behaviour and attitudes that the ancient Greek tragedies give centre stage in their representations of the aftermath of armed conflicts and wars? High up on the list come the moral degradation and crime of *hybris* committed by the victors followed by dramatized accounts of the suffering and humiliation representatives of the defeated are forced to undergo. Rancor, xenophobia and hate are richly represented attitudes. Likewise rape and other forms of degrading abuse and violence, including bondage and the most horrendous forms of religiously motivated forms of abuse, such as ritual killing, human sacrifice and prohibition against burying one's loved ones. Among patterns of attitude and behaviour associated in these plays with war-veterans returning from combat to a life called 'normal' count existential solitude, social isolation and alienation; the incapacity to talk ('the wall of silence'); survival guilt, remorse and shame; loss of meaning and self-respect; domestic violence (including different forms of parricide); dependence on alcohol and other stimulants to handle life; and finally, 'the way of no return' – self-slaughter.

[4] http://www.heraclitusfragments.com/.

7.5 Patterns of Behavior in the Wake of War: Distilled Representations in Greek Tragedy

7.5.1 *First Representation: When the Home Front Becomes the Battlefront*

We encounter a dramatic representation of the home-coming war-veteran in Sophocles' play *Ajax* (Sophocles 1994, hereafter referred to as *Ajax*). The play starts with a conversation taking place outside Ajax's tent, during the siege of Troy, between the goddess Athena – the daughter of Zeus – and Odysseus, the legendary Greek king of Ithaca and hero of Homer's epic poem the *Odyssey*. In this play he is depicted as the subject of Ajax's most deep-felt rancor. The topic of the conversation is the sudden madness that has taken possession of Ajax. Odysseus has been sent by the Greek kings and war leaders, Menelaus (king of Mycenaean Sparta) and his brother Agamemnon (king of Argos), to find out whether Ajax is the vicious killer of the cattle that the Greeks had taken captive from the Trojans. Athene confirms Odysseus' suspicion and unveils to him the cause behind Ajax's madness: "He was stung by anger on account of the arms of Achilles" (*Ajax*, lines 40–41). The reason behind the rage of Ajax is that the armor of the dead Achilles, the most formidable of the Greek warriors, even in the eyes of Ajax, had been awarded to Odysseus instead of to himself. Ajax feels betrayed by Menelaus and Agamemnon:

> I well know, that if Achilles were alive and were to award the prize of valour in a contest for his own arms, no other would receive them but I. But now the sons of Atreus have made them over to an unscrupulous fellow, pushing aside this man's mighty deeds. (*Ajax*, lines 441–445)

He swears to take revenge and in the dead of night he sets out secretly to trace and kill Odysseus, the undeserved heir of Achilles' armor, as well as the brother kings. However, Athena steps in and deludes Ajax into attacking instead the cattle that the Greeks had taken from the Trojans. The play provides with surgical precision an account of the delusional killings:

> It was I [Athena] that held him back from his intolerable delight, casting upon his eyes mistaken notions, and I diverted him against the herds and the various beasts guarded by the herdsmen [...] here he fell upon them and hacked the horned beasts to death, cleaving their spines all around him; [...] And as the man wandered in the madness that afflicted him, I urged him on and drove him into a cruel trap. Then when he rested from this work he tied up those of the cattle that were still alive and all the sheep, and brought them home, thinking he had men there, and not the horned creatures that were his prey, and now he is torturing them, bound as they are, inside his dwelling. (*Ajax*, lines 51–64)

When Ajax comes to his senses and realizes the "mighty deeds" he had performed "among beasts that frightened no one", he is overwhelmed by shame. His self-respect is put in peril, his dignity likewise. And his mind is dominated by the feeling of having become a complete ridicule and outcast in the world of humans and gods. He can't go home again – not ever:

> Alas! Who ever would have thought that my name would come to harmonise with my sorrows? For now I can say 'Alas' a second time, I whose father came home from this land of Oda having won the army's first prize for valour, and bringing home every kind of fame [...] And now what must I do, I who patently am hated by the gods, and loathed by the army of the Greeks, and hated, too, by Troy and by these plains? Shall I cross the Aegean sea, leaving behind the station of the ships and the sons of Atreus, and go home? And what kind of face shall I show to my father Telamon when I appear? However shall he bring himself to look at me when I appear empty-handed, without the prize of victory, when he himself won a great crown of fame? The thing is not to be endured. (*Ajax*, lines 430–434, and lines 457–465)

There is for him only one viable option left, self-slaughter, by his two-edged sword. The sword was originally owned by Hector, the Trojan prince and commander of the Trojan army, but was given as a gift to Ajax by Hector in exchange for Ajax's belt, after a duel between them which none of them was able to bring to victory (*Ajax*, lines 1025–1030). This gift provides Ajax with the solution which for the morality of a noble warrior seems to be the only possible one:

> The killer stands where it will be sharpest, if one has time to work it out, a gift of Hector, the acquaintance I most hated, and whose sight I most detested; it stands in the enemy soil of Troy, newly sharpened with a whetstone that cuts away the iron. And I have planted it there with care, so that it may loyally help me to a speedy death [...].
> O light, O sacred plain of my own land of Salamis, O pedestal of my native hearth, and you glorious Athens, and the race that lives with you, streams and rivers here, and plains of Troy do I address; hail, you who have given me sustenance! This is the last word Ajax speaks to you; the rest I shall utter in Hades to those below. (*Ajax*, lines 815–819, and lines 860–865)

The play does not end with the self-slaughtering of Ajax; it provides in addition a dramatic representation of the deep grief and despair of Tecmessa, the war trophy and slave-concubine of Ajax, who now risks becoming a complete outcast herself with nowhere to seek shelter for herself and their son, Eurysaces. Tecmessa was the daughter of Teleutas, king of Phrygia, and her fate had been sealed during the Trojan war when Ajax killed the king and took his daughter captive. In Tecmessa's own words to Ajax before his suicide, her fate is thus described:

> Lord Ajax, there is no greater evil for men than the fate imposed by compulsion. I was born of a father who was free, greatest of all the Phrygians, and now I am a slave; that was the will of the gods, and in particular of your strength. (*Ajax*, lines 485–489)

After having been exposed directly in their own home to Ajax's delusional killings of the cattle he had brought back with him, and in addition having herself received "awful threats" from the mad-man (*Ajax*, line 312), she attempts to stop Ajax from committing suicide by reminding him that she and their son's life will be put in extreme danger from the day he commits such an act (*Ajax*, lines 490–504, 510–519):

> For on the day when you perish and by your death abandon me, believe that on that day I shall be seized with violence by the Argives together with your son and shall have the treatment of a slave [...] pity your son, my lord, thinking how much harm you will cause to him and to me by your death, if he is robbed of his early sustenance and must live bereft of you, placed under unfriendly guardians! For I have nothing to look to except you; you devastated

> my country by violence, and another fate took my mother and my father in death to live in Hades. What country, what riches can there be for me but you? On you rests all my safety.

Tecmessa also pleads with Ajax to show regard for his parents by instead hanging on to his life and thereby also making possible the fulfillment of his mother's prayers for many years that her son may return home again alive (*Ajax*, lines 505–508). But alas to no avail, for Ajax the only possible place to dwell now is Hades.

The fate of the bodily remains of Ajax is the focus of dramatic attention in the last part of the play. This is the conflict topic from which also Sophocles' play *Antigone* is woven, i.e. the treatment – and mistreatment – of corpses of fallen warriors. Teucer, the half-brother of Ajax, tries to rescue the remains of Ajax from the revenge of the brother kings, but Menelaus orders him to leave the body uncovered to serve as food for the birds (*Ajax*, line 1064). Menelaus tries to justify his cruel order by recalling Ajax's attempted plan of murdering his own allies and military leaders and his refusal "to obey those in authority". He also makes reference to the importance of upholding control in the army through the cultivation of fear and respect (*Ajax*, lines1052–1076). Teucer challenges Menelaus' arguments and when Agamemnon tries to follow up the case of his brother by using a combination of threats and allusions to Teucer's ignoble background (he was himself the son of a captive woman), he stands by his determination, as did Antigone, of having his (her) brother buried even if that would cost him (her) his (her) own life (*Ajax*, lines 1300–1315). Finally it is Odysseus, the man subject of Ajax's most deep-felt rancor, who by reference to justice and the laws of the gods manages to bring the conflict to a solution and safeguards an honourable burial of Ajax:

> Violence must not so prevail on you that you trample justice under foot! For me too he was once my chief enemy in the army, ever since I became the owner of the arms of Achilles; but though he was such in regard to me, I would not so far fail to do him honour as to deny that he was the most valiant among the Argives, except Achilles. And so you cannot dishonour him without injustice; for you would be destroying not him, but the laws of the gods. It is unjust to injure a noble man, if he is dead, even if it happens that you hate him. (*Ajax*, lines 1332–1345)

7.5.2 Ancient Views and Forms of Behaviour in Modern Wars: The Ghost of Ajax

In his fascinating book, *Theater of war*, Bryan Doerries tells about his experience with exposing US war veterans to Sophocles' play. Here are some of his observations:

> Standing before a war-weary infantry of soldiers after a reading of Sophocles' *Ajax* on a U.S. army installation in Southern Germany, I posed the following question, one that I have asked tens of thousands of service members and veterans on military bases all over the world: "Why do you think Sophocles wrote this play?"[…]. The play was written nearly twenty-five hundred years ago […] And yet the story is as contemporary as this morning's

> news. According to a 2012 Veterans Affairs study, an average of 22 U.S. veterans take their lives every day. That's almost one suicide every hour.
> A junior enlisted soldier, seated in the third row, raised his hand and matter-of-factly replied: 'He wrote it to boost morale'.
> I stepped closer to him and asked, 'What is morale-boosting about watching a decorated warrior descend into madness and take his own life?'.
> 'It's the truth', he replied – subsumed in a sea of green uniforms, 'and we're all here watching it together'.
> The soldier had highlighted something hidden within *Ajax*: a message for our time. This wasn't government-sponsored propaganda. Nor was his play an act of protest. It was the unvarnished truth. And by presenting the truth of war to combat veterans, he sought to give voice to their secret struggles and to convey to them that they were not alone. (Doerries 2016, 2–3)

According to Doerries the message of Sophocles' *Ajax* for the audience of his time as well as for our time is the following: "Even the strongest of warriors can be taken down, long after the battle has been lost or won. The violence of war extends far past the battlefield. Not only was psychological injury, it seems, a persistent and universal problem for warriors twenty-five centuries ago, but – like Americans today – the ancient Greeks must have struggled with the violence of war, on and off the battlefield" (Doerries 2016, 70–71). In his book Doerries provides moving accounts from several U.S war veterans and their spouses of how they found comfort in the way Sophocles gives expression to the impact of war on and beyond the battlefield on individuals, families and communities, and how the experiences of Ajax and Tecmessa resonated with their own experiences of coping with the emotional reactions and moral injuries following in the wake of war.

7.5.3 Second Representation: The Fate of Women and Their Offspring in the Wake of War

The impact of war on and off the battlefield on women and children is, as we have seen above, given dramatic attention in *Ajax* through the fates of Tecmessa and their son Eurysaces. But in *Ajax* this topic does not occupy centre stage as is the case in Euripides' plays *Andromache*, *Hecuba,* and *The Trojan women*. In these three plays, unvarnished versions of the horrors women and children are subjected to as a consequence of war are dramatically displayed. Hecuba, the queen of Troy and wife of Priam the Magnificent, is the main character in the play of her name as well as in *The Trojan women*, while in the third play the lead role is held by Andromache, the widow of Hector, the fallen Trojan hero and son of Hecuba. All three plays deal with the human aftermath of the conquest of Troy, and notably with particular focus on the fates of the leading women and their children, i.e. Queen Hecuba, her daughters Cassandra and Polyxena, and her son Polydorus, as well as her daughter-in-law Andromache, her son with Hector, Astyanax, and Molossus, the son Andromache gave birth to in captivity. Instead of providing a condensed account of each of these plays I suggest a 'synoptic' approach, i.e. to look for recurrent story fragments and narrative patterns that Euripides uses to dramatize the plights of these victims of war.

7.5.4 Women as War Trophies

While the fate of Tecmessa as a war trophy and slave-concubine to Ajax serves as a narrative backdrop for the plot in Sophocles' play *Ajax*, Euripides bases his plots in *Andromache*, *Hecuba,* and *The Trojan women* directly on the fates of these women and their offspring. Among these three plays perhaps the most heart-breaking narrative of what it entails for a woman to become a war trophy occurs in *Andromache* (Euripedes 1998, hereafter referred to as *Andromache*):

> If any woman was born to be broken on the earth's turning wheel,
> I am she. I watched my husband Hector die
> under Achilles' hands, and on that day
> the Greeks swarmed Troy,
> I watched my son flung from a tower – my son, Astyanax!
> And I – the daughter of a royal house –
> Packed off to Greece and bonded,
> A plum for Achilles' son, Neoptolemus
> The island prince. Andromache, his Trojan trophy. (*Andromache*, lines 6–15)

The fall into misery of Andromache here displayed does not only concern a former princess having lost all her royal privileges and living as a slave concubine at the mercy of the son of her husband's killer, Achilles. In addition she is exposed to the jealous rage and death threats of Hermione, Neoptolemus' wedded wife, who hates the "slave bitch" and war souvenir of the island prince because of her own barrenness (*Andromache,* line 155). The extent of the emotional horror under which Andromache is doomed to live is, however, not fully spelled out in the play, since it is not mentioned that her father and her seven brothers also had perished at the hands of Achilles (*Iliad,* Book 6). In addition the play is mute with regard to the tradition that it was Neoptolemus, the man whom she is forced to sleep with and to whom she unwillingly had born a child, who had caused the death of Astyanax, her son with Hector. In the play, there are only two lines alluding to the fate of her previous child (*Andromache*, lines 11 and 392). Although these accounts are not textually present in the play, there are good reasons to believe that they were emotionally present in the minds and memories of the ancient Greek public when they were watching the play.

While Euripides in *Andromache* focuses the attention in particular on the fate of Andromache and her offspring, *The Trojan women* (Euripedes 2008, hereafter referred to as *The Trojan women*) follows in addition the fates after the fall of Troy of the dethroned queen Hecuba, her oldest daughter Cassandra, her youngest daughter Polyxena and her youngest son Polydorus. The queen herself is to be given away as a slave to Odysseus, who the play attributes with the decision to kill her grandson *Astyanax* (for this, see later), while her oldest daughter, Cassandra, the cursed soothsayer, is to become the "bride of desire" of king Agamemnon. The curse, according to the tradition, had been caused by the god Apollo, who spellbound by the beauty of Cassandra had granted her the gift of foretelling the future. However, when Cassandra did not return his infatuation, he made that nobody believed her predictions – thinking she was mad – while she at the same time was doomed to foretell the future and endure the pain and frustrations of doing it to no avail. In the play this gift is alluded to by Cassandra expressing a morbid delight in her fate, since she, thanks to her gift, is able to foresee that her becoming the concubine of Agamemnon will lead to his death and the total destruction of the house of Atreus:

> Mother, come! Wrap my head with wreaths of victory.
> Dress me up like a bride. Be happy for me, be happy for my royal wedding!
> Come, send me off to the bridegroom [...]
> [...] I swear by Apollo
> that my marriage to Agamemnon, to that ... *sarcastically* ... glorious king of the Greeks, will come to an end more bitter than that of Menelaus and Helen!
> I will kill him, mother!
> I will destroy his city, mother, and I will avenge the murders of my father and my brothers!
> But enough of this lament for now.
> I will not tell now of the axe that will fall upon my neck and upon the neck of others. Nor will I tell about the matricide that my marriage will cause or the destruction of the house of Atreus.
> I will show them that our city is more blessed than any city in Greece, mother! (*The Trojan women*, lines 353–367)

For the ancient Greek audience familiar with the different legends and stories of the fortunes and fate of the house of Atreus,[5] of which Aischylos' trilogy, *Oresteia* (Aeschylus 1991), probably was the best known,[6] when exposed to this part of the play they would immediately link the prophecy about the killing of Agamemnon and a forthcoming matricide to the accounts about the death of *Agamemnon* at the hands of his wife Clytemnestra and to Orestes' slaying of his mother to avenge the murder of his father. The fate of Andromache the *woman* is given less attention in the play compared to the attention paid to her fate as a mother, in the sense that it is only stated that Achilles' son Neoptolemus has taken her as his "special prize" (*The women of Troy*, line 273). Andromache pleads to her beloved husband Hector to return from Hades to protect her from this dire fate, and she makes the promise never to put Hector out of her mind and heart or turn her love to the murderer she now is doomed to share bed with (*The Trojan women*, lines 660–668).

[5]The expression «the house of Atreus» refers to Atreus, king of Mycene, who according to the tradition was the son of Pelops and Hippodamia and the father of Agamemnon and Menelaus.

[6]The *Oresteia* consists of the following three plays: *Agamemnon*, *The libation-bearers* and *Eumenides*.

7.5.5 The Fate of Children of Female War Trophies

Another topic, besides the war trophy topic, that occupies centre stage in the three plays here considered, is the plight of the children of the noble widows of Troy and their deceased husbands. Since the fate of Hecuba's daughter Cassandra has already been addressed, I now turn the attention to her youngest daughter, Polyxena. When Hecuba asks Talthybius what will happen with Polyxena she receives an enigmatic answer:

> *Hecuba:*
> Tell me, then, Talthybius, who has drawn my unfortunate daughter, Cassandra?
> *Talthybius:*
> She was Agamemnon's special prize.
> [...]
> *Hecuba:*
> And the other one? The last daughter you took from me? What has become of her?
> Talthybius:
> Who do you mean, Polyxena or some other one?
> *Hecuba:*
> Yes, Polyxene, that one. Who has drawn her name?
> *Talthybius:*
> Her draw is to serve Achilles' tomb.
> *Hecuba:*
> My daughter? To serve a tomb? Is this a Greek custom or some sort of law?Tell me, friend!
> *Talthybius:*
> Just be happy for your daughter. Her Fate is good. That's all you need to know.
> *Hecuba:*
> "Her Fate is good?" What do you mean by that? Is she still alive? Can she still look upon the light?
> *Talthybius:*
> She's in the hands of Fate, so she is released from pain. (*The women of Troy*, lines 247[...]-270)

This answer prepares the audience for Hecuba's emotional reactions when the horrible news will be disclosed to her later in the play through the words of Andromache. The audience, however, is aware of what has happened with Polyxena, since her fate is disclosed already at the outset of the play:

> The river Scamandros echoes violently with the sounds of the crying women who must wait for Fate to tell them whose slave they are going to be.
> Fate has declared that some of them will serve the men of Arcadia while others will be slaves to the men from Thessaly. Others still, will be slaves to the sons of Theseus, the king of Athens.
> Then there are those who haven't been told their lot yet. These are the choicest of all the Trojan women. They are those picked for the army's top soldiers. That lot of women is waiting here, in these huts. Among them is Helen, daughter of Tyndareus, king of Sparta. Now, that woman is no greater than any of the other slaves. One of a great many captives. Quite right, too.
> (*Indicating Hecuba:*) And, if anyone cares at all about that one there, the queen of this city, well, there she is, Hecuba! The poor wretch is lying there, by her city's gates, shedding floods of tears. Her grief is great. The disasters that befell her many. Her daughter, Polyxene,

was gruesomely slaughtered, upon Achilles' grave. Slaughtered as a sacrificial offering to Achilles. (*The women of Troy,* lines 29–39)

A substantial part of the play is dedicated to Hecuba and Andromache lamenting the fall of Troy and the loss of their loved ones, and their conversation almost turns into a competition between them about which of them fate has struck hardest. It is during this part of the play that Andromache breaks the terrible news about Polyxena's destiny (*The women of Troy,* lines 610–647, and, lines 680–685).

So far in the play it is the misfortune of Andromache the widowed woman and war trophy that has been staged, but now follows the disclosure of the fate of her son Astyanax. As mentioned in the previous paragraph there are only two lines in *Andromache* alluding to the fate of the child she had given birth to before the fall of Troy. The focus in these lines is on the mother's grief following the brutal death of the son she had with Hector. No explanation is provided as to *why* Astyanax had to be killed. In *The women of Troy* such an explanation is provided; i.e. that it would be risky business to let the son of a Trojan noble grow into a man (*The Trojan women*, lines 717–722).

A few stanzas later Andromache herself breaks the horrible news to her little son (*The Trojan women*, lines 740–763), and the grief of Hecuba in the face of this imminent disaster is also spelled out:

Hekabe:
No! No! O, my son! Son of my ill-fated son!
It's unfair! These evil men have torn away your life from me and from your mother, my little boy!
How can I endure this? How can I help you my poor boy, unfortunate boy? (*The Trojan women*, lines 790–796)

Talthybius' disclosure to Andromache that Odysseus is the mastermind behind the decision to kill her grandson, makes her misery even worse in the minds and hearts of the audience watching the play, since this means that it is the man she now is doomed to live with that has instigated this evil.

In *Hecuba*, (Euripedes 1998, hereafter referred to as *Hecuba*), the third play of Euripides addressing the plight of women and children in the wake of war, the role of Odysseus in exacerbating Hecuba's misery is dramatically heightened through the disclosure that it was him who had convinced the Greeks of the necessity of sacrificing Polyxena on Achilles' tomb:

Chorus:
Until he broke in
That sweet-talking, forked tounged,
glad-handling son of Laertes, Odysseus.
Until Odysseus harangued the crowd, asking
If one slave woman's little life counted as much
as the glorious honor of Achilles.
He said he was ashamed to imagine
One of their valorous fallen brothers
Complaining in Hades that Greeks
Failed to thank the heroes
who died for victory

on the bloodied plains of Troy. (*Hecuba*, lines 168–180)

While the first part of the play provides a much more detailed representation than is the case in *The Trojan women* of the fate of Polyxena and the role Hecuba's new master, Odysseus, plays in the sacrifice of her youngest daughter, it is the destiny of Polydorus, "the last prince born to Hecuba and Priam", that occupies centre stage in the remaining part of the play (*Hecuba*, line 6). In the play's opening (*Hecuba*, lines 8–18), the ghost of Polydorus tells that when his father feared the fall of Troy he had his son smuggled to his old ally and friend together with a fortune in gold, so that in case of defeat, his surviving children would have something to live on (*Hecuba*, lines 19–39).

While Hecuba is still lamenting the loss of Polyxena, the body of Polydorus, which has been washed up on shore, is brought to her. First she thinks it is the body of Polyxena or of her daughter Cassandra. Upon recognizing her son whom she thought safe, Hecuba reaches new heights of despair. And when Polymestor's treason of the house of Priam is disclosed to her – according to the tradition his wife, Ilione, was the eldest daughter of Hecuba and king Priam – her inconsolable grief turns into an uncompromising intention to avenge the unspeakable, unbelievable, ungodly and unbearable crime committed by Polymestor:

Is this what friendship means?
You monster!
You child-murderer?
You hacked him up like this?
You killed our son with your sword? (*Hecuba*, lines 920–927)

Hecuba pleads with Agamemnon to help her avenge the slaying of her son and the "even more ungodly" act following the murder, i.e. that Polydorus' body was left unburied and thrown away into the sea (Hecuba, lines 1053–1056). Agamemnon, who has taken her daughter Cassandra as his "bride of desire", agrees reluctantly to assist Hecuba in setting up a trap against Polymestor. But since the Greek army considers Polymestor an ally he insists that no information about this must be disclosed to the army. Polymestor arrives with his sons pretending he is still a dear friend of the house of Priam and that he mourns with Hecuba the fall of Troy and the recent death of Polyxena (*Hecuba*, lines 1269–1299). Hecuba conceals her knowledge of Polydorus being the murderer of her son and asks Polymestor how her son is. Polymestor assures her that he is absolutely fine, and he adds: "In him you have good luck" (*Hecuba*, line 1328). Hecuba tells Polymestor she knows where the remaining treasures of Troy are hidden and she offers to share the secret with Polymestor so that he can disclose to Polydorus their whereabouts (*Hecuba*, lines 1354–1361). She persuades Polymestor that in case something should happen with him his sons should also know where the treasures are located. When Polymestor in his greedy eagerness to get hold of the treasures asks her whether she has more to say, Hecuba tells that she has managed to hide her personal jewels in a tent nearby. She makes Polymestor believe that she wants him to take care of them as well, and invites him and his sons to follow her into the tent. With the help of other female slaves from Troy who have been hiding in the tent, Hecuba kills Polymestor's sons and stabs Polymestor's eyes (*Hecuba*, lines 1397–1409).

The blinded king of Thrace cries in despair out for help to his Thracian guards and to the sons of Atreus, i.e. Agamemnon and Menelaus (*Hecuba*, lines 1482–1488). Agamemnon re-enters the stage escorted by Greek soldiers angry with the uproar which has disturbed the piece of his soldiers. Agamemnon pretends to be shocked by the sight of the blinded and bleeding Polymestor and the slayed sons, and he asks who the perpetrator is. Polymestor tells it is the vile deed of "Hecuba and those other Trojan she-devils" to revenge his killing of Polydoros. He pleads Agamemnon to lead him to her so that he can "tear her into thousand pieces!" (*Hecuba*, lines 1517–1518 and 1528–1530). Agamemnon says he is going to judge fairly between them after both of them have stated their case. Polymestor is first out, arguing that his killing of Polydorus was for the sake of preserving peace and stability (*Hecuba*, lines 1538–1558).

Hecuba delivers a rebuttal arguing that Polymestor's defense speech was a disgusting attempt at white-washing himself and at hiding the underlying motive for the slaying: "You killed my son for gold" (*Hecuba*, line 1675). Agamemnon sides with Hecuba and concludes that justice has been served by her revenge. Polymestor, in a fit of rage, foretells that Hecuba's death is imminent; she will drown before the ships of the army reaches Greece. Following this doomsaying he also predicts the forthcoming deaths of Cassandra and Agamemnon at the hands of his wedded wife Clytemnestra (*Hecuba*, lines 1773–1778, and 1808–1825). Agamemnon reacts with a mixture of anger and fear and orders his soldiers to gag Polymestor and take him away to "some deserted island where no one will hear his wretched lies!" (*Hecuba*, lines 1840–1843). Polymester assures Agamemnon that even if he took to killing him this would not save him "from the bloodbath of homecoming" in wait for him (*Hecuba*, lines 1828–1829). Soon after, the wind finally rises again, the Greeks will sail, and the Chorus goes to an unknown, dark fate:

> *Chorus:*
> We must go
> to our masters' tents.
> Nobody knows why
> what will happen to us
> there must happen.
> From the harbor
> we must voyage
> to life upon the shore
> of bondage. Nobody
> knows why this must be.
> Fate knows no mercy
> Necessity is hard.
> Why must everything
> happen as it must?
> What is this "must,"
> and why? Nobody knows
> Nobody knows. (*Hecuba*, lines 1852–1868)

7.5.6 *Ancient Views and Forms of Behavior in Modern Wars: The Fate of Women and Their Offspring*

Women's experiences of abduction and bondage, of systematic rape and sexual slavery, of extermination of their offspring, of forced displacement, marriage and impregnation, of religiously motivated forms of killing and sacrilege of human remains, as well as of other forms of extreme cruelty, have been there from the very start. That is, hardly any example of armed conflict exists in human history where such experiences were not – and still continue to be – abundantly represented (UNICEF 1996; Amnesty International 2004; Smith-Park 2004; Khan 2011; Wallace 2011). And this was exactly the kind of material Euripides, Sophocles and Aeschylus made use of to weave their war-plays and forge a universal moral language enabling any audience at any time and space to understand the disastrous effects such conflicts have on women's and children's lives. A moving illustration of the timelessness of these plays is *The Queens of Syria*, a Developing Artists' project where 50 Syrian women, all refugees living in Amman, Jordan, were given 6 weeks to prepare and perform their own adaptation of Euripides' play *The Trojan women* to an audience in the UK (Developing Artists 2013). None of the women had any previous experience of acting. They were all amateurs, trying to make sense of a play written nearly 25 hundred years ago. Here are some of their reactions after working with the play: Woman 1: "Troy's story is very similar to Syria's story; its women, its children, the country that was destroyed. So when they offered us this text and this play we were very keen to participate because we all lived the real experience. It's not like we needed to write a new story, whatever happened in Troy was documented, but it's no more than what happened in Syria". The same woman a little later in the presentation of the project: "This part of the play makes me cry a lot [the stanza she is referring to is the following: "*You are living a painful present while your soul yearns for a happy past*']. And she continues: "We left our hometown, there was a lot of shelling. I wanted to find a better life for my children. The play talks about something real to us. It's old but history repeats itself". Woman 2: "Hecuba is just like me. She was the wife of the king of Troy. Then she lost everything she owned. She lost loved ones and family. It's like us, she was a queen in her home. Hecuba said: '*I used to run this place but now I am nothing*'. That's us now". Woman 3: "I would like to go to London to deliver the message about our life and the conditions we live in. We want the whole world to hear that. I mean, the whole world is not treating us as humans. Some people ran away from death only to meet death. Some drowned in the sea while they ran away from death. Some people were trying to cross illegally. They died on the borders. What is happening to the Syrians?" Woman 4: "It is not enough that you see the things through the television or the radio or other media. You have to meet this people, speak with them and understand them. Then you can decide what's the wrong and what's the right. I would like to thank each and every person who do help any refugee, ever, because it is very good. I know why you did that, because you are human. And we are human. And you break all the walls and you just stand and say 'I am a human and these people are human and we should help them'."

7.6 Concluding Remarks

The Greeks in antiquity did not make a sharp distinction between human disasters and natural disasters, and notably for the simple reason that a third causal factor was always implicated; the Greek gods and deities in their different forms and formats of defence and revenge. In spite of this apparent out-datedness with regard to conceptual clarity and refinement, I believe there are good reasons to argue that the ancient Greek playwrights had a better grasp of what it morally speaking entails for human beings to be hit by disasters than what empirical evidence and theoretical accounts are able to provide. The aim of this chapter has been to come up with arguments for such a position using the narratives of ancient Greek tragedy as a telling source with regard to the different ways human lives might be blown apart in the wake of armed conflicts. For these reasons I believe a narrative approach to disaster bioethics deserves more attention than what has hitherto been the case.

References

Aeschylus. 1991. Oresteia: Agamemnon, Libation-Bearers, Eumenides. In *Aeschylus. Plays: Two*, ed. J.M. Walton. London: Methuen.

Amnesty International. 2004. *Lives blown apart. Crimes against women in times of conflict.* London: Amnesty International Publications.

Aristotle. 1984. Poetics; Nicomachean ethics; politics. In *The complete works of Aristotle. The revised Oxford translation*, ed. J. Barnes. Princeton: Princeton University Press.

Burian, P. 1997. Myth into muthos: The shaping of tragic plot. In *The Cambridge companion to Greek tragedy*, ed. P.E. Easterling, 178–208. Cambridge, UK: Cambridge University Press.

Developing Artists. 2013. *Queens of Syria.* Accessible at: http://www.developingartists.org.uk/our-projects/queens-of-syria:-jordan-&-uk-theatre-tour.

Doerries, B. 2016. *The theater of war: What ancient tragedies can teach us today*. London: Knopf Doubleday Publishing Group.

Euripedes. 1998. Medea, *Hecuba, Andromache, the Bacchae*, ed. D.R. Slavitt and P. Bovie. Philadelphia: University of Pennsylvania Press.

———. 2008. *The Trojan women*. Trans. G. Theodoridis. Accessible at: http://www.poetryintranslation.com/PITBR/Greek/TrojanWomen.htm.

Gellrich, M. 1988. *Tragedy and theory. The problem of conflict since Aristotle*. Princeton: Princeton University Press.

Khan, M. 2011. Why are women used as trophies in war? Or how to win the battle against rape. *Al Arabiya*. Accessible at: http://english.alarabiya.net/articles/2011/06/23/154403.html.

Kuhn, H. 1941. The true tragedy. On the relationship between Greek tragedy and Plato, I. *Harvard Studies in Classical Philology* 52: 1–40.

Lattimore, R. 1964. *Story patterns in Greek tragedy*. London: The Athlone Press.

Nussbaum, M.C. 1986. *The fragility of goodness: Luck and ethics in Greek tragedy and philosophy*. Cambridge, UK: Cambridge University Press.

Østerud, S. 1976. Hamartia in Aristotle and Greek tragedy. *Symbolae Osloenses* LI: 65–80.
Rivier, A. 1944. *Essai sur le tragique d'Euripide*. Lausanne: F. Rouge & Co.
Schütrumpf, E. 1989. Traditional elements in the concept of *hamartia* in Aristotle's poetics. *Harvard Studies in Classical Philology* 2: 137–156.
Smith-Park, L. 2004. How did rape become a weapon of war? Accessible at: http://news.bbc.co.uk/2/hi/4078677.stm.
Solbakk, J.H. 2004. Therapeutic doubt and moral dialogue. *Journal of Medicine and Philosophy* 29 (1): 93–118.
———. 2006. Catharsis and moral therapy II: An Aristotelian account. *Journal of Medicine Healthcare and Philosophy* 9 (2): 141–153.
Sophocles. 1994. Ajax; Electra; Oedipus Tyrannus. In *Sophocles I*, ed. H. Lloyd-Jones. Cambridge, MA/London: The Loeb Classical Library, Harvard University Press.
Sorabji, R. 1980. Tragic error. In *Necessity, cause and blame. Perspectives on Aristotle's theory*, ed. R. Sorabji, 295–298. London: Gerald Duckworth & Co. Ltd.
Stinton, T.C.W. 1975. Hamartia in Aristotle and Greek tragedy. *Classical Quarterly, NS* 25: 221–254.
UNICEF. 1996. Sexual violence as a weapon of war. In *State of the world's children 1996*. Accessible at: http://www.unicef.org/sowc96pk/sexviol.htm.
Wallace, A. 2011. *Colombian women treated as 'war trophies'*. BBC Mundo, Bogota. Accessible at: http://www.bbc.com/news/world-latin-america-14988443.
Wolfe, T. 1934, 2011. *You can't go home again*. New York/London/Toronto/Sydney/New Dehli: Scribner.

Chapter 8
Conceptualizing Disasters from a Gender Perspective

Ayesha Ahmad

Abstract This chapter focuses on how disasters are conceptualized from a gender perspective and will explore concepts such as violence and death against the backdrop of gender inequalities. It will critically examine the conceptualization of a disaster in terms of humanitarian response and execution of policies that aim to protect individuals in disaster situations and mediate the risks that emerge during certain contexts, such as refugee or internally displaced camps. Finally, it will be concluded that disasters, as conceptualised from a gender perspective, still need a more all-encompassing theoretical framework to account for the lived experiences of individuals in terms of their gender identity in societies during times of disasters.

Keywords Disasters · Gender · Gender-based violence · Humanitarian crisis and response · Culture · Vulnerability

8.1 Introduction

This chapter focuses on how disasters are conceptualized from a gender perspective and will explore concepts such as violence and death against the backdrop of gender inequalities. It will critically examine the conceptualization of a disaster in terms of humanitarian response and execution of policies that aim to protect individuals in disaster situations and mediate the risks that emerge during certain contexts, such as refugee or internally displaced camps. Finally, it will be concluded that disasters, as conceptualised from a gender perspective, still need a more all-encompassing theoretical framework to account for the lived experiences of individuals in terms of their gender identity in societies during times of disasters.

A. Ahmad (✉)
Institute for Medical and Biomedical Education, St George's University of London, London, UK
e-mail: aahmad@sgul.ac.uk

D. P. O'Mathúna et al. (eds.), *Disasters: Core Concepts and Ethical Theories*, Advancing Global Bioethics 11, https://doi.org/10.1007/978-3-319-92722-0_8

8.2 The Global Disaster of Gender?

"ISIS are afraid of girls" (Deardon 2015) is a title of a recent newspaper article depicting interviews with Kurdish female fighters in Northern Syria. The statement is placed against the backdrop of an extreme religious ideology that claims a Muslim man who is killed by a woman will not enter heaven. Since the conflict is characterised as a Holy War by ISIS fighters, and motivated by a vision of the afterlife, the prospect of being killed by a woman is significant. This significance can be viewed from different temporal perspectives; the first is in terms of the factors that contributed to the formation of both the belief and the way that the conflict has subsequently developed. The continuum between society and conflict illustrates a central tenet of the way disasters, which often include conflict, are structured and conceptualized from a gender studies perspective. In this sense, societal processes during peace times are reflected during times of conflict, with the norms and practices associated with peace times becoming magnified. Furthermore, the comment made by the female Kurdish fighters is laden with normative values that are drawn from lived experiences and symptomatic of gender equality conflicts within the region. Thus, one conflict is never an isolated conflict but surrounded by meta-conflicts originating from meta-narratives. This chapter is an attempt to explore the conceptualization of disasters from a gender studies perspective. To develop this analysis, time must first be committed to understanding why a gender studies concept has developed in the way it has and what it means in the context of disaster research.

8.3 Gender Studies: How Are Disasters Conceptualized?

The contributions in this chapter from gender theorists involve individuals whose work may not have initially or primarily been geared towards responding to disasters. The field of gender studies refers to a dynamic and multi-disciplinary group of researchers. A gender studies perspective views disasters as gendered-constructed processes. This understanding has carried with it a very important normative message: that to respond to those in need during a disaster, gender needs to be considered as an integral factor. Thus, the conceptualization of disasters in gender studies has been tasked with providing argumentation on the gendered aspects of a disaster.

This chapter will also explore a further element in how disasters are conceptualized in gender studies by asking why gender researchers have been involved significantly and increasingly in disaster risk, reduction, and response. A deconstruction of the origin of the interaction between gender and disaster traces the question of how are disasters conceptualized within gender studies to the ethical issue of addressing and responding to gender during disasters. Contributions from feminist perspectives, for example, have pushed for disasters to be understood in terms of the weaknesses and determinants within a society that determines the nature of the disaster; in other words, the disaster is occurring prior to the event(s) that trigger a humanitarian emergency crisis. The consequences of a gender-neutral framework of disasters and a binary approach towards disaster and non-disaster or vulnerable and non-vulnerable settings and populations are negative. Enarson and Pease (2016, xviii) have critically reflected on the normative aspect of disasters bracketing out the 'unheard voices' of a disaster. They write how "singular problems arise from genders being taken as 'natural', fixed or physically based, when so much is done to craft them in service of vested interests and institutional values and goals", and then how "emergencies can potentially be opportunities for lasting change and improvement. But also, as in so many global change issues, this may not suit vested interests. They get busy, sometimes violently, trying to restore, even exaggerate, pre-disaster gender relations" (Enarson and Pease 1998, xviii). Conceptualising disasters from a gender perspective requires understanding that governments, local policy-makers, or certain groups within a society for example will be potentially in contrast with aspects of a generalised humanitarian intervention premised on equality of human life, without factoring in differences in decision-making related to gender identity. During the Taliban regime, for example, women were forbidden to be examined by male doctors (Iacopino 1998, 58). A gender-neutral disaster framework will therefore lead to the overlooking of the gendered nature of the body during conflict, and its impact on the provision of healthcare to women. In turn, a failure to address gender will reduce the efficacy of a disaster response in addressing the needs of the entire affected population.

Disasters, then, occupy a space in which policy-based responses and interventions are potentially at risk of being centred on reinforcing a return to the "things that are actually hidden" (Enarson and Pease 2016, xviii). On the other hand, disasters can be an "opening for other genders" but by virtue of this opening being created, the dominant pre-existing gendered terrain such as masculinity as in Enarson and Peases' example becomes threatened. In this view, a conceptualization of disasters from a gender studies perspective refers to a shift in social landscapes, as well as physical ones. This is the meaning of the embodiment of a terrain as gendered; our landscapes are the site of our lived experiences, memory, and future discourses some of which will involve conflicts or movements towards social justice or restructuring of cultural, religious, or gender norms and values. Disasters become case studies that lead to critical developments for social change.

8.4 Basis for Disasters

Disasters-especially disasters that were considered as 'natural'-have traditionally been subjected to narratives that refer to actions of deities or spirits or curses, which in turn are in response to some aspect of human action within the affected population. Typically, such rhetoric reflects pre-existing understandings of localised views of the surrounding world. In a study exploring images of God in participant narratives following Hurricane Katrina, a collection of both positive and negative associations was reported. Images of God were categorised as "(a) Omnipresent God, (b) Omnipotent God, (c) Distant God, (d) Personal God, (e) God in Others, (f) God as Judge, (g) God of Lessons, and (h) God as Loving Father Figure" (Aten et al. 2008, 249). The meaning of these images to the participants revealed paradoxical and contradictory understandings and experiences of the ways individuals related themselves to God and the associations that connected their lived experiences with the event of the disaster. From a gender perspective, the lack of coherence in the way that images of God were envisioned by the participants show the difficulty in making generalized and absolutist claims about the impact of the event. Furthermore, the notion of a disaster as being detached from values or actions within a community is challenged by how the internalization of narratives relates to lived experiences of underpinning narratives. For example, individuals may receive distress related to their status as a man or woman, or other identity if situated in a society that is structured on highly prescribed and strict gender roles. Disastrous events potentially confirm negative beliefs towards a particular gender; following the earthquake in Afghanistan in October 2015, societal interpretations, used on an anecdotal basis for this chapter, of the earthquake that resulted in over 1500 deaths attributed blame to women for wearing un-modest dress. In turn, this served to reinforce ideologies that prescribed wearing religious garments to protect the honor related to the woman, her family, and the wider society. By taking a gendered perspective to a disaster, the response should address both needs directly related to the disaster itself and needs related to long-term issues, especially related to the recognition of human rights standards. This is the basis for much of the work (Fordham 2003; Enarson and Fordham 2001) that has been developed by gender researchers arguing that a short-term acute and emergency approach to disasters does not address or recognize that the real disaster for women is in the long-term effects.

8.5 Contextualizing Disasters: Who's Ground Is It?

Gender analysis and frameworks have worked to improve theoretical approaches to disasters that have traditionally treated disasters as stand-alone events with clearly defined phases in terms of crisis and recovery. In turn, an ethical issue has been highlighted in the way that relief agencies were initially reluctant to examine disaster management and response polices (Comfort et al. 1999). By pushing a gender-based conceptualization of a disaster into policy agenda through analysing the circumstances that create or contribute to conditions that result in human communities, disasters have gradually been reframed.

Disasters are a social phenomenon and social processes become more visible in times of crisis. This means that societal, cultural, and religious norms and values are evident in the nature of a disaster and shape the needs and risks of affected individuals. Gender is an organising principle in society, which is explored throughout this chapter, and thus disasters are not gender neutral.

Disasters are international frontlines where a society is shown to the rest of the world in its most fragile and bare state. Societal structures, depending on the extent of the disaster, are laid out in its skeletal form. In this sense, disasters viewed from a gender perspective are vital and fertile ground for both deconstruction and reconstruction. Furthermore, the way that gendered bodies impact on disasters reflects the social construction perspective of a disaster. For example, a woman's capacity and resources and approaches towards a disaster symbolise a specific context and time (Enarson and Chakrabarti 2009). Yet, in parallel, such social processes are evident of the need to develop a systematic approach towards understanding disasters as more than an event. Disasters become expressions, and reflections, on current situations that a community, society and nation are facing. In this sense, this chapter will highlight the relationship of disasters to social transformation, which is especially important from a gender studies perspective to reconstruct societies to have greater gender equality. Social transformation is perhaps an integral reason why gender studies have contributed so much to disaster research because of the potential to respond to disasters in a way that helps reforms that are addressing gender injustices to develop and be sustained in viable conditions. Much of this chapter will focus on the ways that perspectives from gender studies on disasters have been segregated from disaster studies and the ways that integration attempts are currently being taken forward and why.

8.6 Disasters: Processes Not Events

The changing and evolving landscape of how disasters are conceptualized by researchers has gradually come to align more closely with the view of disasters from a gender studies perspective. As understandings about disasters have increased, there has been greater acceptance of a disaster being informed by and underpinned by social problems theory, particularly during the late 1980s and the 1990s, which the United Nations called the International Decade for Natural Disaster Reduction (Kreps and Drabek 1996).

Earlier phases of gender studies criticised disaster research for overlooking the effects of gender and gender relations and furthermore, bypassing the role of women's involvement in disaster-affected households and communities (Peacock et al. 1997). An initial way of conceptualizing disasters through a gender studies perspective, then, was to create systematic argumentation for how to situate gender in disaster research discourses. By the 2000s both gender studies and disaster research began to call for more substantial recognition of gender-sensitive disaster relief.

In part, the development of conceptualizing disasters through a gender lens has come from qualitative research that has primarily been with women. The goal of this research has been to bring women's subjectivities to the forefront of considering how to respond to disasters. In a paper exploring the experiences of women in the wake of Hurricane Mitch in 1998 (Cupples 2007), the argument attempts to persuade disaster management actors to incorporate a more nuanced focus on the complexities of gender identity and relations between genders. This argument is evidence of the polarization of women either in terms of their vulnerabilities or in terms of their capabilities in both gender and disaster literature.

Furthermore, criticisms from gender studies perspectives of attempts to integrate gender into disaster management have been in the form of, for example, "if addressed at all, gender has been integrated into disaster research and practice as a demographic variable or personality trait and not as the basis for a complex and dynamic set of social relations" (Enarson 2002, 5). In this sense, the argument, then, is to create a conceptual framework where gender relations and disasters "are socially constructed under different geographic, cultural, political-economic and social conditions and have complex social consequences for women and men" (Ibid.). A long-standing criticism is in the way that women's lives have been reduced to that of disaster victims.

8.7 Understanding Gender in Disaster Response: The Normativity of Humanitarian Interventions

A recent study from Iran concluded that different aspects of a disaster were manifested through different aspects of gender. In the context of recent earthquakes in Iran, it was described that a woman is present in society in different ways; namely, as an individual who experiences the disaster, as a member of a family, and as part of a community (Nakhaei et al. 2015). Using these themes, Nakhaei et al. (Ibid) could identify key needs of Iranian women affected by the earthquakes. By understanding the status of gender within the Iranian context, an appropriate disaster response could be tailored. A major concern of affected women was to be resettled into a permanent home, which reflected the status of the woman in the family structure as needing to mediate the changes that occurred in their family including separation and loss of male family members. This poses practical challenges for a woman's everyday life in a society where liberty is restricted based on gender as well as the emotional impact of the bereavement and reorganization of family life. Finding ways to recover from a disaster may be at odds with the ideas of progression and modernity that humanitarian workers have as their ideals and markers of a functioning society. This gap in perception and goals for planning needs to be addressed. Often it can lead to an uncomfortable prescription of imposing normative values or realigning gender roles and requirements onto a foundation that is not sustainable.

Positive social transformation related to gender is possible in the context of disaster settings. The Nepalese civil war conflict offers a long-standing example. Traditionally Nepalese widows were required to wear a white sari. However, following an armed conflict lasting from 1996 to 2006 and causing over 15,000 deaths, many women became widows. During the post-conflict era, widows challenged the centuries-old entrenched belief system surrounding the status of women and resisted the practice of the 'white sari' (Yadav 2016). Here the complexity of a disaster is witnessed. The conflict became the context for social transformation from a form of gender discrimination to gender equality.

8.8 Developing Vulnerability

Previous work on vulnerability in disaster research (Cannon 1994; Perloff 1983) towards women during disasters that has reduced women to passive victims has gradually been challenged through contributions in gender studies. An alternative strategy has emerged, namely the consideration of a disaster as an opportunity for social justice. From a gender lens, therefore, vulnerability is temporal and linked to social justice and development. In this sense, development programmes in both disaster and non-disaster settings focus on providing skills for resilience and increased capability to manage complex and challenging situations. In a similar vein, disaster research scholars called for integration between gender, disaster and development (Pelling 2003), which represents an intersectionality in addressing vulnerability as a form of disaster response. Challenges remain, however, for those working from a gender perspective framework. Providing immediate relief and physical alleviation of suffering, including saving lives, conflicts with development programmes that were ongoing prior to disasters. These projects are then disrupted or terminated due to lack of collaboration and differing priorities plus different time-frames for their interventions. On this pragmatic level, the conceptualization of disasters from gender studies suffers from different viewpoints from other disciplines whereby gender may be overlooked or not considered at all. These are viewpoints that situate gender into a sub-category or additional feature of a specific event such as a disaster. Gender studies on the other hand views the disaster entirely from a framework of the gender norms of a society. In this sense a disaster is framed in terms of gender relationships, or rather, the imbalance of gender inequalities. The disaster that is shaped by an earthquake or a famine, for example, is the way in which gender roles have been structured and organized in a way that creates risk and vulnerability. Risk and vulnerability are the two components that shape an individual's health needs during disastrous events. The disaster is the inequality in society, and not specifically the catastrophe of a natural and/or man-made event.

Vulnerability has become central to gender discourses in analysing disasters. Vulnerability, though, was first argued to be key to conceptions of gender in discussions about violence (Hollander 2001). During risk analysis of violence, it was found that men in the United States of America have a higher risk of experiencing violence but the fear of experiencing violence is greater for women. In response to this disparity, Hollandar (2001) argued that femininity has become associated with vulnerability whereas masculinity is paired with dangerousness. Vulnerability, then, is personified as a core component of being female (ibid). In turn, however, violence against women and girls has become polarised in a binary victim and perpetrator relationship. Thus, in dominant feminist narratives about vulnerability, it is in this context that the male perpetration of violence is assigned. However, the tension and complexity of conceptualizing vulnerability in disasters serves a twofold purpose; namely to assess risk in terms of vulnerability but also to develop empowerment and deconstruct victimization in development following disasters. Fundamentally, the discourse of vulnerability illustrates a rhetoric of the body that is gendered, and it is this gendered body that determines whether an event is a disaster based on the needs that result.

8.9 Deconstructing Disasters from a Vulnerability Perspective: Inserting Intersectionality

Within a gendered framework, vulnerability is a temporal phenomenon. Vulnerability is addressed to identify strategies to counteract the social factors that are structuring the ways that vulnerable groups are susceptible to risk and harm. Following on, vulnerability highlights that there are two elements to consider from a gender studies perspective about disasters; namely that the disaster is gendered and the experience of the individual during the disaster is gendered.

A very contemporary aspect of disasters through a gender framework is the systematic recognition of multiple identities. The base-line of gender is a determinant of needs, risks or vulnerabilities during and beyond a disaster and/or humanitarian crisis. Invariably, a gender perspective has viewed disasters as an "intersecting dimension of human life" (Enarson et al. 2007, 130). In this sense, the concept of disaster continues to develop in terms of its larger narratives that embody lived experiences and a continuous spectrum of social processes. The notion of intersectionality offers a more nuanced cutting-edge platform to launch dialogues via research and collaboration via multiple sectors of disaster planning, response and evaluations. But the difficulty is that when the categories of a gender-based social science theory of disasters are implemented, they become weighted down by their own internal structures. Health, for example, is undergoing a transformation taking it from its medicalised home within the clinic into a greater societal situatedness where there is resistance against reducing health as an isolated and measurable quality of an individual. The inter-connectedness of health is important because it links to the Intersectionalities of disasters: namely that there is motivation for health too to be conceptualised from a gender perspective.

8.10 Mental Health in Disasters; Challenges in Assessing Needs from a Gender Perspective

A gendered conceptualization of disasters has called for greater attention to the experiences of those whose lives and livelihoods are affected during a disaster, and for the overlooking of women's experiences to be counteracted. Feminist theory from disaster mental health research identified geographical differences in the way that women's experiences were accounted for and have tried to respond to this discrepancy. U.S.-focused research has examined and utilised the conservative agenda of a disaster, covering topics related to disaster policy, management organizations and warning systems (Bolin et al. 1998). Research, however, on disasters and the impact of the lived experience during a disaster, more readily included theoretical advances from feminist and gender studies including the effects of disasters on women and disadvantaged groups (Bolin et al. 1998). An explanation for this differentiation could be that researching disasters in other contexts highlighted cultural variations and promoted the need to learn from communities, which in turn created the space for a more diverse range of voices and dialogue.

Understanding mental health to a significant extent is dependent on narrative and attention to the disaster recovery period. However, despite disaster mental health gaining greater ground in recent years and featuring the agenda of disaster responders, barriers exist when trying to gain a fuller picture of a survivor's mental health. From a disaster research perspective, mental health is understood to be significant for the recovery process. However, in line with a gender studies concept of a disaster, mental health should be stream-lined in terms of challenges present in the society pre (and post) disaster. Presently, there is a dominant view of disaster mental health that has been limited to negative consequences from a traumatic stress perspective (Joseph and Jaswal 2014). In part, the privileging of a trajectory focused on trauma in terms of disaster mental health conforms to an aspect of disaster conceptualization that has been consistently challenged by those working in some capacity within gender studies and other disciplines. Fordham (1999, 15) writes that those who have been affected by a disaster are classified as "belonging to a homogenous group called victims". Following on from such a perspective, the limitations of understanding disaster mental health as victims suffering from trauma means that this "apparent similarity conceals considerable difference: difference in terms of gender, class, race/ethnicity, age, sexual orientation, physical and mental ability, culture, etc." (ibid). A gender studies perspective is therefore not only concerned with gender but with raising awareness and calling for systematic analysis and addressing of other differences within groups of people who become classed as belonging to a specific category such as "victims".

The gender studies concept of disasters as being fundamentally concerned with social justice is essential for the development of disaster mental health understanding. Given the treatment gap for global mental health, feminist approaches towards health research have been suggested (Chiumento et al. 2016) due to an emphasis on a form of social justice that emphasises "multiple and complex structures of inequality and power" (Rogers and Kelly 2011, 397). Considering this, Fordham continues to argue that "recognizing difference in disaster is part of the solution, not the problem" (Fordham 1999, 15). In the context of mental health, individuals suffering from mental disorders are subjected to varying degrees of stigmatization and discrimination and the recognition of other voices is instrumental to reduce marginalization. Gender studies is an area within disaster research that seeks to create a more nuanced approach to disaster management such as in disaster mental health and its instrumentalisation as part of the post-disaster recovery process.

On a more applied level, a gender conceptualization of disasters in relation to mental health is linked to the designing and implementation of mental health recovery programmes. In a retrospective study conducted 6–11 months following the Great East Japan Earthquake and Tsunami, a total of 42.6% of the respondents, who were all residents and survivors of the disaster, were identified as having moderate or serious mental health problems (Yokyama et al. 2014). Furthermore, the same study showed that women were significantly affected by mental health problems following the disaster. Health complaints, severe economic status, relocations and lack of social networks were found to be important risk factors for mental health. Interventions that respond to these risk factors are important for the reduction of mental health problems after the disaster—for example, interventions for men that focused on economic support. These findings gain more traction when combined with the theoretical aspects of a gender framework to conceptualize disasters. Hence there arises pressure for the roles of researcher and activist when conceptualizing disasters from a gender perspective.

8.11 Expanding Horizons: The Forming of Violence from Disasters

The significance of disasters as a precursor for an increase in violence including domestic violence, sexual violence, and child abuse, neglect, and exploitation (WHO 2005) has prompted a discourse within gender theory to respond proactively to disaster-related violence across all sectors and phases of disasters and disaster management. However, more epidemiological studies are needed to investigate the association between natural disasters and violence (Rezaeian 2013).

Increased risk of gender-based violence during disasters is linked to gender inequality. A disaster is not isolated from the social and cultural factors that underpin gender inequality and structure gender-based violence. In the context of the tsunami in Sri Lanka in 2004, a preliminary study exploring the needs of women helped to inform a community based programme to reduce the incidence of sexual and gender based violence in post-tsunami Sri Lanka (Rees et al. 2005). The programme enabled the strengthening of communities and social support networks for women including resources to formally document incidences of violence. A further aspect of the programme targeted the need for women to be centralised in social and political movements in preventing violence and improving gender equality in the long term. A gender studies perspective holds that women need to be represented more in prevention of violence interventions and this includes disaster response programmes.

Having made significant transformations in the moral viewing of disasters from a gender studies perspective, conventional views that a disaster is a natural phenomenon and a devastating event, which result in a generalised vulnerability of the affected society, are weakened. Gender studies continues to highlight areas of disasters that are subject to complex social processes and indirect ways that disasters impact on individuals depending on different aspects of their identity such as gender.

A study was undertaken following the Deepwater Horizon oil spill (DHOS) that explored the relationship between oil spill exposure and mental health among women in the southern coastal Louisana parishes affected by the DHOS (Rung et al. 2016). As part of a telephone interview with 2842 women between 2012 and 2014 following the DHOS, women were asked about depression, mental distress, domestic conflict and exposure to the oil spill. Sixteen percent reported an increase in the number of fights with their partners, and 11% reported an increase in the intensity of partner fights. In addition, 13% reported severe mental distress and 28% reported symptoms of depression; these results of poor mental health outcomes following the DHOS referred to different psychological consequences of the disasters, and to the breakdown of livelihoods and families, and the deterioration of mental health. In terms of disaster mitigation, it was understood that exposure to the DHOS was a significant predictor of both domestic violence and associated mental health distress. Given that the southern coastal Louisiana region is disaster-prone this information is important for future disaster responses and the detection of aspects of the disaster that require specific attention in both the short and the long term. This combination of different lived experiences conforms to a gender studies view of disasters that women experience the effects of a disaster some time after the immediate and identified point of the disaster, and that social processes such as violence towards women increase in times of crisis.

8.12 Conclusion

The conceptualization of disasters from a gender theoretical analysis continues to influence the framework of disaster risk, reduction, and response and the network of disaster and gender studies is expanding. This is not to say that a gendered understanding of disasters is not without its challenges; but the advocacy and focus towards sustainable and long-term approaches towards providing social justice in the form of gender equality is persistent and overcoming shortfalls in disaster mediation that have previously been encountered. Thus, the view that women be represented in disaster interventions is central to the discourse of disasters in gender studies and widening the critical analysis to impact on other genders such as masculinities in the assessment of risk and vulnerability when the status of a discriminated group is elevated. On a final note, this chapter has emphasised that societies experience disasters on different structural levels and different points of a disaster impact on specific groups of people at different times per the nature of the cultural and social factors that are pre-existing in the disaster context. Disaster responses must be community-based and nuanced to account for gender as the organizing principle of a disaster as a continuous process.

References

Aten, J.D., M. Moore, R.M. Denney, T. Bayne, A. Stagg, S. Owens, S. Daniels, S. Boswell, J. Schenck, J. Adams, and C. Jones. 2008. God images following hurricane Katrina in South Mississippi: An exploratory study. *Journal of Psychology & Theology* 36 (4): 249–257.

Bolin, R., M. Jackson, and A. Crist. 1998. Gender inequality, vulnerability, and disaster: Issues in theory and research. In *The gendered terrain of disaster: Through women's eyes*, 27–44. Westport: Praeger.

Cannon, T. 1994. Vulnerability analysis and the explanation of 'natural' disasters. *Disasters, Development and Environment* 1: 13–30.

Chiumento, A., M.N. Khan, A. Rahman, and L. Frith. 2016. Managing ethical challenges to mental health research in post-conflict settings. *Developing World Bioethics* 16 (1): 15.

Comfort, L., B. Wisner, S. Cutter, R. Pulwarty, K. Hewitt, A. Oliver-Smith, J. Wiener, M. Fordham, W. Peacock, and F. Krimgold. 1999. Reframing disaster policy: The global evolution of vulnerable communities. *Environmental Hazards* 1 (1): 39–44.

Cupples, J. 2007. Gender and Hurricane Mitch: Reconstructing subjectivities after disaster. *Disasters* 31 (2): 155–175.

Deardon, L. 2015. "Isis are afraid of girls": Kurdish female fighters believe they have an unexpected advantage fighting in Syria. Independent. https://www.independent.co.uk/news/world/middle-east/isis-are-afraid-of-girlskurdish-female-fighters-believe-they-have-an-unexpected-advantage-fighting-a6766776.html. Accessed 9 Sep 2018.

Enarson, E. 2002. Gender issues in natural disasters: Talking points and research needs. In *Crisis, women and other ender concerns*, 5–12.

Enarson, E., and M. Fordham. 2001. From women's needs to women's rights in disasters. *Global Environmental Change Part B: Environmental Hazards* 3 (3): 133–136.

Enarson, E., A. Fothergill, and L. Peek. 2007. Gender and disaster: Foundations and directions. In *Handbook of disaster research*, 130–146. New York, NY: Springer.

Enarson, E., and P.D. Chakrabarti. 2009. *Women, gender and disaster: global issues and initiatives*. New Delhi: SAGE Publications India.

Enarson, E., and B. Pease. 2016. *Men, masculinities and disaster*. New York: Routledge.

Fordham, M. 1999. Balancing resilience and vulnerability. *International Journal of Mass Emergencies and Disasters* 17: 15–36.

———. 2003. Gender, disaster and development. In *Natural disasters and development in a globalizing world*, ed. Mark Pelling, 57–74. London: Routledge.

Hollander, J.A. 2001. Vulnerability and dangerousness: The construction of gender through conversation about violence. *Gender & Society* 15 (1): 83–109.

Iacopino, V. 1998. The Taliban's war on women: A health and human rights crisis in Afghanistan [Vinvent Iacopino; a report by Physicians for Human Rights]. *Afghan Digital Libraries*.

Joseph, J., and S. Jaswal. 2014. Disaster recovery and mental health: The lived experiences of survivors. *Social Work Practice in Mental Health: Cross-Cultural Perspectives* 1: 214.

Kreps, G.A., and T.E. Drabek. 1996. Disasters as non-routine social problems – 2. *International Journal of Mass Emergencies and Disasters* 14 (2): 129–153.

Nakhaei, M., H.R. Khankeh, G.R. Masoumi, M.A. Hosseini, Z. Parsa-Yekta, L. Kurland, and M. Castren. 2015. Impact of disaster on women in Iran and implication for emergency nurses

volunteering to provide urgent humanitarian aid relief: A qualitative study. *Australasian Emergency Nursing Journal* 18 (3): 165–172.
Peacock, W.G., B.H. Morrow, and H. Gladwin. 1997. *Hurricane Andrew: Ethnicity, gender, and the sociology of disasters*. New York: Psychology Press.
Pelling, M. 2003. *The vulnerability of cities: Natural disasters and social resilience*. London: Earthscan.
Perloff, L.S. 1983. Perceptions of vulnerability to victimization. *Journal of Social Issues* 39 (2): 41–61.
Rees, S., E. Pittaway, and L. Bartolomei. 2005. Waves of violence: Women in post-tsunami Sri Lanka. *Australasian Journal of Disaster and Trauma Studies* 2005: 1–6.
Rezaeian, M. 2013. The association between natural disasters and violence: A systematic review of the literature and a call for more epidemiological studies. *Journal of Research in Medical Sciences: The Official Journal of Isfahan University of Medical Sciences* 18 (12): 1103.
Rogers, J., and U. Kelly. 2011. Feminist intersectionality: Bringing social justice to health disparities research. *Nursing Ethics* 18 (3): 397–407.
Rung, A.L., S. Gaston, E. Oral, W.T. Robinson, E. Fontham, D.J. Harrington, E. Trapido, and E.S. Peters. 2016. Depression, mental distress, and domestic conflict among Louisiana women exposed to the Deepwater Horizon oil spill in the WaTCH study. *Environmental Health Perspectives* 124 (9): 1429–1435.
WHO. 2005. *Violence and disasters*. http://www.who.int/violence_injury_prevention/publications/violence/violence_disasters.pdf.
Yadav, P. 2016. White sari—Transforming widowhood in Nepal. *Gender Technology and Development* 20 (1): 1–24.
Yokoyama, Y., K. Otsuka, N. Kawakami, S. Kobayashi, A. Ogawa, K. Tannno, T. Onoda, Y. Yaegashi, and K. Sakata. 2014. Mental health and related factors after the Great East Japan earthquake and tsunami. *PLoS One* 9 (7): e102497.

Chapter 9
Bio-ethical Considerations for Public Health in Humanitarian Action

Siri Tellier

Abstract The objectives and operational norms of public health are explicitly and strongly based on bio-ethical principles, involving many dilemmas. To a great extent, these principles remain the same when dealing with public health in humanitarian action (PHHA), but their application may involve even more excruciatingly difficult decisions and dilemmas. This chapter reflects on what those principles and dilemmas are, and how they have changed over time. It describes how the global health situation has changed dramatically over the last decades, and what implications that has for health in emergency situations. It also addresses the changing nature of disasters, including more protracted emergencies involving long term displacement, fragile contexts as well as the effect on the capacity of health systems as they are under increasing pressure and attack. Finally, it notes some of the major improvements in humanitarian response, including development of widely accepted guidelines and coordination mechanisms, and how this has contributed to improvements in saving lives and preventing morbidity.

Keywords Public health disaster · Health risk reduction · Displacement · Fragile contexts

9.1 Introduction

The objectives and operational norms of public health are explicitly and strongly based on bio-ethical principles, involving many dilemmas. To a great extent, these principles remain the same when dealing with public health in humanitarian action (PHHA), but their application may involve even more excruciatingly difficult decisions and dilemmas.

S. Tellier (✉)
Health in Emergencies and Refugee Health, School of Global Health, University of Copenhagen, Copenhagen, Denmark
e-mail: stellier@sund.ku.dk

D. P. O'Mathúna et al. (eds.), *Disasters: Core Concepts and Ethical Theories*, Advancing Global Bioethics 11, https://doi.org/10.1007/978-3-319-92722-0_9

To support these statements, and to point to some of the most acute bio-ethical dilemmas, we will build upon a review of changes over the last two centuries, in particular:

1. What is a public health disaster?
2. What is the overall objective of PHHA?
3. How has the global health situation changed?
4. How have those changes influenced the health impact of disasters?
5. How has the global approach to public health changed?
6. How has that influenced the approach to PHHA?

The final section explores

7. Personal reflections: some bio-ethical challenges and dilemmas.

PHHA is an action-oriented field. Therefore, both theoretical concepts and operational norms will be discussed.

9.2 What Is a Public Health Disaster?

The United Nations Office for Disaster Risk Reduction (UNISDR) has defined a *disaster* as '*A serious disruption of the functioning of a community or a society at any scale due to hazardous events interacting with conditions of exposure, vulnerability and capacity, leading to one or more of the following: human, material, economic and environmental losses and impacts*', with the annotation that this may test or exceed the capacity of the affected society to cope with its own resources, and require external assistance (UNISDR 2016). In the following, we will use that as a working definition.

The Centre for Research on the Epidemiology of Disasters (CRED), which maintains one of the most widely used databases on disasters, records an event as a '*disaster*' if it conforms to at least one of the following criteria:

- Ten or more people dead
- One hundred or more people affected
- The declaration of a state of emergency
- A call for international assistance (CRED)

There are many definitions of a *public health disaster*. However, most of them base themselves on the concept that a hazard has caused '*excess mortality*', that is, additional deaths above the '*baseline*', pre-disaster level.

In 1990 Toole and Waldman proposed that 'excess mortality' be seen as a defining characteristic for identifying a state of emergency. To arrive at a quantitative metric, they proposed that a doubling of the baseline mortality should be considered as the threshold value. They took that baseline to be the average mortality for developing countries as a whole in 1990, arriving at a threshold crude mortality rate of 1 death per 10,000 population per day. This threshold was supplemented by a specific metric for children aged under 5 years of age, since that population is most at risk for excess mortality[1] (Sphere Project 2004; Toole and Waldman 1990).

Measures of mortality are often supplemented by a quantitative measure of *malnutrition* in children aged under 5 years, which is seen as a proxy for the overall health of the population. Usually the threshold level for classifying a situation as a serious emergency is that the prevalence of *global acute malnutrition*[2] in children aged 6–59 months is above 10% (UNHCR 2018).

Another term has been added more recently: a '*Public Health Emergency of International Concern*' (with the somewhat unfortunate abbreviation 'PHEIC'). The 2005 WHO International Health Regulations (IHR) define a PHEIC as

> *an extraordinary event which is determined:*
>
> – *to constitute a public health risk to other States through the international spread of disease; and*
> – *to potentially require a coordinated international response.* (WHO 2008 p9)

Notably, the IHR are legally binding – that is, all States are obliged to report to WHO on health events (both communicable disease but also for example radiation), and represent a major strengthening of the reporting system (Baker and Fidler 2006). The IHR provides a framework for on-going, early warning surveillance – a cornerstone of public health. It involves on-going analysis to determine whether any given report may be considered to be irrelevant noise, or worrying enough to follow closely, or sufficiently extraordinary to warrant being classified as a PHEIC. This thinking is not unique. Many countries have a system for reporting disease on a regular (e.g. weekly) basis. The DEWS (Disease Early Warning System which tracks communicable disease), GLEWS (Global Early Warning System which tracks animal-ecosystem-human health interactions) or FEWS (Food Early Warning System) point to the significance attached to identifying potential emergencies.

That is, from a public health point of view, but arguably also from the wider humanitarian action point of view, disasters are conceptualised in terms of the level of excess mortality they cause, and humanitarian action in general is judged in terms of how well it succeeds in saving lives.

Finally, '*public health*' is defined as '*all organized measures (whether public or private) to prevent disease, promote health and prolong life among the population as a whole*' (WHO Glossary, p3). This definition includes both modifiable environmental or individual determinants of health (preventive measures) as well as essential health services (treatment and care measures) (Koplan et al. 2009).

This is not to say that morbidity is absent from humanitarian mind-sets. However, it has taken time to achieve prominence, both in humanitarian and other situations (see the discussion on DALYs below).

---

[1] Mortality exceeding 1 death per 10,000 population per day, or 2 children aged 0–4 per 10,000 children aged 0–4 per day. In 1990, that threshold represented a doubling of the baseline mortality for developing countries.

[2] Global Acute Malnutrition (GAM) is calculated with the Z-score defined as a weight-for-height index less than −2 standard deviations from the mean weight of a reference population of children of the same height and/or having oedema.

9.3 What Is the Overall Objective of PHHA?

A significant milestone in humanitarian action was the creation of the International Committee of the Red Cross in 1863. A central objective of that organisation was to provide health care to wounded soldiers, and to create the humanitarian space for health workers to be able to do so. That is, as mentioned above, from the beginning of humanitarian action, 'saving lives' was one of its central objectives and ethical mandate.

Bringing mortality down to the 'baseline', pre-disaster level remains a key objective, not only for health workers, but for all humanitarian response. The 2011 Sphere Handbook, which represents widely used standards for humanitarian action, states that 'saving lives with dignity' is a central purpose for all humanitarian action, and notes that the standards are 'a set of minimum standards in key life-saving sectors … water supply, sanitation and hygiene promotion; food security and nutrition; shelter, settlement and non-food items; and health action' (Sphere Project 2011, p. 4).

9.4 How Have the Baseline Health Problems Changed?

One of the most central bio-ethical approaches of public health is that it must prioritise action in order to address the most important public health problems. Therefore, it is essential to establish what those health problems are.

Those problems have changed over time. The health impact of disasters is highly dependent on the baseline health situation of the affected population before disaster struck. Therefore, in the following we will list important characteristics of that baseline global health situation and recent trends.

9.4.1 The Baseline: Global Life Expectancy Has Increased Dramatically

In the year 1800, global life expectancy was estimated at around 28.5 years (Riley 2005). With industrialisation, it began to improve. By 1950[3] the global average had reached 47 years (United Nations 2017). By 2017 the estimated average global life expectancy was 72 years, that is, an increase of more than 4 months per year since 1950, with no upper limit in sight (Christensen et al. 2009; United Nations 2017) (Table 9.1).

[3] The estimates are given for a 5-year period, e.g. 1950–1955, but are listed here for single years for easier reading, e.g. 1950.

Table 9.1 Life expectancy in high, middle and low income countries (HMLICs, 1950–1955 and 2015–2020 United Nations 2017)

	1950–1955	2015–2020	Increase
World	47	72	25
HIC	65	81	16
MIC	43	71	28
LIC	35	63	28

Table 9.2 Burden of disease, different types of disease, 1990 and 2015 (Global Burden of Disease Study 2013 Collaborators 2015)

	Types of disease	1990	2015
Group 1	Communicable diseases, nutritional, maternal and perinatal conditions	34%	20%
Group 2	Non-communicable diseases (including cancer, heart disease, diabetes, chronic lung disease)	57%	70%
Group 3	Injury (including suicide, homicide, mass violence, accidents, force of nature)	9%	10%

9.4.2 Disparity Between Countries Has Narrowed, But Some Still Lag

Life expectancy in High Income Countries increased by 16 years in the period 1950–2015. In Low and Middle Income Countries the increase was 28 years. Thus, the gap narrowed. However, so-called fragile states and contexts saw less progress than the average (World Bank).

9.4.3 The Causes of Death Have Also Changed over This Period

Historically, the top causes of deaths were communicable diseases and starvation. However, already by 1990 we had become better at controlling those diseases (called ‘Group 1’ in the table above) (Table 9.2).

Today, Group 1 causes only 20% of deaths. The proportion of deaths attributed to non-communicable diseases (Group 2 above) has increased from 57% to 70% This shift is referred to as the ‘epidemiologic transition’ (Omran 1971).

Table 9.3 Demographic shifts, 1950–2015, Japan, Somalia and the World (United Nations 2017)

	Japan		Somalia		World	
	1950–5	2015–20	1950–5	2015–20	1950–5	2015–20
Crude birth rate (births/1000/year)	23.6	8.1	48.9	42.9	36.9	18.6
Total fertility (births/woman)	3.0	1.5	7.3	6.1	5	2.5
Crude death rate (deaths/1000/year	9.1	10.8	29.8	11.0	19.1	7.7
Life expectancy	63	84	34	57	47	72
% of population aged 0–4	14	4	17	18	13	9
% of population aged 65+	5	28	3	3	5	9

9.4.4 *The Age Group Experiencing Most Improvement Is Children Under 5*

In 1950, at the global level 21.5% of children died before they reached the age of 5. In 2017 it was 4.3% (United Nations 2017). Young children are the ones most vulnerable to Group 1 diseases, and they have benefited the most from improvements.

9.4.5 *The Demographic Transition Has Accentuated Shifts in Health*

The 'demographic transition' occurs as countries move from the high death and birth rates common around 1800. Often, declines in mortality, in particular under-5 mortality, are followed a few decades later by declines in birth rates. The result is temporary rapid population growth and long term ageing of the population.

Thus, in a country such as Somalia, which is in the early stages of both the epidemiologic and demographic transitions, children under 5 constitute 21% of the population, whereas in Japan, which began the transition around 1950, the proportion is around 4% (Table 9.3).

The two transitions, demographic and epidemiologic, interact with each other. Thus Somalia, with a high proportion of young children, has a higher burden of group 1 diseases, whereas in Japan, with an older population, most deaths are attributed to Group 2 diseases.

9.4.6 *Urbanization Also Has Significant Health Implications*

In 1950, 30% of world population resided in urban areas, while by 2008 it was more than half (UN 2014). An increasing number is living in low elevation coastal zones (LECZ), vulnerable to inundation, and the number living in slums remains close to a billion (UN 2015). Urban living provides potential for improvements in health, but also for increased risk factors: poor water, sanitation and hygiene (WASH), crowding, less access to healthy food, unhealthy life styles, and violence/dangerous traffic/job conditions. This may cause a 'triple burden of disease' from the three above-mentioned disease groups.

9.4.7 *A New Metric: Beyond Mortality to Healthy Life Years*

As indicated above, the health of populations is often measured in terms of *mortality*. The 'global burden of disease study' (GBD), first published in 1994 (Murray et al. 1994) introduced a metric to measure *morbidity*: the Disability Adjusted Life Years (DALY). This measures not only how many years people live, but how many years they live in good health. The metric was introduced partially because, with a growing burden of chronic Group 2 diseases, growing numbers of people were living with chronic disabilities. It was a milestone in the conceptualization of health, partially because it drew attention to the burden of disease due to mental illness, which rarely causes death, but causes much ill health.

9.5 How Have Those Changes Influenced the Health Impact of Disasters?

9.5.1 *Mortality Due to Disasters Is Now Relatively Modest*

Globally, there are 55–60 million deaths annually (United Nations 2017). At present, only a small proportion of that number is a result of disasters.

This was not always so. With respect to armed conflict, tens of millions died in the two world wars of the twentieth century. The 1994 Rwanda crisis is estimated to have resulted in over half a million deaths (Global Burden of Disease 2015 Mortality and Causes of Death Collaborators 2016). Data on deaths due to violence in Iraq are hotly contested, but most estimates are in the range of a few hundred thousand over several years (Burnham et al. 2006; Tapp et al. 2008). The same holds for Syria (Price et al. 2014). On average, deaths to collective violence average 200,000–300,000 per annum.

For natural disasters, outbreaks of epidemics or starvation historically caused dramatic spikes in mortality. Starvation in Ireland killed about an eighth of the population in the middle of the nineteenth century (Ó Gráda 2009). The global influenza epidemic of 1918 killed more people than the First World War (1 estimate is 50 million) (Taubenberger and Morens 2006). In recent decades, the average annual number of deaths due to natural disasters is around 100,000, and whereas malnutrition seems to be on the rise since 2016, mass starvation is rare.

Individual populations can experience overwhelming impact, for example male life expectancy in Syria is estimated to have dropped from 73.9 to 62.6 since 2010 (Global Burden of Disease 2015 Mortality and Causes of Death Collaborators 2016). However, this is still less than the 20-year drop in life expectancy in some sub-Saharan countries due to AIDS (United Nations 2017).

Thus, in general, the proportion of deaths which are due to disasters is lower than was historically the case, and other causes of death are more prominent. However, even though a high-profile epidemic like Ebola caused 'only' around 11,000 deaths, it caused great international havoc (duBois et al. 2015).

9.5.2 The Causes of Death in Disasters Have Followed the Epidemiologic Transition

In parallel, the causes of death in disasters have also changed over time. Over the course of the twentieth century it became clear that, although combatants were at special risk for Group 3 diseases (injury), civilian populations, especially those forcibly displaced, were at risk for Group 1 diseases. That is, although the epidemiologic transition meant better control of communicable diseases, when the preconditions for good health disappeared, for example WASH, nutrition and shelter, the epidemiologic transition was reversed. In particular, young children, who are the most vulnerable to Group 1 diseases, were at great risk for excess mortality.

Gradually, awareness has grown that natural disasters (e.g. hurricanes) do not necessarily result in outbreaks of communicable diseases if the health system is more or less intact and 'herd immunity' is high (that is, a high proportion of the population is immune, for example because they have been vaccinated) (Sphere Project 2011). Thus, the Kobe earthquake in Japan did not cause major outbreak of communicable disease; neither did the 2004 Indian Ocean tsunami in the affected countries.

Attention to mental health had already begun to increase in the 1990s, as awareness of chronic conditions and disabilities increased. However, until recently other Group 2 diseases, that is NCDs such as diabetes or heart disease, received little attention (Demaio et al. 2013). This changed with the Syrian crisis. The baseline population in Syria before the crisis was older, more urbanised and more affluent than the affected populations in most of the crises of the previous two decades. They had very high levels of some of the risk factors for NCDs, such as obesity, but had survived due to good health care. As half the Syrian population is displaced, it has become a challenge to provide people living with chronic NCDs with continuous, expensive treatment (Rabkin et al. 2016; Ruby et al. 2015).

In general, disasters have a different impact on different population groups, which is an essential realisation for public health prevention and care.

As mentioned above, young children are at special risk for Group 1 diseases. Older people are sometimes at special risk: 71% of those who died in the wake of

Hurricane Katrina in 2005 were 60 years and older (Adams et al. 2011). Women tend to be at somewhat higher risk in natural disasters, whereas men are generally more at risk in many conflict related settings (Eklund and Tellier 2012; Tellier 2014). Displaced persons, in particular those who are internally displaced (IDPs), are at particular risk, as their usual means of preventing disease (food, WASH, shelter) are disrupted (CRED 2013; Spiegel et al. 2010).

9.6 How Has the Baseline Approach to Public Health Changed?

9.6.1 Some Milestones in Conceptualisation and Bio-ethical Standards in Public Health

The thought that health was not only an individual issue between doctor and client, but a bio-ethical issue where society or the State could, and should, intervene, took time to develop, with what might be called a 'big bang' around 1850.

The industrialization of the nineteenth century saw significant societal changes in Europe and North America. Trade was globalising, and travel accelerating with steamships, railroads and building of the Suez Canal. Populations were urbanising, and exposed to crowding and other health risks (Ersoy et al. 2011; Howard-Jones 1975). Seeing these developments, the German physician Rudolph Virchow in a seminal article in 1848 proposed that the medical profession had a special obligation to be the advocates for the poor, but also that health was an interdisciplinary issue, in particular requiring political will including to reduce risk factors (e.g. sanitation) (Virchow 1848).

The societal changes brought successive cholera pandemics – early examples of what would now be called 'Public health emergencies of international concern'. This resulted in what was arguably the first global health initiative: the Sanitary Conference in Paris in 1851. The conference was unsuccessful, as agreement could not be reached on what caused cholera, and therefore what the solution should be (Ersoy et al. 2011; Howard-Jones 1975). Fourteen such conferences were held between 1851 and 1936.

A better understanding came in 1854. John Snow in London mapped *who* died during a cholera epidemic, from *where* they drew their water, and *when* they died (Brody et al. 2000). He used these empirical epidemiological tools to identify a polluted water source as the risk factor, and to mobilise political will to prevent its use. Robert Koch's microscopic isolation of the bacterium causing cholera in 1884 identified the bio-medical cause of the disease. Together, these discoveries contributed to improvements in WASH in many European cities, and major improvements in population health, even before the advent of medical approaches to prevention and treatment, for example vaccination or antibiotics (McKeown and Brown 1955).

The establishment of the United Nations brought a recognition of health as a human right, therefore underlining the ethical principle of equality, in the WHO Constitution (WHO 1946) and the Universal Declaration of Human Rights (UN 1948). In 1966 a review of the Covenant on Economic, Social and Cultural Rights helped identify health risk factors and the obligation of States to act to improve population health (UN 2000).

The decades of the 1950s–1970s brought a milestone – the eradication of smallpox. An essential precondition for that success was the strategy: 'surveillance and containment'. This entailed targeted vaccination of those who might have come into contact with infected individuals, so that only a few per cent of a population needed to be vaccinated, rather than trying to reach everyone, saving both money and health system capacity (Fenner 1988; Foege et al. 1975).

In 1978 the Alma Ata conference on primary health care set a goal of 'Health for All by 2000', therefore further operationalising the bio-ethical value of equal access to basic health care (WHO 1978). It also made explicit the idea that the preconditions for health go beyond the health sector, including community participation and education.

However, the financial crisis of the 1980s resulted in 'structural adjustment'. In that optic, public health was seen as an expensive, non-essential consumer good. This resulted in 'selective primary health care', focusing on inexpensive targeted interventions, for example immunization of children (Cash et al. 1987).

The 1993 World Bank report 'investing in health' brought back the idea of health as an investment which was a necessary precondition for development (World Bank 1993). It was a further significant shift when the Commission on Macro-economics and health in 2001 elaborated on this, identifying a low level of cost (30–40 USD per year) for a basic health package, thus maintaining the thought that cost must be contained, but also going beyond the narrow targeted approach (WHO 2001).

Inherent in this history is the on-going dispute about the respective benefits of so-called 'vertical' versus 'horizontal' approaches. The vertical approach targets a particular disease, whereas the horizontal focuses on how to build up health systems which can respond to any health hazard and improve overall wellbeing.

The Millennium Development Goals (MDGs), launched in 2001, had a primarily vertical approach on health, addressing individual diseases such as HIV/AIDS. There has been much progress on the MDG health targets since 2000 (UN 2015). However, health systems were not prioritized.

In 2007 WHO launched a description of what is called the '6 building blocks of health systems' (WHO 2007):

1. Leadership and Governance
2. Service delivery
3. Health information
4. Human Resources
5. Medicines and Technologies
6. Financing

These building blocks are now widely used as conceptual framework. The Sustainable Development Goals (SDGs), launched in 2015, take an explicitly horizontal approach, both in the health goals ('wellbeing throughout the life cycle') and the proposed solutions, including Universal Health Coverage (UHC), defined as: *'all people obtain the health services they need without suffering financial hardship to pay for them, a well-run health system, a system for financing, access to essential medicines and technologies, and well trained health workers'* (WHO 2014).

The reader may be struck by the constant referrals to WHO standards, but as will be explained below, they form the basis for widely accepted PHHA guidelines.

The above history has helped develop some key characteristics of Public health, which are also central in PHHA (Koplan et al. 2009):

- *Population* rather than individual focus
- *Evidence* based – epidemiology and surveillance as cornerstones of public health – the ethical obligation to seek scientifically founded solutions
- *Equality* (a human rights approach)
- Reducing modifiable *risk* factors – prevention as well as health care, and therefore an inter-sectoral approach and responsibility
- *Efficiency and prioritization* – prioritising the most serious health issues, developing and adjusting strategy to get the biggest 'bang for the buck'

These characteristics and bio-ethical norms become particularly relevant for humanitarian action, where there may be overwhelming health issues, where basic preconditions for survival and health systems may have been destroyed, and where there is a risk of sometimes deliberate exclusion of vulnerable groups from health care.

9.7 How Has That Influenced the Approach to PHHA?

9.7.1 The Evidence Base: Surveillance and Assessment

As mentioned above, surveillance and epidemiological data are cornerstones of public health.

In a disaster, this is even more crucial. There are several reasons for this, including:

- Guiding the response (assessing the problem, and the evolving effectiveness of the response strategy)
- Reporting to the outside world (gaining political and financial support)
- Underpinning the bio-ethical principles of impartiality and human rights (some groups may need assistance more than others. However, what is seen as responding to need by one actor may be seen as political favouritism by another. Assessment can help establish needs, in a manner perceived to be as objective as possible).

There are many guidelines for such assessments. They recommend undertaking assessments as a priority, before action is decided, and coordinating among actors (MSF 1997; Sphere Project 2011). A key recommendation is to collect data in a prioritised, phased and pragmatic manner: using rules of thumb, accessing available secondary data to establish the baseline situation, and following up with whatever primary data can be conveniently gathered. Individually, these data may not be representative, but when the information is triangulated (compared among different sources) they can still give a useful picture. Clear, simple case definitions used for screening (e.g. 'have you seen cases of acute, watery diarrhea?') can be useful to involve a wide range of actors, including local populations, in surveillance (Parham 2016; Tellier 2014). Only longer term should large-scale studies collecting high quality primary data be undertaken (Tellier and Roche 2017).

As the Non-Governmental Organisation (NGO) Assessment Capacities Project (ACAPS) suggests:

- *know what you need to know*
- *better to be approximately right than precisely wrong*
- *make sense not data.* (Tellier 2014)

Or, as Gilbert Burnham from Johns University told the author in a personal communication: '*public health is about making decisions on incomplete information*'. The bio-ethical imperative is to *act* (since not doing so might lead to death and suffering) in a timely, impartial and effective manner, but also to *learn* from mistakes, with accountability to supporters and affected populations. Assessments are essential for this.

Despite the many guidelines, this remains an area with many issues.

Technically, primary data collection can be difficult, time consuming, expensive and dangerous, both for researchers and beneficiary populations. For example, asking women about sexual violence can lead to their being socially ostracised (Sriram et al. 2009).

Reviews of humanitarian response repeatedly show a lack of coordination amongst different humanitarian actors, with each collecting their own data, and using methods and metrics which are not comparable. Data on injuries in Haiti used divergent definitions, making assessment difficult (PAHO 2011).

The reasons for this multiplicity of surveys are speculative. Beyond the technical difficulties, the usual coordination difficulties may come into play. Competition may also be a factor, particularly if donors have the impression that organisations with the most impressive data are the most worthy of financial support (Knox and Campbell 2015; Tellier and Roche 2017). A review by Active Learning Network for Accountability and Performance in Humanitarian Action (ALNAP) found that many field staff of humanitarian organisations had the impression that data were produced for headquarters' advocacy and fund-raising work, rather than operational field activities (Knox and Campbell 2015).

9.7.2 Risk Reduction and Prevention

PHHA is to a great extent concerned with modifiable risk factors, both environmental and individual. As mentioned above, improvements in WASH as well as nutrition have historically had great influence on mortality. This is explicitly indicated in guidelines for PHHA, including those of Médecins sans Frontières (MSF) (1997), Johns Hopkins/International Federation of Red Cross (IFRC)/Red Crescent Societies (Johns Hopkins and IFRC 2007) or the Sphere project (2011). The thought that the risk of excess deaths is not inevitable, but rather a function of several modifiable factors is sometimes expressed as a 'risk equation'. Here, we will use the one introduced by Boudreau and modified by Johns Hopkins/IFRC:

$$R = H \times E \times V / C$$

(Boudreau 2009; Johns Hopkins and IFRC 2007)

To explain this equation, we will give an example.

The *risk* (R) that a young child will die from measles is a function of whether or not there is a hazard (H) (the measles virus is present in the population), how *exposed* (E) the child is to the virus (the severity of infection is influenced by the amount of viral exposure, and this may be increased in crowded conditions). The risk is exacerbated by the *vulnerability* (V) of the child (e.g. malnutrition), or mitigated by the *coping* capacity (C) of the child, e.g. due to vaccination. The example of measles is often given, since measles is one of the most contagious diseases known. Measles case fatality[4] for children in non-conflict settings is less than 1%, while in conflict settings it is up to 30%, for the reasons mentioned above (UNICEF 2016).

A bio-ethically and technically well-founded approach would call for addressing all the contributing factors. In the immediate aftermath of a disaster, a decision might be taken to prioritise vaccination, because it is faster and less expensive than improving nutritional levels. Longer-term, it would be essential to improve the nutritional status, for general health and wellbeing as well as to prevent measles deaths (UNICEF 2016).

Overall, targeted risk reduction strategies, building on lessons from centuries of public health, have resulted in greatly reduced mortality. For example, after the 1991 hurricane in Bangladesh, it was clear that women were dying at higher rates than men. One of the measures taken was to expand the radio system, so that women in their homes could hear about the approaching disaster and seek shelter (Eklund and Tellier 2012).

---

[4] Case fatality: the proportion of persons who die from a disease (number who die divided by the number of diagnosed cases). Most usefully applied to monitor short duration illness, such as measles, as opposed to AIDS or cancer.

9.7.3 Prioritisation and Efficiency

As mentioned repeatedly above, prioritisation is a fundamental bio-ethical concern in public health: which health problems are most pressing? Which resources should be used to address them? Which groups should be targeted? This has developed over time.

As mentioned above, the Red Cross in 1864 focussed on group 1 disease – injury in victims of armed conflict.[5]

During the twentieth century, humanitarian response broadened, including civilian victims as well as 'natural disaster'. The priority of PHHA began to shift to Group 1 diseases (communicable, nutritional, maternal conditions). Successive Sphere Manuals have emphasized both risk factors (for example WASH and nutrition) and response (for example outbreak control). Reproductive health was added as a focus area in 1996 (IAWG 2010).

In the last decade, there is a growing interest in Group 2 (non-communicable diseases). In 2008, agreement was reached on an approach for mental health and psycho-social support (IASC 2007). For other non-communicable diseases, the author experienced strong resistance by colleagues, and by medical journals, when she brought it up as a bio-ethical challenge in 2009, with some of the reasons given that it was too expensive or complicated to address. In the last few years, it is increasingly recognized (possibly influenced by the Syrian crisis), but guidelines have still to be fully developed (Demaio et al. 2013).

This gradual shift of focus reflects both the changing baseline burden of disease, as well as changing characteristics of populations affected by disasters.

'Triage' is a basic approach, often used in surgery, but with wider application. It is used to describe how treatment of patients is prioritised. Any prioritisation involves bio-ethical considerations, and these decisions can be difficult, despite the availability of agreed technical standards. For treatment of injury, in cases of 'multiple casualties', which stretch but do not overwhelm the capacity of the health system to respond, the priority may be to serve those in most imminent danger of dying. In cases of 'mass casualties', where the health system is overwhelmed and not able to respond according to 'normal' standards, this prioritization may be turned on its head, with priority placed on serving those who are most likely to survive (Tellier and Roche 2017). As mentioned above, this may be one reason NCDs (Group 2) have only slowly been prioritised, as it is rare they cause massive sudden death, and their treatment is complex and expensive.

[5] Reference is made to the disease groupings given in Sect. 2.3–1,2 and 3.

9.7.4 Coordination: Health Cluster

Coordination is a central concern in humanitarian action. Going back to the definition of disasters, the concept is that the affected community or country cannot cope. The question then is, if the national government does not have the capacity to coordinate international humanitarian organizations, who does?

The 1991 46/182 UN General Assembly Resolution for strengthening response to disasters was a milestone, intended to address that problem (UN 1991). It established a UN humanitarian coordinator, as well as an Inter-Agency Standing Committee (IASC), which coordinates approaches and establishes standards and guidelines. After the 1994 Rwanda crisis, the Red Cross/Red Crescent and a group of NGOs united in producing the 'Sphere Project', with a humanitarian charter and minimum standards for humanitarian response (stating that populations affected by disasters have rights).

Another milestone in humanitarian action was in 2005, with the creation of what often is referred to as the IASC 'cluster system'. So far there are 11 clusters at global level, and WHO is the global lead for the health cluster (IASC 2015).

The vision of the cluster is to reduce avoidable mortality, morbidity and disability, and restore the delivery of, and equitable access to, preventive and curative health care as quickly as possible and in as sustainable a manner as possible (IASC 2008). Reviews indicate that the cluster system has resulted in improvements in coordination, with less overlap or gaps (IASC 2015; Olu et al. 2015). They also indicate that for the first decade of implementation the focus has been too much on process and too little on results, and that one of the most difficult areas seems to be coordination with local actors, including handing over to them when humanitarian actors leave (IASC 2015; Olu et al. 2015).

9.7.5 Preparedness

As for most humanitarian action, preparedness is essential for PHHA. Many humanitarian actors adopt an 'all-hazards' approach, that is, making preparations which can be applied in the early stages of a wide variety of disasters. They have a blueprint nature, since it is difficult to make plans for all situations. The approach is then phased over time: in principle action is modified, as the situation evolves, better information becomes available, and there is less time pressure (again underscoring the importance of continuing assessment and prioritisation).

For example, the IASC health cluster has developed Interagency Emergency Health Kits, which are stored (in humanitarian jargon: 'pre-positioned') for example in the UNICEF warehouse in Copenhagen. Such kits may be prepared to meet the needs of a standard population: for example 10,000 people for a period of 3 months. The kits are painfully wasteful because they have not been targeted and therefore contain commodities that will never be used. However, when a massive emergency occurs and commodities have to be shipped, pre-packaging reduces the reaction time, and increases what is termed 'surge capacity' – that is, the ability to react speedily, massively and, hopefully, meaningfully.

Another example is Emergency Medical Teams (EMTs), until recently named Foreign Medical Teams. A major bio-ethical issue in the past has been that unqualified and ill-equipped health workers have arrived, without procedures for screening them, with inadequate or non-existent equipment and support systems, and potentially causing more harm than good. A certification process, including detailed technical standards and a classification system, was introduced by WHO in 2013. EMTs are expected to come as a team, have quality training, as well as equipment/supplies in order to successfully respond rather than be a burden on the national system. The lead of the health cluster at country level is expected to help local authorities check those qualifications (Norton et al. 2013).

A recent review finds a continuing competence gap – well-established EMTs keep improving, but unprepared and poorly equipped teams continue to arrive, overwhelming affected countries. Deployment to date has concentrated on surgical teams, which are expensive and may not correspond to main needs. Another issue is a need for better legal and procedural preparedness at the national level to facilitate the entry and coordination of the EMTs (WHO 2017).

9.7.6 Building on Local Systems and Exit Strategy

The concepts and norms are clear: international humanitarian action in disasters is informed by the understanding that the affected community temporarily 'cannot cope'.

Equally important is the understanding that the role of any outsiders is to plan their action in a manner that at least does not weaken local structures, but supplements and ideally strengthens local capacity. For the health field, this means building on the local health system, and that can be particularly complex. One key feature of health systems is that they have a method of referring complicated cases from the simplest, primary level (e.g. a local clinic) to a higher, more sophisticated level (e.g. a 'tertiary' hospital). All levels must function at the same time, making them different from, for example, educational systems (IASC 2008; IFRC 1996; UN 1991; UNISDR 2005). This makes harmonisation even more challenging.

IASC guidelines on health recovery emphasize that programming for development needs to begin at the earliest possible stage of relief work (IASC 2008). The guidelines suggest using the six building blocks of health systems (see above under Sect. 4.1) as an analytical framework for situation analysis and response planning. Lessons are becoming clearer on do's and don'ts.

For example:

- Governance: in emergency situations, a segmented approach is often adopted, depending on access to unsafe areas, areas controlled by different groupings or different approaches by different international actors. This makes it more difficult to establish a national plan, functioning at all the levels mentioned above, as in Afghanistan (Newbrander et al. 2014)
- However, disasters can also be opportunities for management reform (Boin et al. 2005). A study by Nyenswah et al. from Liberia describes how governmental structures were made more effective in the Ebola crisis, as those workers who did not perform were dismissed, whereas those who remained were able to build leaner, flatter decision-making structures (Nyenswah et al. 2016). The main concern identified by the article is that the system will revert to old habits one the emergency is over.
- Human resources: in Cambodia internationals trained 59 different categories of health workers, which met their immediate needs but did not correspond to local standards of qualifications and therefore could not be integrated into the national system when internationals left (Nabarro and Evans 2005). A frequent problem is that internationals pay salaries are not sustainable by local organizations.
- Service delivery: in Afghanistan a basic package of health services (BPHS) was developed, based on the above-mentioned six building blocks of health systems. It was budgeted at a low cost, with funding committed by three major donors, yet faced challenges in implementation (Edward et al. 2011; Health and Fragile States Network 2009; Newbrander et al. 2014).
- Vaccines and medicines: essential drugs programmes can be easier to introduce in countries where there is no well-established commercial drug industry (IASC 2008).

9.7.7 An Example of Sectoral Guidelines

One key role of the IASC is to develop norms in the form of technical guidelines, to encourage better quality and coordination. Here we will give one illustrative example: reproductive health. The IASC sets out a minimum initial service package (MISP) to be implemented in the first 3 months after a disaster strikes, before it may have been possible to do a detailed situation assessment:

1. Identify a coordinator
2. Initiate action to prevent avoidable maternal and neonatal mortality
3. Prevent and treat HIV/AIDS
4. Prevent and treat gender based violence
5. Plan for integration into local services, to allow for a broader approach

This reflects the bio-ethical principles mentioned above: strict prioritisation of life-saving interventions, acknowledgement that action may be taken even without full assessment, acknowledging the importance of coordination, and the beginnings of an exit strategy. Health kits have been developed to support the indicated activities (IAWG 2010).

9.8 Personal Reflections: Some Bio-ethical Challenges and Dilemmas

Public health has strong, strikingly clear and consistent bio-ethical values, with the utilitarian goal of improving health as much as possible for as many people as possible. These values hold, sometimes in exacerbated form, in humanitarian situations. But many dilemmas occur.

1. *Prioritisation*: prioritisation (including triage) is at the heart of public health action. Prioritising one activity necessarily means deprioritising another. The bio-ethical choice can be excruciatingly difficult to make, professionally, politically and personally. Professional decisions can be difficult, but the political perception of that choice, by populations and authorities, can be even more so. If one population group is more at risk than another, and humanitarians prioritise interventions for that group, this may cause political problems. A choice not to give antibiotics to a population struck by cholera may be perceived as giving treatment which is second best, even though technical evidence shows it is as effective as the lower cost Oral Rehydration Therapy. Many professionals have informed me that their most recurrent nightmares were remembering the patients they had to deprioritize for lack of capacity.
2. *Business continuity*: people continue to have health problems not associated with the disaster, for example traffic accidents or obstetric emergencies. Yet, the local health system may have been incapacitated, meaning it cannot maintain business continuity. Funding for humanitarian action does not always provide for treating health problems not associated with the disaster, and local laws or organizational guidelines may disallow it. Should humanitarians treat them nevertheless? What if donors do not allow it?
3. *Standards*: health is a comparatively regulated field, and most countries have standards for protected medical professions and treatments. Health humanitarians also have an ever-expanding set of standards. However, not all countries live up to those standards, and humanitarians do not always follow them if they find them inappropriate. In the case of controversial issues such as abortion, national laws may be at direct odds with personal or organisational bio-medical ethics and professional standards (for example, five countries do not allow abortion even to save the life of the mother). One large donor variously permits, or does not permit, funding of organisations which treat or refer patients for abortion, including where national laws permit it.
4. *Exit Strategy*: the IASC guidelines for health recovery propose that services and staff training should be in accordance with the six building blocks of the local

health system in order to facilitate post-emergency handover to local institutions. However, in an emergency, if you need to make rapid decisions about prioritisation, e.g. measles vaccination, there may not be time to train staff, say, in the full job description of a community health worker. In the Haiti earthquake, the policy before the 2010 earthquake was based on fee-for-service. During the disaster, it is difficult for an emergency surgical team to ask for payment. However, it made the post-disaster return to the national policy more difficult (PAHO 2011)

5. *Access/security*: health humanitarians are faced with the same problems as other humanitarians: they may not be able to access the groups which need them the most. There seem to be increasing numbers of targeted attacks on local and international health providers. It is an eternal dilemma to decide under which conditions services should be continued.
6. *Coordination*: humanitarian actors sometimes are criticised for acting in a chaotic manner, or not planning for the longer term. The solution is sometimes seen as developing more guidelines and policies to improve coordination, technical quality and planning. For example, there is an exhortation for community participation, 'localisation' (channelling funding as directly as possible to local organisations), yet this may pose bio-ethical dilemmas in living up to principles of neutrality and impartiality (Brown and Donini 2015; Cohn and Kutalek 2016; duBois 2016; Schenkenberg 2016). Humanitarian work is riddled with dilemmas, but as one observer notes, the dilemmas that humanitarian workers experience cannot be remedied by declaring ever-expanding sets of principles to dictate practice (Hilhorst and Jansen 2013; Valbak 2016). This author would suggest better analysis of why bio-ethical principles and guidelines are not followed, rather than producing more guidelines. Possibly that is more difficult – guidelines are something authorities can delegate to staff, whereas analysis of why they are not followed may identify issues where authorities themselves need to change.
7. *Funding*: this relates to the omnipresent issue of funding –perhaps the most pressing problem. Humanitarian action is often based on raising funding after action has begun. All the above dilemmas and ethical choices are deeply dependent on funding decisions, many of which may be unpredictable and incomprehensible for field workers.

The former Emergency Relief Coordinator, Jan Egeland, sometimes quoted a famous aphorism: We try, we fail. We try again, we fail better.

Or, in another medium:

References

Adams, V., S.R. Kaufman, T. van Hattum, and S. Moody. 2011. Aging disaster: Mortality, vulnerability, and long-term recovery among Katrina survivors. *Medical Anthropology* 30 (3): 247–270. https://doi.org/10.1080/01459740.2011.560777.

Baker, M.G., and D.P. Fidler. 2006. Global public health surveillance under new international health regulations. *Emerging Infectious Diseases* 12 (7): 1058–1065. https://doi.org/10.3201/eid1207.051497.

Boin, A., P. Hart, E. Stern, B. Sundelius, and M. Inambao. 2005. *The politics of crisis management*. Cambridge, UK: Cambridge University Press.

Boudreau, Tanya. 2009. Solving the risk equation people-centred disaster risk assessment in Ethiopia. Humanitarian Practice Network Network Paper. http://odihpn.org/wp-content/uploads/2009/06/networkpaper066.pdf. Accessed 16 Apr 2018.

Brody, H., M.R. Rip, P. Vinten-Johansen, N. Paneth, and S. Rachman. 2000. Map-making and myth-making in Broad Street: The London cholera epidemic, 1854. *Lancet* 356 (9223): 64–68. https://doi.org/10.1016/S0140-6736(00)02442-9.

Brown, Dayna, and Donini, Antonio. 2015. Rhetoric or reality? Putting affected people at the centre of humanitarian action. ALNAP Study. http://www.alnap.org/resource/12859. Accessed 16 Apr 2018.

Burnham, G., R. Lafta, S. Doocy, and L. Roberts. 2006. Mortality after the 2003 invasion of Iraq: A cross-sectional cluster sample survey. *Lancet* 368 (9545): 1421–1428. https://doi.org/10.1016/S0140-6736(06)69491-9.

Cash, Richard A., Gerald Keusch, and Joel Lamstein. 1987. *Child health and survival: The UNICEF Gobi-FFF program*. London: Room Helm.

Christensen, K., G. Doblhammer, R. Rau, and J.W. Vaupel. 2009. Ageing populations: The challenges ahead. *Lancet* 374 (9696): 1196–1208. https://doi.org/10.1016/S0140-6736(09)61460-4.

Cohn, S., and R. Kutalek. 2016. Historical parallels, ebola virus disease and cholera: Understanding community distrust and social violence with epidemics. *PLOS Currents Outbreaks* 8. doi:https://doi.org/10.1371/currents.outbreaks.aa1f2b60e8d43939b43fbd93e1a63a94.

CRED. 2013. *People affected by conflict 2013 – humanitarian needs in numbers*. CRED. http://reliefweb.int/sites/reliefweb.int/files/resources/PubID303ConflictReport.pdf. Accessed 16 Apr 2018.

———. Frequently asked questions. http://www.emdat.be/frequently-asked-questions. Accessed 16 Apr 2018.

Demaio, A., J. Jamieson, R. Horn, M. de Courten, and S. Tellier. 2013. Non-communicable diseases in emergencies: a call to action. *PLoS Currents* 6: 5. https://doi.org/10.1371/currents.dis.53e08b951d59ff913ab8b9bb51c4d0de.

duBois, Marc. 2016. Be careful what you wish for – will local NGOs fall into the same trap as their northern cousins? *World Humanitarian Summit* 2016: 20160808.

duBois, Marc, Wake, Caitlin, and with Sturridge, Scarlett, and Bennett, Christina. 2015. The ebola response in West Africa exposing the politics and culture of international aid. HPG Working Paper. https://www.odi.org/sites/odi.org.uk/files/odi-assets/publications-opinion-files/9903.pdf. Accessed 16 Apr 2018.

Edward, A., B. Kumar, F. Kakar, A.S. Salehi, G. Burnham, and D.H. Peters. 2011. Configuring balanced scorecards for measuring health system performance: evidence from 5 years' evaluation in Afghanistan. *PLoS Medicine* 8 (7): e1001066. https://doi.org/10.1371/journal.pmed.1001066.

Eklund, Lisa, and Siri Tellier. 2012. Gender and international crisis response: Do we have the data, and does it matter? *Disasters*. https://doi.org/10.1111/j.1467-7717.2012.01276.x.

Ersoy, Nermin, Gungor, Yuksel, and Akpinar, Aslihan. 2011. *International sanitary conferences from the Ottoman perspective (1851–1938)*.

Fenner, Frank. 1988. Development of the global smallpox eradication programme. Smallpox and its eradication In *History of international public health, No. 6*, 366–418. Geneva: WHO.

Foege, William H., J.D. Millar, and D.A. Henderson. 1975. Smallpox eradication in West and Central Africa. *Bulletin of the World Health Organization* 52 (2): 209–222. NA (Bulletin only began attributing DOIs in 2006).

Global Burden of Disease 2015 Mortality and Causes of Death Collaborators. 2016. Global, regional, and national life expectancy, all-cause mortality, and cause-specific mortality for 249 causes of death, 1980-2015: A systematic analysis for the Global Burden of Disease Study 2015. *Lancet* 388 (10053): 1459–1544. https://doi.org/10.1016/S0140-6736(16)31012-1.

Global Burden of Disease Study 2013 Collaborators. 2015. Global, regional, and national incidence, prevalence, and years lived with disability for 301 acute and chronic diseases and injuries in 188 countries, 1990–2013: A systematic analysis for the Global Burden of Disease Study 2013. *Lancet* 388: 1545–1602. https://doi.org/10.1016/S0140-6736(15)60692-4.

Health and Fragile States Network. 2009. *Health systems strengthening in fragile contexts: A report on good practices and new approaches*. London. http://gsdrc.org/document-library/health-systems-strengthening-in-fragile-contexts-a-report-on-good-practices-and-new-approaches/. Accessed 16 Apr 2018.

Hilhorst, Dorothea, and Bram J. Jansen. 2013. Humanitarian space as arena: A perspective on the everyday politics of aid. *Development and Change* 41: 1117–1139. https://doi.org/10.1111/j.1467-7660.2010.01673.x.

Hopkins, Johns, Bloomberg School of Public Health, and IFRC. 2007. *The Johns Hopkins and Red Cross red crescent public health guide in emergencies*. Vol. 2. Geneva: International Federation of Red Cross and Red Crescent Societies.

Howard-Jones, Norman. 1975. *The scientific background of the international sanitary conferences (1851–1938)*. Geneva. Electronic document, Accessed.

IASC. 2007. IASC guidelines for mental health and psycho-social support in emergencies. http://www.who.int/hac/network/interagency/news/iasc_guidelines_mental_health_psychososial.pdf?ua=1. Accessed 16 Apr 2018.

———. 2008. Health cluster guidance note on health recovery. http://www.who.int/hac/global_health_cluster/guide/117_iasc_global_health_cluster_recovery_strategy_guidelines.pdf. Accessed 16 Apr 2018.

———. 2015. Reference module for cluster coordination at country level. http://who.int/health-cluster/about/cluster-system/cluster-coordination-reference-module-2015.pdf. Accessed 16 Apr 2018.

IAWG, Inter-agency Working Group on Reproductive Health in Crises. 2010. *Inter-agency field manual on reproductive health in humanitarian settings – 2010 revision for field review*. Geneva: United Nations. http://www.who.int/reproductivehealth/publications/emergencies/field_manual_rh_humanitarian_settings.pdf. Accessed 16 Apr 2018.

IFRC. 1996. *Key factors for developmental relief*. International Review of the Red Cross. Geneva. http://www.icrc.org/eng/resources/documents/article/other/57jmvw.htm. Accessed 16 Apr 2018.

Knox, Clarke Paul, and Campbell, Leah. 2015. Exploring coordination in humanitarian clusters. https://reliefweb.int/sites/reliefweb.int/files/resources/study-coordination-humanitarian-clusters-alnap-2015.pdf. Accessed 16 Apr 2018.

Koplan, Jeffrey P., T. Christopher Bond, Michael H. Merson, K. Srinath Reddy, Mario Henry Rodriguez, Nelson K. Sewankambo, and Judith N. Wasserheit. 2009. Towards a common definition of global health. *The Lancet* 373 (9679): 1993–1995. https://doi.org/10.1016/S0140-6736(09)60332-9.

McKeown, T., and R.G. Brown. 1955. Medical evidence related to English population changes in the eighteenth century. *Population Studies* 9: 119–141. https://doi.org/10.2307/2172162.

MSF. 1997. *Refugee health: an approach to emergency situations*. London: Macmillan.

Murray, C.J., A.D. Lopez, and D.T. Jamison. 1994. The global burden of disease in 1990: summary results, sensitivity analysis and future directions. *Bulletin of the World Health Organization* 72 (3): 495–509.

Nabarro, David, and T. Evans. 2005. Guide to health work force development in post-conflict environments. Geneva: World Health Organization. http://apps.who.int/iris/bitstream/handle/10665/43243/9241593288_eng.pdf;jsessionid=BA0246B50164AF0731A674BE8EEA7E4C?sequence=1. Accessed 16 Apr 2018.

Newbrander, W., P. Ickx, F. Feroz, and H. Stanekzai. 2014. Afghanistan's basic package of health services: its development and effects on rebuilding the health system. Global Public Health 9 (Suppl 1):S6–S28. https://doi.org/10.1080/17441692.2014.916735.

Norton, I., J. von Schreeb, P. Aitken, P. Herard, and C. Lajolo. 2013. Classification and minimum standards for foreign medical teams in sudden onset disasters. Health Cluster. Geneva: WHO. http://www.who.int/hac/global_health_cluster/fmt_guidelines_september2013.pdf?ua=1. Accessed 16 Apr 2018.

Nyenswah, Tolbert, Cyrus Y. Engineer, and David H. Peters. 2016. Leadership in times of crisis: The example of ebola virus disease in liberia. *Health Systems & Reform* 2 (3): 194. https://doi.org/10.1080/23288604.2016.1222793.

Ó Gráda, Cormac. 2009. *Famine – a short history*. Princeton/Oxford: Princeton University Press.

Olu, O., A. Usman, S. Woldetsadik, D. Chamla, and O. Walker. 2015. Lessons learnt from coordinating emergency health response during humanitarian crises: A case study of implementation of the health cluster in northern Uganda. *Conflict and Health* 9: 1. https://doi.org/10.1186/1752-1505-9-1.

Omran, A.R. 1971. The epidemiologic transition. A theory of the epidemiology of population change. *Milbank Memorial Fund Quarterly* 49 (4): 509–538. https://doi.org/10.1111/j.1468-0009.2005.00398.

PAHO. 2011. Health response to the earthquake in Haiti, January 2010 – lessons to be learned for the next massive sudden-onset disaster. Washington, DC: Pan American Health Organization. http://reliefweb.int/sites/reliefweb.int/files/resources/Full_Report_3342.pdf. Accessed 16 Apr 2018.

Parham, Nic (ACAPS). 2016. Flying blind? Gathering and using quality information in situations of constrained access. Third webinar of the ALNAP Bridgoin the evidence gap series. Online event (webinar), ALNAP.

Price, Megan, Gohdes, Anita, and Ball, Patrick. 2014. *Updated statistical analysis of documentation of killings in the Syrian Arab Republic*. UNHCR. http://www.ohchr.org/Documents/Countries/SY/HRDAGUpdatedReportAug2014.pdf. Accessed 16 Apr 2018.

Rabkin, M., F.M. Fouad, and W.M. El-Sadr. 2016. Addressing chronic diseases in protracted emergencies: Lessons from HIV for a new health imperative. *Global Public Health* 1–7. doi:https://doi.org/10.1080/17441692.2016.1176226.

Riley, James C. 2005. Estimates of regional and global life expectancy, 1800–2001. *Population and Development Review* 31 (3): 537–543. https://doi.org/10.1111/j.1728-4457.2005.00083.x.

Ruby, Alexander, Abigail Knight, Pablo Perel, Karl Blanchet, and Bayard Roberts. 2015. The effectiveness of interventions for non-communicable diseases in humanitarian crises: A systematic review. *PLoS One* 10 (9): e0138303. https://doi.org/10.1371/journal.pone.0138303.

Schenkenberg, E. 2016. *Emergency gap: The challenges of localised humanitarian aid in armed conflict*. Médecins Sans Frontières. https://arhp.msf.es/sites/default/files/MSF_EGS03_The%20challenges%20of%20localised%20humanitarian%20aid%20in%20armed%20conflict_november%202016_0_0.pdf. Accessed 16 Apr 2018.

Sphere Project. 2004 *Humanitarian charter and minimum standards for disaster response*. Geneva: The Sphere Project. http://ocw.jhsph.edu/courses/RefugeeHealthCare/PDFs/SphereProjectHandbook.pdf. Accessed 16 Apr 2018.

———. 2011 *The sphere handbook: Humanitarian charter and minimum standards for disaster response*. Geneva: The Sphere Project. http://www.ifrc.org/PageFiles/95530/The-Sphere-Project-Handbook-20111.pdf Accessed 16 Apr 2018.

Spiegel, P.B., F. Checchi, S. Colombo, and E. Paik. 2010. Health-care needs of people affected by conflict: future trends and changing frameworks. *Lancet* 375 (9711): 341–345. https://doi.org/10.1016/S0140-6736(09)61873-0.

Sriram, C.L., C.J. King, Julie A. Mertus, Olga Martin-Ortega, and Johanna Herman. 2009. *Surviving field research: Working in violent and difficult situations*. London: Routledge.

Tapp, C., F.M. Burkle Jr., K. Wilson, T. Takaro, G.H. Guyatt, H. Amad, and E.J. Mills. 2008. Iraq war mortality estimates: A systematic review. *Conflict and Health* 2: 1. https://doi.org/10.1186/1752-1505-2-1.

Taubenberger, J.K., and D.M. Morens. 2006. 1918 Influenza: The mother of all pandemics. *Emerging Infectious Diseases* 12 (1): 15–22. https://doi.org/10.3201/eid1201.050979.

Tellier, Siri. 2014. *Technical brief: Demographic profile using secondary data*. Geneva: ACAPS. https://www.acaps.org/sites/acaps/files/resources/files/demographic_profile_using_secondary_data_august_2014.pdf. Accessed 16 Apr 2018.

Tellier, Siri, and Roche, Niall (eds). 2017. Basic concepts and current challenges of public health in humanitarian action. In *International humanitarian action*, ed. H.-J. Heitze and P. Thielbörger, 229–320. Springer.

Toole, M.J., and R.J. Waldman. 1990. Prevention of excess mortality in refugee and displaced populations in developing countries. *The Journal of the American Medical Association* 263 (24): 3296–3302. https://doi.org/10.1001/jama.1990.03440240086021.

UN. 1948. Universal declaration of human rights, United Nations General Assembly in Paris on 10 December 1948 (General Assembly resolution 217 A).

———. 2015. *The millennium development goals report 2015*. New York: United Nations. http://www.un.org/millenniumgoals/2015_MDG_Report/pdf/MDG%202015%20rev%20(July%201).pdf. Accessed 16 Apr 2018.

UN, Committee on Economic, Social and Cultural Rights. 2000. General comment no. 14, the right to the highest attainable standard of health (article 12 of the international covenant on economic, social and cultural rights). http://tbinternet.ohchr.org/_layouts/treatybodyexternal/Download.aspx?symbolno=E%2fC.12%2f2000%2f4&Lang=en. Accessed 16 Apr 2018.

UN, Department of Economic and Social Affairs, Population Division. 2014. *World urbanization prospects: The 2013 revision, highlights*. New York: UN, Department of Economic and Social Affairs, Population Division. http://esa.un.org/unpd/wup/. Accessed 16 Apr 2018.

UN, General Assembly 78th Plenary meeting. 1991. Strengthening of the coordination of humanitarian emergency assistance of the United Nations, A/RES/46/182. General Assembly, 78th Plenary meeting. http://www.un.org/documents/ga/res/46/a46r182.htm. Accessed 16 Apr 2018.

UNHCR. 2018. *Emergency handbook*. Geneva: UNHCR. https://emergency.unhcr.org/entry/86022/acute-malnutrition-threshold. Accessed 16 Apr 2018.

UNICEF. 2016. Two-thirds of unimmunized children live in conflict-affected countries. *Press release*, 24–30 Apr 2016.

UNISDR. 2005. Hyogo framework for action 2005–2015: Building the resilience of nations and communities to disasters. *United Nations*. http://www.unisdr.org/files/1037_hyogoframeworkforactionenglish.pdf. Accessed 16 Apr 2018.

———. 2016. Terminology: Disaster. https://www.unisdr.org/we/inform/terminology#letter-d. Accessed 26 Apr 2018.

United Nations, Department of Economic and Social Affairs Population Division. 2017. *World population prospects: The 2017 revision*. New York: United Nations. http://esa.un.org/unpd/wpp/. Accessed 16 Apr 2018.

Valbak, Iben Gejl. 2016. The everyday practices of aid: A phenomenological analysis of international humanitarian aid workers' experiences of collaborating with Nepalese government officials following the Nepal earthquake 2015. University of Copenhagen.

Virchow, Rudolf. 1848. Die Medizinische reform. In *1941, medicine and human welfare, Henry Ernest Sigerist*. New Haven: Yale University Press.

WHO. 1946. Preamble to the constitution of the world health organization as adopted by the international health conference. New York, 19–22 June, 1946; signed on 22 July 1946 by the representatives of 61 States (Official Records of the World Health Organization, no. 2, p. 100) and entered into force on 7 April 1948. New York.

———. 1978. Declaration of Alma-Ata. International Conference on Primary Health Care, Alma-Ata, 6–12 September 1978, USSR, 1978.
———. 2007. *Everybody's business: Strengthening health systems to improve health outcomes. WHO's framework for action.* Geneva: WHO. http://www.who.int/healthsystems/strategy/everybodys_business.pdf. Accessed 16 Apr 2018.
———. 2008. International health regulations 2005. http://apps.who.int/iris/bitstream/handle/10665/246107/9789241580496-eng.pdf?sequence=1. Accessed 16 Apr 2018.
———. 2014. What is universal health coverage? http://www.who.int/features/qa/universal_health_coverage/en/. Accessed 20170115. Accessed 15.01 2017.
———. Glossary – public health. http://www.who.int/healthsystems/hss_glossary/en/index8.html. Accessed 16 Apr 2018.
WHO, Commission on Macroeconomics and Health. 2001. Macroeconomics and health: Investing in health for economic development. http://apps.who.int/iris/bitstream/handle/10665/42435/924154550X.pdf?sequence=1&isAllowed=y. Accessed 16 Apr 2018.
WHO, IFRC. 2017. The regulation and management of international emergency medical teams. http://www.ifrc.org/PageFiles/115542/EMT%20Report%20HR.PDF. Accessed 16 Apr 2018.
World Bank. 1993. *World development report 1993: Investing in health.* New York: Oxford University Press. https://openknowledge.worldbank.org/handle/10986/5976. Accessed 16 Apr 2018.
———. Indicators. https://data.worldbank.org/indicator/. Accessed 16 Apr 2018.

Part II
Moral Theories and Response to Disasters

Chapter 10
Disaster Consequentialism

Vojin Rakić

Abstract In this chapter I will give an interpretation of the role consequentialist ethics can have in disaster settings. I will argue that consequentialist ethics is most appropriate when decisions are taken that affect not single individuals but larger numbers of people. This is frequently the case in political decision making, especially when powerful states act in the domain of international relations, but also in disaster settings. I will focus on the latter settings and argue that in those contexts consequentialism is most adequate as a moral theory. I will also contend that different situational settings require different ethics. The moral relevance of these situational settings is primarily dependent on the number of people affected by morally relevant decisions. The formulation of my position will be preceded by a brief review of the historical development of consequentialism, primarily related to disaster settings. In order to make my arguments as vivid as possible I will use four vignettes. In two of them consequentialist ethics is appropriate, while in the other two deontology is a more reasonable moral theory. In the former two we deal with large numbers of people in disaster settings; in the latter two with "regular" settings that do not affect the lives of many individuals.

Keywords Disaster consequentialism · Consequentialist ethics · Disaster settings · State consequentialism · Deontology · Ultimate harm · Situational settings

---

I am indebted to Bert Gordijn and Donal O'Mathuna for their insightful comments on this chapter. My work on this chapter has been supported by COST Action 1201 and Project # III 41003 of the Serbian Ministry of Education, Science and Technological Development.

V. Rakić (✉)
Center for the Study of Bioethics, Institute of Social Sciences, European Division of the UNESCO Chair in Bioethics, University of Belgrade, Belgrade, Serbia

D. P. O'Mathúna et al. (eds.), *Disasters: Core Concepts and Ethical Theories*, Advancing Global Bioethics 11, https://doi.org/10.1007/978-3-319-92722-0_10

10.1 Introduction

Consequentialism argues that the morality of an action is contingent upon the action's outcome or consequence. Hence, a morally right action is one that produces a good outcome or consequence. The more people are affected by such an outcome, the better it is.

Consequentialist ethics is essential in the context of disasters. The reason is that disasters frequently affect large numbers of people. Accordingly, the focus is often not on the individual, but on the consequences for larger numbers of people. Hence, consequentialism is an approach to ethics that appears to fit the context of minimisation of deaths and suffering in disaster settings.

But how did consequentialism come about as a theory and how has it tried to address disasters? In what follows I will address a number of the main consequentialist approaches to disasters, some of them in their historical contexts. These approaches are contingent upon two issues: first, various types of consequentialist ethics, and second, the historical development of a range of disasters humanity has been facing.

To some extent I will structure my chapter on the basis of these two issues, at the same time being very selective and focusing only on those consequentialist approaches that are either the most relevant ones or directly related to disasters. An extensive analysis of various variants of consequentialism will remain outside this chapter's scope. Thus I will not go into any details and specificities of rule consequentialism, two-level consequentialism, motive consequentialism, negative consequentialism, the "acts and omissions doctrine," etc.[1]

I will conclude that different situational contexts sometimes require different ethical approaches. These situational contexts are not so much culturally determined as they are contingent upon the existence of a disaster setting marked by (medical) emergencies in which multiple lives are at stake and in which there is a shortage of resources that are needed to save those lives. Furthermore, I will conclude that consequentialist ethics is often the most acceptable (least unacceptable) approach when decisions have to be made about many individuals. Such decisions are frequently taken in disaster settings.

First I will give a very brief overview of the development of consequentialist ethics and refer to a contemporary debate regarding consequentialism through the example of a theory that addresses the issue of major disasters. Almost needless to say, this will only be a background sketch for the theme of this chapter and by no means something that will even resemble exhaustiveness.

---

[1] These types of consequentialism are being examined in various studies on ethical theories, starting from corresponding sections in the Stanford Encyclopedia of Philosophy, to Mizzoni (2010) and Hooker (2000).

10.2 Mohist Consequentialism

The first form in which consequentialism appeared was state consequentialism, notably *Mohist consequentialism* (fifth century BC, named after the Chinese philosopher, Mozi). It appeared precisely as an attempt to address disaster settings. All this occurred long before the emergence of utilitarianism as a moral theory that focuses on individuals.

Mohist ethics had many elements of a political theory. During Mozi's era, war and famines were common in China, and population growth was seen as a moral necessity for a harmonious society. Mohist consequentialism evaluates moral values on the basis of how they contribute to the interests of a state. Hence, it defines the interests of the state (i.e., the good) through social order, material wealth, and population growth (Loewe and Shaughnessy 1999). In other words, it tries to encapsulate the social order of that time in a moral and political theory that is deemed to be the most appropriate one for addressing the challenges of that order. Mohist consequentialism is therefore based on a plurality of intrinsic goods taken as constitutive of human welfare in the context of the Chinese state of Mozi'stime, a state that was partially marked by disaster settings. In sum, consequentialism initially appeared as state consequentialism in the form of a moral theory that attempted to address disasters.

10.3 Consequentialism in European Antiquity

Although various types of consequentialist ethics were debated in Ancient times (e.g., in Plato's dialogues, with Thrasymachus from the *Republic* as one of the prototype consequentialists), I will refer here only to hedonistic, egoistic and ascetic moral theories. The reason for mentioning them is not only their importance in Ancient times, but also the fact that these theories are types of consequentialism that have the individual rather than the state in their focus, departing in that way from State-centred approaches, such as Mohist consequentialism.

Hedonist theories argue that pleasure is the most important pursuit of humankind, while individuals should make an effort to maximise pleasure and minimise pain, i.e., achieve a net balance of pleasure and pain in which the former dominates the latter (Tannsjo 1998). One of the most well-known Ancient hedonistic theories is *Epicureanism*. This type of moderate hedonism seeks to maximise happiness, but defines happiness more as a state of tranquillity than pleasure (Evans 2004).

Egoist theories hold that an action is morally right if it maximises the good for oneself. Hence, egoism might justify actions that are good for the individual, but detrimental to the general good (ibid.).

Asceticism, on the other hand, promotes a life characterised by abstinence from egoistic pleasures. Its aim is generally the achievement of a spiritual objective. Ascetic theories have also influenced the concept of the moral good in early Christian and Medieval times (Clark 1999).

All these individual-based consequentialist theories are not very well suited to addressing disasters. The reason is that they are embedded in rather different contexts, contexts in which philosophers contemplate about the good life of individuals.

10.4 Machiavellianism

With Machiavelli we see a revival of state consequentialism. The historical context of his moral theory was the context of potential disasters. Machiavelli's perspective is one of an adviser to an absolutist ruler of his time. Clearly, a small city state on the Apennine peninsula that is determined to preserve itself against predatory empires surrounding it has to employ various cunning tactics. As its government is absolutist, the interest of the state and the interest of the ruler are perceived as identical (*'l'Etat c'est moi'*). The means the absolutist ruler employs are justified by their consequences. These consequences should consist of disaster prevention in the ruler's principality that is to make sure not to be overrun by a predatory empire determined to enslave it and subjugate to its own rule and culture. As enslavement is a consequence that is highly detrimental to the interests of the people living in Machiavelli's city state, the absolutist ruler has the moral right to employ a wide variety of means (some of them with immediate immoral impact) in order to avoid disastrous outcomes for the state.

It ought to be noted that Machiavellianism has modern variants that are neither embedded in the context of absolutist states, nor in the context of disasters. The *Raison d'Etat* is frequently employed in international relations by democratic states that do not face disasters. The justification for this type of morality is frequently some sort of pragmatic moral theory. One such theory is promoted by Benjamin Barber, who argues that morality is constructed in the political realm. It is, as it were, some kind of added value to politics. Barber is therefore aversive towards philosophers deciding about what will count as moral (Barber 1989). Note the similarity with Machiavelli:

> But since it is my intent to write something useful to whoever understands it, it has appeared to me more fitting to go directly to the effectual truth of things than to the imagination of it. And many have imagined republics and principalities that have never been seen or known to exist in truth. For it is far from how one lives to how one should live. That he who lets go of what is done for what should be done learns his ruin rather than his preservation. (Machiavelli, The Prince, Chapter 15).

Both Machiavelli and Barber commit a typical is-ought mix-up by assuming that prescription is to be based on description, that ethics is to be founded on existing reality (in their view this reality is politics). But the interest of the state does not necessarily have to be anything morally desirable, especially if the means for achieving it are immoral. In a liberal state, moreover, the interests of the government and the state certainly do not have to coincide. Hence, Machiavelli might be right that "letting go of what is done for what should be done" brings about the ruler's "ruin rather than his preservation", but that does not mean that "what is done" is moral. Still, Machiavelli's position can be justified by the context of an absolutist ruler trying to preserve his state (frequently meaning his rule) from the disaster of its disappearance. Barber's state (the U.S.) is a democratic state that does not face an imminent disaster of that type. Hence, Machiavelli's pragmatic consequentialism has a moral justification in small absolutist states. Such type of consequentialism is more difficult to justify in contemporary political theory in democratic contexts, as in these contexts the preservation of a government and the state do not coincide.

All in all, pragmatic consequentialism as a *moral* theory faces serious difficulties in non-disaster settings. As a *political* theory it is however entirely justified as a means of maximising the power of the state vis-a-vis other states. We see here therefore how wrong it would be to reduce the moral to the political. Such a reductionism can be justified if the state is in danger of disappearance or if the state and/or society is in danger of facing another type of disaster of similar magnitude, but under "regular circumstances" reducing the moral to the political can hardly survive as a coherent ethical theory.

10.5 Utilitarianism

The emergence of utilitarianism was a landmark event in the development of consequentialist ethics. Though not fully articulated until the nineteenth century, utilitarian stances can be encountered throughout the history of ethical theory (e.g., see Gill 2006).

Although there are many varieties of utilitarianism, it is generally considered to be the view that an action is morally right if its consequences produce the most good, i.e. the greatest happiness of the greatest number of people. Utilitarianism holds that happiness is the maximisation of pleasure and the minimisation of pain. According to utilitarians, the idea that the moral worth of an action is solely determined by its contribution to overall utility (maximising happiness or pleasure, minimising pain) applies to all individuals. Hence, in utilitarianism it is the *total utility of individuals* that is important.

Utilitarianism holds that pleasure (happiness) is intrinsically valuable, while pain (suffering) is intrinsically disvaluable. Consequently, everything else has value only to the extent that it contributes to happiness and the prevention of harm. In that sense, as with all other types of consequentialism, utilitarianism is instrumental: it justifies a broad spectrum of means leading to a desirable end, defined by utilitarians as a maximisation of pleasure.

Utilitarianism favours equal consideration of interests, rejecting any differentiation among individuals as to who is worthy of concern. It does not discriminate among individuals. Utilitarianism does however support the idea of declining marginal utility, recognising that the same thing can serve the interests of a well-off individual to a lesser degree than it would serve the interests of a less well-off individual.

The origins of utilitarianism are often traced back to Epicureanism. But as a specific school of thought, it is generally attributed to the founder of utilitarianism in England, Jeremy Bentham (e.g., Bentham 1789), as well as to John Stuart Mill (e.g., Mill 1861). Arguably the most influential contemporary utilitarian, Peter Singer, expands the principle of utility from humans to a continuously expanding circle of beings with moral status, specifically animals (Singer 2011).

Finally, let it be noted as well that utility, after which utilitarianism is named, is a measure in economics pertaining to the relative satisfaction and desirability of the consumption of goods. Utilitarianism can therefore be seen as a quantitative approach to ethics, in which the maximisation of pleasure/minimisation of pain is the common denominator of the moral value of the consequences of our actions.

10.6 A Contemporary Debate: "Ultimate Harm"

Much of contemporary ethical thought has some form of utilitarianism/consequentialism as its grounding rationale. It would be far beyond the purposes of this chapter to go into the debates on this issue or even to give an adequate review of the themes that are at stake. I will limit myself therefore to one highly influential consequentialist theory in bioethics that has a lowering of the likelihood of disasters as its grounding rationale. Igmar Persson and Julian Savulescu have promoted a theory in recent years which argues that humanity has adapted its morality through evolution to what is considered as right and wrong in small close-knit societies. In such societies not much attention is being paid to broader communities and the non-immediate future. Hence, the morality of such societies is "myopic". With the rapid development of new technologies, however, humanity faces the danger of large-scale disasters, some of which may either annihilate humankind or make worthwhile life on this planet forever impossible. Persson and Savulescu call this scenario "ultimate harm". As humanity is "morally myopic" and hence incapable of truly understanding and preventing the danger of ultimate harm, it is in need of moral bioenhancement: an improvement of its moral character by biomedical means (Persson and Savulescu 2012). They initially argued that the state ought to make this kind of moral enhancement mandatory (Persson and Savulescu 2008), while in their later writings they have not adopted a decisive stance on that issue (Persson and Savulescu 2012).

The relevant point for the purposes of this chapter is that Persson and Savulescu do not justify moral bioenhancement by some intrinsic good that is contained in morality, but by its consequences. These consequences consist in a lowering of the likelihood of disasters, especially a major disaster that would in one form or another practically annihilate human life, or at least worthwhile human life. In line with much of consequentialist thinking, they justify the strategy they propose by its consequences for large numbers of people.

Persson and Savulescu have been criticised by various scholars for a multitude of reasons, ranging from the argument that cognitive enhancement is sufficient for moral betterment and that moral bioenhancement is therefore superfluous (Harris

2011) to the argument that moral bioenhancement is to be aspired, but only under the condition that it is elective[2] (Rakić 2014).[3]

A scholar who cogently brought into question the consequentialism contained in the argument of Persson and Savulescu was Harris Wiseman. He argued that the whole conception of seeking a grounding rationale for moral enhancement in the lowering of the likelihood of ultimate harm was misguided. In actual fact, Wiseman brought into question the entire consequentialist strain of Persson and Savulescu's position. He argued, namely, that the morality of actions ought not to be justified merely by their consequences, even if they are as dramatic as is ultimate harm (Wiseman 2014).

10.7 Different Games, Different Moral Rules

Utilitarianism is an appropriate moral theory irrespective of the fact whether the context is regional (earthquakes, tsunamis, hurricanes) or global (ultimate harm disasters included) – as long as it deals with many people rather than a single individual. Similar to other types of consequentialism, utilitarianism might be entirely appropriate in disaster settings, at the same time being a much less adequate moral theory in "normal", non-disaster and non-emergency settings. Let us look at the following examples.

Example 1 Terrorists have detonated a bomb in the main hall of an airport. There are a few dozen fatalities and hundreds of wounded people. Some of them are severely injured with a very low likelihood of survival, others are severely injured with moderate chances of survival, a third group of people are severely injured with a high likelihood of survival, another group have no life threatening injuries but require immediate medical care, and yet another group of people have mild injuries. There is a shortage of medical staff at the scene, people are panicking, and immediate action is required. In such a disaster setting, a consequentialist approach would be entirely appropriate. Medical staff would have to make triage decisions: resources should be spent on those who are severely injured, but with a reasonably high likelihood of survival. If those resources were spent on the injured victims with a low likelihood of survival, fewer lives would be saved as a consequence.

Example 2 Two armies face off in the battlefield. One of the two has many killed and wounded soldiers and its commanders order a withdrawal. As a consequence of a shortage of logistical resources, some wounded soldiers have to be left behind.

[2] This also raises doubts about the relevance of the theory of Persson and Savulescu for the disasters which are most common: those that do not affact the whole globe, but that are limited to certain regions of the world. I am indebted to Dónal O'Mathúna for this insight.

[3] A similar but less emphatic stance in favor of voluntary moral enhancement can be found in Douglas (2011) – published before Rakić's work.

Triage follows. Such triage might resemble the one from Example 1, but it could also have other specificities. For instance, preference might be given to preserve the lives of medical staff in order to have as many people as possible who can save the lives of those wounded soldiers who will not be left behind. This is a typical consequentialist logic that is fully justified in the described setting.[4, 5]

These two examples of consequentialist logic, even if justified in the cases the examples refer to, would be inappropriate in a non-disaster and non-emergency setting. Triage based on consequentialist ethics is something that is unlikely to occur under regular circumstances in a hospital with sufficient medical resources. In such circumstances the moral logic of the physician is usually a deontology that is based on his professional virtues – the duty to provide the best possible medical care to the particular patient whom the doctor is treating. A utilitarian logic in such circumstances might be ludicrous. Take the following well-known example.

Example 3 David, Klaas and Hakan are terminally ill. In order to survive, David needs a heart transplant, Klaas a liver transplant, while Hakan can only be saved if his pancreas is being transplanted. Nemanja and his wife visit their friends. To his surprise and dismay Nemanja's wife tells her beloved husband that he has the moral duty to save these three lives, sacrificing his own, by donating his heart to David, liver to Klaas and pancreas to Hakan. Nemanja, a utilitarian, is at pains to persuade his wife that in this particular instance the morally justified net utility does not consist in saving three lives by sacrificing one life (his own life).

Let us now expand on some of the derisory absurdities of utilitarianism (and other sorts of consequentialism) in certain contexts, on the basis of the following example.

Example 4[6] Mr. Prokic is a hard-working husband and father of two children, who lives in country A. He has a mediocre marriage. His wife perceives him as unromantic and generally uninspiring, while both his son and daughter think he is outright dull. Mr. Prokic makes nobody particularly happy or unhappy. At one point he meets a refugee from country B, Mr. Bajic. Mr. Bajic is a consequentialist. He was a colonel in the army of the Communist state Y, taught Marxism at the military academy and

---

[4]This is however not without debate. A number of authors argue that a purely consequentialist approach needs to be balanced with other ethical approaches (Petrini 2010). See also Ten Have (2014) and Barilan (2014).

[5]The moral principles from Examples 1 and 2 are of course nothing new. They are taught at medical schools throughout the world within subjects that deal with urgent and war surgery. They are one more indication that in those specific contexts it is consequentialist ethics that is being applied as a rule.

[6]The characters in this example are people I personally know. I have changed their names and some of their essential peculiarities in order to make them both unrecognizable to the reader, as well as to make the point as strong as possible (zoophilia being made up as one of their characteristics). The substance of their moral character and a variety of the situational contexts in which they operated have however been left unchanged.

worked for the army's counter-intelligence service, mainly by reporting politically suspect conversations conducted by his comrades and friends to his superiors. After the breakup of Y, Mr. Bajic joined a paramilitary group. When this rogue army started to withdraw from the parts of B where Mr. Bajic originated from, he began to claim first a C and later a B origin of his last name, but he remained nonetheless unaccepted as their kin by both the members of ethnic group C and ethnic group B. Finally Mr. Bajic decided to flee to A where he retired from the army and registered as a refugee.

Mr. Bajic is also a zoophile. He became that as a juvenile in his village in B in which there were only 20 households. His life as a goat herder contributed to him developing a sexual interest in goats. He never married. After registering as a refugee in A he purchased a house in a village near A's capital and bought dozens of goats from his retirement money that was being paid regularly to him by the army. He took good care of his goats and continued to acquire satisfaction by being sexually intimate with them.

Mr. Bajic had a long lasting interest in ethics. He masqueraded before his friends, some of whom were his former students, as a deontologist – in order to make more efficient use of his hidden consequentialist inclinations. However, to Mr. Prokic he did not masquerade as a deontologist. Mr. Bajic explained to Mr. Prokic that he leads a morally more laudable life than Mr. Prokic. His argument was that he contributes to net happiness in the world more than Mr. Prokic does: he is happy, his goats are happy, he does not harm anyone, he has fun with his friends and neighbours, while on the other hand, Mr. Prokic makes nobody happy. Mr. Prokic was perplexed.

But that was not the end of the story. Mr. Bajic introduced Mr. Prokic to his good friend, Mr. Bobanic, a zoophile Mr. Bajic knew from his childhood life in rural B, and also a petty criminal. Mr. Bobanic left B for A right after the beginning of the war and was very critical of A for not being able to carry out an efficient draft and swift occupation of B. Mr. Bobanic, who maintained tight connections with the secret police for which he worked in the communist period, soon became the director of a ruined company from the socialist period. The state tolerates the existence of this company as it employs a few hundred people, paying them minimal salaries. Mr. Bobanic is involved in various petty criminal activities, primarily low-level corruption. As he does not steal a lot, the dominant political party signals to the police and public prosecutor to leave Mr. Bobanic and the company he runs at peace.

At one point Mr. Bajic opened his heart to Mr. Prokic in the following way: "You see, even Mr. Bobanic is more moral than you are; he is even more moral than I am, as he contributes most to the net balance of happiness – Mr. Bobanic makes both himself happy because he can realise his zoophilia, he steals to the extent that this makes him happy, his company employs hundreds of people who live in poor conditions but are happy for not being hungry, and as a petty thief he does not cost the state too much. In conclusion, if we classify the morality of the three characters in this example in a utilitarian fashion, we will get the following list in decreasing order of morality: Mr. Bobanic, Mr. Bajic, Mr. Prokic.

Intuitively, however, most of us would be inclined to morally prefer Mr. Prokic's dullness and the fact that he does not make anyone too happy or too sad, to Mr. Bajic's zoophilia, hypocrisy and a general dishonesty pervading his entire life (all of which goes unnoticed), and especially to the corrupt "businessman", petty criminal and zoophile Mr. Bobanic who appears to contribute most to the net balance of happiness at the expense of unhappiness by both his zoophilia (that brings Mr. Bobanic a lot of joy) and his position in the state socialist company that he runs and in which his employees are spared of extreme existential hardships (for which some of them even glorify Mr. Bobanic).[7]

Examples 1 and 2 favour consequentialism, while Examples 3 and 4 are intended to describe contexts in which utilitarianism and any other sort of consequentialism appear to be defective moral theories. Especially the last somewhat extravagant example is designed in a way that shows a whole range of issues that bring into doubt a utilitarian/consequentialist ethics in that specific context.

10.8 Disaster Bioethics as Disaster Consequentialism

In disaster settings in which decisions have to be made that are based on triage aimed at saving the largest possible number of lives with insufficient resources, the number of lives saved trumps respect for cultural conventions. The reason is that saving lives is a universal moral value. It is morally more significant than a culturally determined convention that is relevant only in a specific context with relative rather than universal values.

One among many examples is the following. Disaster responders have saved lots of people's lives by performing amputations. Although the amputees have been ostracised in some of the cultures they originated from, ending up starving, this has not resulted in disaster responders ceasing to perform amputations. The reason is that in certain cases amputations can save lives.

A dogmatic sacralisation of cultural specificity is immoral if it means that we ought to discriminate between people on the basis of some type of social status or other trait and infer from that that some lives ought to be preferred to other lives. The extent to which cultural values are to be respected is a matter of degree. That is why their value is relative rather than universal. They are conventions.

Certain moral values, on the other hand, are more than conventions. Treating human lives equally is one such value. Still, even here there can be exceptions. One of them has been addressed in this chapter: disasters. In disaster settings, namely, the value of equal treatment of human lives can sometimes be relativised. It might

[7] Of course, various problems might be opened if we try to calculate utility in a different way, e.g. by arguing that the state and its citizens would be better off if Bobanic and similar characters were fired and arrested. That might very well be the case, but in our example the state does not maintain such a logic. Hence, Mr. Bajic is entirely right when arguing from his consequentialist standpoint that Mr. Bobanic is a morally laudable personality.

be morally justified to "let go" of a life in order to save more lives. In cases in which decisions are being taken about multiple lives, while medical resources are insufficiently available, disaster respondents might have a moral duty not to treat a patient who is unlikely to survive – in order to save *more* lives. Examples 1 and 2 illustrate such cases. In those settings consequentialism turns out to be a superior moral theory.

In non-disaster settings, on the other hand, deontology (Example 3) or virtue ethics (Example 4) are the ones that are being preferred. In Example 3, Nemanja does not have a moral duty to sacrifice his life by donating his organs to other people. Moreover, neither his wife nor the treating physician of the three patients has a moral duty to demand this from him. The treating physician has a moral duty to employ other means to help his three patients. Hence, consequentialism is out of the question here as an acceptable moral doctrine. Similarly, in Example 4 consequentialist ethics results in absurdities. In this example it is the virtues of the three characters that we apparently value much more than the consequences of their deeds. Here it is virtue ethics that appears superior.

All in all, in different situational settings different moralities are being preferred. Settings in which consequentialist ethics is preferred are those in which decisions have to be taken about multiple lives. Disasters generally belong to them. It can therefore be concluded that disaster settings appear to require *disaster consequentialism*.

References

Barber, B.R. 1989. *The conquest of politics: Liberal philosophy on democratic times*. Princeton: Princeton University Press.

Barilan, Y.M. 2014. Triage in disaster medicine: Ethical strategies in various scenarios. In *Disaster bioethics: Normative issues when nothing is normal*, ed. D.P. O'Mathúna, B. Gordijn, and M. Clarke, 49–63. Dordrecht: Springer.

Bentham, J. 1789. *An introduction to the principles of morals and legislation*. Oxford: Clarendon Press. 1907.

Clark, E.A. 1999. *Reading renunciation: Asceticism and scripture in early Christianity*. Princeton: Princeton University Press.

Douglas, Tom. 2011. Moral enhancement via direct emotion modulation: A reply to John Harris. *Bioethics* 27 (3): 160–168.

Evans, M. 2004. Can Epicureans be friends? *Ancient Philosophy* 24: 407–424.

Gill, M. 2006. *The British moralists on human nature and the birth of secular ethics*. New York: Cambridge University Press.

Harris, J. 2011. Moral enhancement and freedom. *Bioethics* 25 (2): 102–111.

Hooker, B. 2000. *Ideal code, real world: A rule-consequentialist theory of morality*. Oxford: Oxford University Press.

Loewe, M., and E.L. Shaughnessy. 1999. *The Cambridge history of Ancient China*. Cambridge, UK: Cambridge University Press.

Macchiavelli, N. 1998. *The Prince*. Chicago: Chicago University Press.

Mill, J.S. 1861. In *Utilitarianism*, ed. Roger Crisp. Oxford: Oxford University Press. 1998.

Mizzoni, J. 2010. *Ethics: The basics*. Chichester: Wiley.

Nussbaum, M.C. 1999. Virtue ethics: A misleading category? *The Journal of Ethics* 3 (3): 163–201.
Persson, I., and J. Savulescu. 2008. The perils of cognitive enhancement and the urgent imperative to enhance the moral character of humanity. *Journal of Applied Philosophy* 25: 162–177.
———. 2012. *Unfit for the future: The need for moral enhancement*. Oxford: Oxford University Press.
Petrini, C. 2010. Triage in public health emergencies: Ethical issues. *Internal and Emergency Medicine* 5 (2): 137–144.
Rakić, V. 2014. Voluntary moral enhancement and the survival-at-any-cost bias. *Journal of Medical Ethics* 40 (4): 246–250.
Singer, P. 2011. *The expanding circle: Ethics, evolution and moral progress*. Princeton: Princeton University Press.
Tännsjö, T. 1998. *Hedonistic utilitarianism*. Edinburgh: Edinburgh University Press.
Ten Have, H. 2014. Macro-triage in disaster planning. In *Disaster bioethics: Normative issues when nothing is normal*, ed. D.P. O'Mathúna, B. Gordijn, and M. Clarke, 13–32. Dordrecht: Springer.
Wiseman, H. 2014. SSRIs and moral enhancement: Looking deeper. *American Journal of Bioethics Neuroscience* 5 (4): W1–W7.

Chapter 11
Disasters, Vulnerability and Human Rights

Henk ten Have

Abstract The concept of vulnerability has been introduced in the bioethical debate recently. In philosophy, vulnerability has been a core notion particularly in Continental schools. In a sense every human being is vulnerable. In bioethics the concept has been introduced initially in the context of clinical research to demarcate groups of individuals or populations as 'vulnerable' and therefore entitled to special protections. With the globalization of bioethics, suffering and risk in the face of medical research, technologies and care have become global realities, so that the concept of vulnerability has emerged as one of the principles of global bioethics, for example in the UNESCO Declaration on Bioethics and Human Rights. The principle of vulnerability is especially salient in the context of global disasters. It points the ethical discourse in specific directions that focus more on ameliorating the conditions that produce vulnerability, rather than on emergency actions focused on saving lives. In this connection, the human rights discourse might be helpful to focus attention and actions in connection to disasters. This discourse can complement the dominant ethical framework of humanitarianism in disaster prevention, relief, and recovery. Both ethical discourses are strongly connected with the notion of vulnerability. Human rights language presents the sufferers of disasters as bearers of rights rather than as victims. It also focuses attention at structural violence, economic injustice and global solidarity. However, this requires a critical reformulation of human rights discourse, since it often adopts a neoliberal approach. It assumes that globalization offers opportunities to strengthen human security and provide basic needs, rather than threatening them. In practice, human rights discourse is no longer used to protect the vulnerable but to legitimize the global practices of neoliberalism. It often shares the vision of progress, growth and development that underlies neoliberal approaches and policies, hardly questioning the negative relationships between social context, trade and human flourishing. Global bioethics, if taken seriously, can redirect human rights discourse to ways to prevent future disasters.

H. ten Have (✉)
Center for Healthcare Ethics, Duquesne University, Pittsburgh, PA, USA
e-mail: tenhaveh@duq.edu

D. P. O'Mathúna et al. (eds.), *Disasters: Core Concepts and Ethical Theories*, Advancing Global Bioethics 11, https://doi.org/10.1007/978-3-319-92722-0_11

Keywords Globalization · Global bioethics · Disaster bioethics · Human rights · Neoliberalism · Vulnerability

11.1 Introduction

Since 2000, several large-scale disasters have hit South-east Asia (2004), the US (2005), Haiti (2010) and Japan (2011). While major disasters happened before and smaller disasters occur almost every day, international concerns with disasters have increased significantly during the last two decades. Many international organizations, from the United Nations to the World Medical Association, are now involved in activities related to prevention of, preparation for, and recovery from disasters. It has also been recognized that there are many ethical issues in disaster management and response. In fact, a new field of bioethical activity has emerged, disaster bioethics (Zack 2009; O'Mathuna et al. 2014; Gluchman 2016). In this field, the main traditions of ethics (virtue ethics, and deontological and consequentialist approaches) are applied to normative questions faced in emergency responses to catastrophes, research with victims, policies of disaster preparedness, and efforts of long-term recovery. Generally, disasters evoke waves of empathy and solidarity across the world. They are often regarded as the best examples of the emergence of global humanitarianism that cares about human suffering everywhere and that takes action to save human lives and protect vulnerable populations. Modern humanitarianism is characterized by a particular moral geography. Care for victims is based on impartiality and neutrality (Walker 1997; ten Have 2014). Humanitarian intervention and assistance are driven by compassion, solidarity and beneficence. Their aim is to rescue the innocent and helpless. The assumption is that a higher moral order is at work. Normally, each government has the duty to protect its citizens. If states are no longer able or willing to protect citizens, and a disaster has annihilated the social infrastructure, others have the duty to help. There is a global moral order that necessitates assistance and intervention to prevent or mitigate evil. Disasters are therefore a common example in the emerging discourse of global bioethics. They are associated with processes and policies of globalization, particularly economic exploitation and climate change, like other global bioethical problems. But they are also calling for a broader ethical framework, going beyond the standard perspective of respect for individual autonomy.

11.2 Global Ethical Frameworks

The Indian Ocean Tsunami in 2004 was one of the worst natural disasters in recorded human history. It had an enormous media impact and humanitarian response. Charitable giving was unprecedented. However, reconstruction has been slow; many victims still are displaced; aid pledged by governments not delivered; donated monies not spent (Lewis 2006; Miliband and Gurumurthy 2015; Barnett and Walker

2015). Calls for reform of international disaster policies and management have been made since the 1970s after disasters such as the Bangladesh cyclone (1970) and the Sahelian drought (1970–1976). The same shortcomings continue to be observed for a long time: a focus on short-term recovery ignoring long-term pre-disaster needs; and poor coordination of many agencies involved in relief efforts (Michell 2001).

The dominant ethical framework for disasters is humanitarianism. Humanitarian assistance in disaster situations is 'ethics in action.' It is motivated by compassion and solidarity. It is first of all emergency ethics. Rescue people and save human lives is the first objective. The basic concern is immediate relief for individual victims. One does not need extensive elaboration of theoretical viewpoints to show what should be done. Humanitarianism illustrates how people care about each other and that they are all equal in their vulnerability. However, it is increasingly recognized that the humanitarian discourse has limitations (Fassin 2007). First, it is focusing on the value of saving human lives but not on other values such as human dignity and justice. The logic of compassion replaces the demand for justice. Second, it is directing its efforts towards individual persons, not on the local context of history, culture and economy that often is unjust, and has produced vulnerability. Third, it focuses on victims. Recipients of aid do not often speak out, they are generally silent and absent; the vulnerable are not given a voice. Finally, emergency ethics does not give equal attention to all lives; not everybody can be equally protected, not everybody can be saved. This focus also makes it difficult to provide structural, long-term aid in order to address the root causes of suffering (such as poverty, malnutrition, and bad governance).

Criticism of the humanitarian framework, especially after the Indian Ocean Tsunami, directed attention to human rights. In disaster situations many violations of human rights may occur. Humanitarian professionals should not only be saviors but also protectors. The right to life can be neglected, as well as the rights to shelter, livelihood, and health. In addition, both populations and individuals can be discriminated against. Governments can neglect their duty to protect citizens. Although many earlier calls have been made to draft an international treaty on human rights to disaster assistance, after 2004 there was a rapid development of normative instruments related to disasters (for example, Operational Guidelines on Human Rights and Natural Disasters adopted by the UN Inter-Agency Standing Committee in 2006; Hurst 2010). United Nations agencies started to connect disasters and human rights approaches. In January 2010, the Human Rights Council organized for the first time a session on the human rights approach to disaster response, recovery, and reconstruction (Abebe 2011). The Council sent a powerful political message to governments that it is important to apply human rights during natural disasters. Protection of human rights is a key component of disaster management. Denial of human rights makes individuals and populations more vulnerable to devastation. In disaster conditions individuals have no control; but they have rights that are not suspended in such situations. On the other hand, governments have obligations to prepare and to protect. The emphasis on human rights was furthermore reinforced by the growing interest in the right to health. Many countries have ratified the International Covenant on Economic, Social and Cultural Rights. This multilateral treaty is in force since 1976 and includes the right to health. States must ensure that everyone within their jurisdiction has access to underlying preconditions of health, such as water, sanitation, food, water and housing. These are essential determinants of health; they are fulfilling basic needs especially in abnormal conditions of disaster (Carmalt 2014). The appeal to the right to health is under threat when natural hazards result in disasters. Human rights protections must be integrated in disaster prevention and planning, humanitarian assistance and rebuilding efforts. Human rights therefore provide another, or at least a complementary ethical framework for disaster bioethics.

Redefining humanitarian aid in terms of rights has several advantages. It is grounded on international human rights law that is not only a moral discourse but is also based on international institutions (cf. Gordijn and ten Have 2014). It implies global obligations and responsibilities. Actors and stakeholders can be held accountable to the international community. Human rights furthermore dignify rather then victimize. Helping people who are suffering from disasters is not merely a matter of compassion and charity; they have rights because they are fellow human beings, regardless of who and where they are. Humanitarian aid is a duty and an issue of global justice.

However, both ethical frameworks of humanitarianism and human rights have been criticized as inadequate and inefficient. The first is a major driving force for global solidarity but often unpredictable and incidental while human rights commit and are permanent obligations. On the other hand, human rights must be implemented by governments. Yet, whilst in disaster conditions governments are sometimes unwilling to discharge their human rights associated obligations, more often they are simply too overwhelmed to do so. From the perspective of global bioethics, however, there is no contradiction or opposition between the two ethical frameworks. In fact, both humanitarianism and human rights are based on the same underlying idea: the notion of vulnerability that constitutes a global moral community or shared humanity.

11.3 Vulnerability as Common Ground

The term ‘vulnerability’ is used in various disciplines ranging from philosophy, theology and ethics to ecology, computer science and physiology. There is an enormous diversity of formulations and interpretations. An interesting approach is proposed from a general system perspective focussing on the conceptual components of the notion, regardless of the domains in which it is used and irrespective of whether it is used for human beings, communities or countries. Neil Adger, climate change researcher from the United Kingdom, defines vulnerability as “the state of susceptibility to harm from exposure to stresses associated with environmental and social change and from the absence of capacity to adapt” (Adger 2006: 268). This is a functional, not a content definition. It does not clarify the fundamental characteristics of vulnerability but shows how the notion functions and relates to other concepts. This approach is useful since it urges us to consider the conceptual elements that we need to take into account in understanding the notion. Vulnerability is regarded as a function of exposure, sensitivity and adaptive capacity.

The first component is exposure. There must be external stresses or perturbations that produce potentially harmful threats. For human beings these threats are hard to avoid since they are continuously exposed to each other and to the social and natural environment.

The second component is sensitivity. This is susceptibility to harm or damage. In a general sense it is "the degree to which the system is modified or affected by an internal or external disturbance or set of disturbances" (Gallopin 2006: 295). From a medical perspective sensitivity is inherent in the body, organs, tissues and cells: they can be affected for example by lack of oxygen. From a general perspective focusing on the human person sensitivity is inherent in the human predicament, existing prior to any exposure.

The third component is the ability to adapt or capacity of response. Sometimes a distinction is made between coping ability and adaptive capacity. The first is the short-term capacity to overcome external stresses, the second is the longer-term adjustments. Human beings are able to cope, adapt and make adjustments; they can resist and overcome threats.

The functional definition underlines that vulnerability exists when all three components are present. For example when there is a threat of an infectious disease, the exposure is in principle the same for everyone, but the sensitivity is different: children and the elderly have more risks if they are affected. The adaptive capacity is better for persons who have access to medical care and medicines. The most vulnerable groups therefore are children and elderly with no, or only inadequate, access to the healthcare system. Another example is that in severe winter conditions, the exposure is in principle the same for everyone, as is the sensitivity. But the adaptive capacity is insufficient for homeless persons. This is what makes them vulnerable to cold injuries.

The use of 'vulnerability' in the scholarly literature is recent. In many cases it is just a descriptive or technical term. For example, a country can be particularly vulnerable to earthquakes. In the context of bioethics however, it has an ethical connotation. Here, the term 'vulnerability' is not a neutral attribute of a particular person or group of persons. Making an observation or giving a description could be done by using words like 'exposed' or 'subject to' in order to indicate that a person is threatened or capable of being wounded. In the discourse of bioethics, and perhaps also in some other discourses, vulnerability has normative implications. Vulnerability evokes a response; it encourages other people to provide assistance; we cannot leave vulnerable persons to their fate. If we can prevent them becoming wounded, we should take action.

Two aspects of the notion explain its normative force. First, vulnerability is conditional. A person is capable of being wounded but the wounds have not yet occurred; they will probably happen unless appropriate measures will be taken. This conditionality generates a responsibility to take care and preventive action. Second, vulnerability is associated with possible harm, not with positive outcomes.

Vulnerability indicates that something negative might happen. The consequence of both aspects is that unless some action is taken a vulnerable person will probably be harmed or wounded. Because vulnerability is a potentiality there is also room for intervention. Perhaps the person can be assisted to protect himself, can be protected by others against harm, or made less vulnerable through various care arrangements. Perhaps harm can be prevented from taking place, or the impact of harm can be mitigated.

11.4 Central Role of Vulnerability

In the discourse of disaster bioethics vulnerability is a core notion. It is frequently used in connection to disasters themselves. It is also linked to theories of human rights. Finally, it has emerged recently as a new principle of bioethics.

11.4.1 Vulnerability and Disasters

Disaster experts regard Indonesia as a disaster-prone country. The eruption of Krakatau in 1883 was one of the most destructive volcanic events in recorded history. A long series of earthquakes and tsunamis has hit the country. Due to its geophysical location the country is more vulnerable than other countries to disasters (Puspita 2010). Other countries and regions are vulnerable to natural disasters for different physical reasons. Oceania for example includes many small island nations that risk disappearing when sea levels continue to rise (Lewis et al. 2013). Another type of vulnerability is social vulnerability. Pre-existing conditions such as poverty, dense populations, deforestation, and inferior building construction make some populations more vulnerable than others. Disasters often have the worst impact on the poor, the elderly and the disabled; they magnify social inequality (Zack 2009, 2014). Disasters are not only unforeseen events that cause damage, destruction and suffering, but they also overwhelm the response capacity of nations and require international assistance. They often hit poor countries that already lack capacity to meet basic needs of the population long before the disaster. They do not have the health infrastructures and treatment possibilities available in developed countries. Vulnerability, therefore, should be assessed at the national level but also for subgroups within populations. Disaster vulnerability furthermore occurs because in disaster situations the enjoyment of human rights is threatened. Disasters are major sources of human rights violations (Hurst 2010). Especially the right to life and security maybe at risk. Many people will be displaced; they are vulnerable to exploitation. They face unequal access to assistance, discrimination in aid provision, unsafe settlement, and lack of property restitution (Brookings-Bern Project 2008). Years after Hurricane Katrina it was concluded that recovery efforts "have not compensated the most vulnerable parts of the population affected by the storm, who had the greatest relative losses" (Zack 2011: 45). Disadvantaged populations were the most victimized, not only by the physical consequences of the disaster but also by the institutional and structural corruption, racism, neglect, fraud and violence during the recovery and reconstruction period (Voigt and Thornton 2015). Human rights violations reinforce various forms of vulnerability.

11.4.2 Vulnerability and Human Rights

Vulnerability is a core notion in international human rights language. Bryan Turner (2006) has developed the theory that the foundation of human rights is our common vulnerability. Human beings are embodied agents. Because of their biological vulnerability humans feel pain, and can suffer. They are also dependent on others to grow and mature, to become autonomous individuals and to be cared for in illness and ageing. They are socially connected because they need social support and legal protection. Vulnerability demands that humans build social and political institutions to provide collective security. Human rights have emerged because human beings have the capacity to recognize pain and suffering in others. Michael Ignatieff defends human rights with the argument of moral reciprocity. Human actions are justified or not because we are able to imagine the pain and degradation done to other human beings as if it were our own (Ignatieff 2001). The emergence of human rights language in the second half of the eighteenth century had been based on philosophical ideas of individual autonomy and equality. People learned to empathize with others and to think of others as equals (Hunt 2007).

Humans are moral agents; they have the capacity of moral empathy, conscience, and agency because they live in what Turner calls "an existential context of shared experiences of pain and humiliation" (Turner 2006: 9). Turner argues that human rights are universal principles because vulnerability is shared and thus constitutes a common humanity. Furthermore, it connects them as rights of individual human beings to social rights of citizens through social institutions and arrangements. However, such arrangements are always imperfect and inadequate, thus precarious. This dimension of precariousness is especially important in disasters. Vulnerability means world-openness. Humans are essentially vulnerable beings. They can never be completely protected and made invulnerable.

11.5 Vulnerability as a Phenomenon of Globalization

Vulnerability is an ambiguous notion for contemporary bioethics because it has emerged in a specific context of globalization. It is argued, for example, that the landscape of medical research has significantly changed (Ten Have 2016b). It is now a global enterprise, requiring a broader ethical framework. Globalization has created an asymmetry of power of which vulnerability is one of the major symptoms. It is also indicated that there is growing vulnerability, especially of women in developing countries, related to neo-liberal, global economic policies (Jaggar 2002). Failing states are blamed for increasing vulnerability due to the persistence of poverty and hunger (Watts and Bohle 1993). And it is observed that the discourse of vulnerability has particularly emerged and expanded in the context of global phenomena such as natural disasters and the pandemic of AIDS (Delor and Hubert 2000).

What exactly is the interconnection of vulnerability and globalization? During the 1990s the term 'globalization' was increasingly used in social sciences and public policy discourse (ten Have 2016a). While there are different interpretations of globalization, the common core of these interpretations has been identified as the operation of a dominant market-driven logic. This logic changed the nature of state regulation, "prioritizing the well-being of market actors over the well-being of citizens" (Kirby 2006: 95). Rules and regulations protecting society and the environment are weakened in order to promote global market expansion. A new social hierarchy emerged worldwide with the integrated at the top (those who are essential to the maintenance of the economic system), the precarious in the middle (those are not essential to the system and thus disposable), and the excluded at the bottom (the permanently unemployed) (Cox 2002). Precariousness, inequality, and exclusion are characteristics of this new social order of globalization.

According to this analysis, vulnerability is the result of the damaging impact of globalization. It is a symptom of social disintegration. As a consequence of this type of globalization, threats to human well-being increased and coping mechanisms eroded. In particular international and intergovernmental organizations are using the language of vulnerability to describe the impact of globalization (Brown 2011). The United Nations Development Program concluded in 1999 that growing vulnerability is the result of globalization: "People everywhere are more vulnerable" (UNDP 1999, 90). While acknowledging the vast progress in human development over the last decades, subsequent UNDP reports continue to use vulnerability as a core notion to pay attention to the weakened position of the most disadvantaged people and to advocate more equitable policies.

Due to increasing risks and lower resilience, people all around the world but especially in developing countries have diminishing abilities to cope with threats and challenges. Mechanisms of social protection are declining. The 'space of vulnerability' has widened (Watts and Bohle 1993). Vulnerability is produced by social, economic and political changes associated with globalization. It is therefore not an individual concern but is socially produced since society itself is affected. Society has become subservient to the needs of the economic system.

Analyzing globalization in this manner may explain the ambiguity of vulnerability for contemporary bioethics. According to the market thinking of neo-liberal globalization the human person is primarily *homo economicus*: a rational individual motivated by minimizing costs and maximizing gains for himself. In this perspective, humans relate primarily to others through market exchanges. Citizenship, the public sphere and social networks erode because social interaction is reduced to individuals and commodities that are traded (Kirby 2006). This economic discourse is not much different from the dominant discourse of contemporary bioethics that considers human beings primarily as autonomous individuals. Being ill, receiving treatment and care, and participating in research are first of all individual affairs; consent and individual decision-making are preconditions for cooperation with others. Precisely such discourse is questioned in the ethical perspective on vulnerability. If the human person is not an economic but a social being, he or she is not primarily motivated by material needs; acquisition of economic possessions is a means to social goods.

This analysis leads to a paradox. Over the past two decades vulnerability has become an important notion in bioethical debates. The focus on vulnerability is associated with globalization, in particular neo-liberal market policies that have exposed more people worldwide to more threats. These policies are based on the assumption that human beings are self-interested, rational individuals. In addressing vulnerability, contemporary bioethics is often using the same basic assumption, arguing that vulnerability should be reduced through empowering individual autonomous decision-makers. It is understandable that bioethics is concerned with the fall-out of globalizing processes for individual persons. But using an individual focus abstracted from the social dimension of human existence, and neglecting the damaging impact of market mechanisms on social life will not allow bioethical policies and guidelines to redress the creation of vulnerability. What is a symptom of the negative impact of a one-dimensional view of human beings is remedied with policies based on the same type of view. As long as the problematic conditions creating and reinforcing human vulnerability are not properly analyzed and criticized, bioethics will only provide palliation.

11.6 Vulnerability and Disaster Bioethics

What are the implications of a broader notion of vulnerability for disaster bioethics? When the vulnerable person is considered as a 'failed' autonomous subject, vulnerability will not only be located in the individual but will also imply a specific practical response, i.e. protection through substituting the lack of capacity through the voice of others. It is clear that this particular framing is normatively driven: it is the result of the primacy of the ethical principle of respect for personal autonomy. What is less clear is that significant dimensions of the notion of vulnerability are left out of consideration. For example, structural, social, economic and political determinants that disadvantage people are not deemed relevant. The focus on individual weakness preempts a social and political perspective that considers vulnerability as the outcome of specific situations; that argues that people are *made* vulnerable in specific contexts; that the notion is more related to the ethical principles of justice, solidarity and equality than individual autonomy. The paradox is that the discourse of vulnerability has developed in association with increasing processes of globalization. It gives voice to today's experience that everyday existence is more precarious, that we are exposed to more hazards and threats, and that our capacities to cope have decreased. The fall-out of these processes for individual persons has correctly instigated bioethics to address the problem of how persons can be protected and empowered. But as long as bioethics does not critically examine the production of vulnerability itself it does not address the root of the problem. Framing vulnerability as a deficit of autonomy not only presents part of the whole story but it also implies a limited range of options and actions. In this sense, mainstream bioethics' interpretation of vulnerability is ideological: it directs theoretical and practical attention away from the circumstances that make subjects vulnerable.

11.6.1 The Need for Global Bioethics

The emergence of the notion of vulnerability is a symptom of a new approach in bioethics, going beyond the limited perspective of mainstream bioethics. The global bioethics advocated by Van Rensselaer Potter is finally coming into existence (Potter 1988; ten Have 2012). The notion of vulnerability is challenging bioethics to develop and expand its theoretical framework beyond the principles and approaches established in the 1970s. It also urges bioethics beyond its initial frame of reference that is heavily influenced by North-American culture and ideology. A lot of theoretical work is currently done to develop such broader theoretical frameworks based on human rights, social justice, capabilities and global care ethics. Bioethics no longer is, as formulated by Albert Jonsen, "a native grown American product" that can be exported to other parts of the world (Jonsen 1998: 377). In this global era the product is essentially transformed. It is facing new problems such as poverty, corruption, inequality, organ trade and medical tourism for which the standard bioethical responses are inadequate. The scope and agenda of bioethics are inescapably widening, and it is precisely the notion of vulnerability that calls for such broader bioethics.

11.6.2 The Critical Discourse of Vulnerability

The notion of vulnerability is able to redirect bioethics debate since it has two significant implications. First, it implies the view that human persons are social beings. It challenges the idea that individual persons are autonomous and in control. Since the human condition is inherently fragile, all human beings are sharing the same predicament. Because our bodily existence is vulnerable, humans have developed institutions and social arrangements to protect themselves. This is neither an individual accomplishment nor a threat. Vulnerability means that we are open to the world; that we can engage in relationships with other persons; that we can interact with the world. It is not a deficit but a positive phenomenon; it is the basis for exchange and reciprocity between human beings. We cannot come into being, flourish and survive if our existence is not connected to the existence of others. The notion of vulnerability therefore refers to solidarity and mutuality, the needs of groups and communities, not just those of individuals. The second implication is that vulnerability mobilises a different response: if vulnerability is a symptom of the growing precariousness of human existence and is exacerbated in certain conditions, the social context can no longer be ignored in bioethical analysis. On the contrary, bioethics should focus on the distribution and allocation of vulnerability at global level. Instead of focusing on individual deficits, analysis should criticise the external determinants that expose individuals to possible damage and harm. It also means that individual responses are insufficient; what is needed is a collective response, in other words social and political action.

Redirecting and broadening the bioethical debate implies that critical analysis is directed on the root causes of bioethical problems. Processes of globalization are strongly influenced by neoliberal market ideology. The market is regarded as the main source of vulnerability and insecurity (Kirby 2006; Thomas 2007). Neoliberal policies are multiplying insecurities: less and more precarious employment, deterioration of working conditions, financial instability, growth of poverty, and environmental degradation. They also lead to the breakdown of protective mechanisms; safety networks and solidarity arrangements that existed to protect vulnerable subjects have been minimized or eliminated. Rules and regulations protecting society as well as the environment are weakened in order to promote global market expansion. As a result, precariousness has generally expanded. This is precisely what the market ideology wants to accomplish: people only flourish if they are confronted with challenges, if there is the possibility of competition. Individual security is "a matter of individual choice" (Harvey 2005: 168). It is exactly this ideological discourse that is replicated in mainstream bioethics' interpretation of vulnerability as deficient autonomy. But if, on the contrary, vulnerability is regarded as the result of the damaging impact of the global logic of neoliberalism, a different approach will emerge. It is not surprising that the language of vulnerability is often used by international and intergovernmental organizations. The devastating effects of neoliberal policies are most visible in the developing world. But nowadays, existential insecurity is everywhere. It is also obvious that market ideology has not in fact enhanced human welfare. It has mainly promoted increasing inequality. It has created a world in which the 85 richest persons have as many financial resources as the 3.5 billion poorest people (Oxfam 2014). A small elite has appropriated the political process and has bended the rules of the economic system for its own benefit. Read the story of Iceland; in the 1970s and 1980s an egalitarian country with a rapidly growing economy. Neoliberal policies and privatization of the banking system in 1998–2003 resulted in fast enrichment of a small elite but massive indebtedness of the country so that in 2004 it had the highest national debt in the world (Reid 2014).

When bioethics discourse was initiated and expanded during the 1970s and 1980s the major moral challenges were related to the power of science and technology. How can patients be protected against medical interference and paternalism? How can citizens have more control over healthcare decisions? In what ways can patients' rights be defined and implemented? These questions have shaped the agenda and methodology of mainstream bioethics, especially in more developed countries. But in a global perspective, many citizens do not have access to modern science and technology. They are marginalized in a system that is increasingly privatized and commercialized. They are exploited in clinical research projects since it is their only change to receive treatment and care. It is obvious that in this perspective, especially since 1990s, the major moral challenges have changed. It is no longer the power of science and technology that produces ethical problems but the power of money. Healthcare, research, education, and even culture and religion are regarded as businesses that are competing for consumers.

The irony is that neoliberalism is not liberal at all. It is increasingly combining market language with security concerns, creating ‘imperial globalism’ (Steger 2009). All citizens everywhere are continuously monitored and surveyed by a class of guardians who are not subjected to any legal regulation. A vast security apparatus has unleashed the techniques of a militarized empire. Nobody seems responsible. Accountability is absent. Political leaders deceive, deny and lie (Bamford 2013). Secret assassination programs with remote controlled killing machines do not follow the legal standards of trial and legal hearing. Talk about individual autonomy, let alone privacy and transparency, in this context seems rather vain. In many countries free market ideology is furthermore easily combined with authoritarian politics, fundamentalist religion or autocratic rule. The vast majority of the poor is shut out of public discourse. It is not want of money that makes people miserable; it is being trapped in a system that is rigged against them (Boo 2012).

When the major bioethical problems of today are produced by the dominance of neoliberal market ideology, bioethics should redefine itself as critical global discourse. Focusing attention on the social context will not be enough. Bioethics must argue for a reversal of priorities in policy and society: economic and financial considerations should serve the principles of human dignity and social justice, and no longer be ends in themselves. This implies specific strategies for social inclusion but also institutional support. It will be necessary to demonstrate more vigorous advocacy and activism, supplementing academic enquiry. Social inequalities and conditions that produce vulnerability are not beyond social and political control. It will also require that the voices of the disadvantaged, the deprived and the vulnerable are more often heard within the bioethical discourse, involving vulnerable groups in policy development and implementation. Global vulnerability is furthermore transforming the significance of cooperation. Forging global alliances and new networks of solidarity is the only way to address global threats. An individualistic perspective makes it impossible to address the root causes of vulnerability. Influencing and changing social conditions requires what Fiona Robinson has called “collective capacity to act” (Robinson 2011: 60). International human rights discourse provides the best approaches and mechanisms to redirect bioethics into this broader activity.

11.7 Human Right Framework for Disasters

When disasters strike, human rights are not lost. Citizens have the same rights as before but it will be more difficult to exercise them, and often there is a need to prioritize them because the circumstances do not make it possible to apply all at the same time. Governments also have the same duty to protect human rights but in disastrous conditions it may be more complicated to exercise this duty. Victims of disasters face various human rights challenges: unequal access to assistance, discrimination in aid provision, unsafe resettlement, property restitution, and displacement. These challenges can occur in different phases of disaster management. Human rights-based approaches should therefore be incorporated in all phases: preparedness, emergency relief and response, reconstruction and recovery. They should offer a holistic approach focused on the basic needs of victims.

It is argued that four categories of human rights are at stake in disasters. First is the right to the protection of life. This is the priority of disaster relief directly after the catastrophe has occurred. It is also, as discussed above, the primary concern of humanitarianism. Second are the rights related to basic necessities such as food, health, shelter and education. These are needs included in the right to health. Third are rights related to more long-term economic and social needs (housing, land, property and livelihood). Fourth are rights related to other civil and political protection needs (documentation, movement, and freedom of expression). While the first two categories of rights are especially relevant during the emergency phase, the two last categories are particularly relevant in the recovery and reconstruction phases (Brookings-Bern Project on Internal Displacement 2008).

This framework of rights shows the characteristics of a human rights-based approach. It emphasizes equality. Assistance should be provided on the basis of need. It is a coherent approach since rights are interconnected. The right to housing is linked with the rights to health and water. Furthermore, the human rights based approach is continuous; implementing the right to shelter demands a transition from rudimentary shelter into longer-term reconstruction or development (Carver 2011). However, in overwhelming situations, rights cannot be applied to everyone and not every right can be applied. This means that priorities have to be selected, and that triage is necessary, not merely at the level of individual victims, but also at the meso- and macro-levels (ten Have 2014). Furthermore, there is a need for interpretation, determining what a specific human right means in local conditions. Displacement is a common and major problem with disasters. The right to shelter means that people can live somewhere in security and dignity. But what is the content of this right in very different countries and who are the rights-holders? Human rights discourse does not specify what kind of shelter needs to be provided.

The human rights framework is particularly advocated for prevention and preparedness. One reason is that disasters will have a disproportional effect on people and populations that are vulnerable. Marginalized populations will suffer most. Pre-existing human rights violations, poverty, and government corruption will also impact outcomes of disaster response efforts. Mechanisms of injustice that exist before disastrous events happen will continue to manifest themselves during disaster response and recovery (Hurst 2010). Chile is a good example of how a human rights-based health system can guide disaster response to protect vulnerable populations such as children. Because of pre-existing programs, children and families could be quickly and efficiently supported after the earthquake of 2010 (Arbour et al. 2011).

International human rights law implies a universal duty to assure health and human dignity (Walker 1997; Gostin and Archer 2007). The idea of a common humanity that underlies the notion of vulnerability not only requests governments to protect the rights of individual citizens, but also implies an obligation for international cooperation and assistance, if governments are failing or neglecting human protection. The emergence of global bioethics demonstrates that human rights are a global concern. For example, prevention of disasters is a governmental responsibility. Governments should protect, as far as possible, the right to life and health of their citizens. Disasters can be prevented and citizens made less vulnerable through reducing exposure, enhancing resilience, and providing effective mitigations. Failure to take feasible measures that would have prevented or mitigated the consequences of foreseeable disasters amounts to human rights violations. A case in point is a judgment of the European Court of Human Rights in the Budayeva case. Mudslides in the Russian town of Tyrnauz killed several people and destroyed many buildings in July 2000. The protecting dams along the river were damaged from previous mudslides but never repaired. A state agency had warned the local ministry but no measures were taken. Claims of survivors were rejected by domestic courts arguing that the causes of death were natural. The European Court argued that Russia had violated the duty to protect life against the consequences of disasters. The state authorities had neglected the duty to take preventive measures against a natural hazard that was clearly identifiable; at the same time effective means to mitigate the risk were available to them. Therefore, the state is responsible and is obligated to compensate the survivors. Deaths caused by man-made or natural disasters can amount to a human rights violation by the state (Kälin and Haenni Dale 2008).

This case demonstrates the power of human rights discourse. Not only do human rights work as safeguards to protect against abuse of government power, they also provide positive entitlements. Rights that exist in normal situations, continue to exist in conditions that are not normal. A human rights-based approach furthermore requires accountability and empowerment. Local communities and people are enabled to claim their rights. Providing shelter is not charity, compassion or favor: it is a universal right. When a disaster takes place and relief is provided, governments can be held accountable (Da Costa and Pospieszna 2015).

At the moment, however, human rights discourse is still weak. Heads of states publicly denounce and ridicule the discourse. Many argue that domestic laws are more important than human rights. It is also weakly defended in practice by states that used to regard themselves as champions of human rights. It is criticized from a theoretical point of view as ideological and ineffective. It is argued that human rights are not universal but an instrument of Western countries to impose their values on the rest of the world. Another argument against human rights is that international human rights law is a great moral achievement with the noble intention of protecting the powerless and the vulnerable, but that in reality it is ineffective and has not improved human wellbeing. All major human rights treaties have been ratified by more than 150 countries, but in many countries the rights articulated in these treaties are continually violated (e.g. non-discrimination of women; prohibition of child labor) (Posner 2014). Even international organizations do not take human right seriously. Recently, for example, the UN Special Rapporteur on extreme poverty and human rights criticized the World Bank for treating "human rights more like an infectious disease than universal values and obligations." (United Nations 2015). They pay lip service instead of making rights operational. This critique in fact implies that human rights discourse can adopt, and perhaps often has, a neoliberal approach. It assumes that globalization offers opportunities to strengthen human security and provides for basic needs, rather than threatening it and making human beings more vulnerable. In this context, human rights are no longer used to protect the vulnerable and to argue that health is more important than trade, but to justify the global policies and practices of neoliberalism. An analogous assumption is that human rights have emerged in the tradition of individualism; they are primarily individual rights and therefore cannot address the structural causes of violence and oppression (Evans 2005).

11.8 Conclusion

Disasters are associated with ethical questions. The dominant framework dealing with these questions is humanitarianism, appealing to values such as saving human life, solidarity and compassion. This chapter argues that this ethical framework should be complemented with the framework of human rights. Disasters, humanitarianism and human rights are interconnected by the notion of vulnerability. Vulnerability reflects the precariousness of the human condition and the fragility of the human species. It is also a reflection of radical changes in contemporary human existence due to processes of globalization. Disasters occur because of (increasing) human vulnerability. At the same time, vulnerability is also the source of human rights. Because every human is vulnerable and there is a constant possibility of harm, human beings need each other and must cooperate. They need institutions such as human rights to survive and flourish. Vulnerability therefore is not just an individual attribute. Mainstream bioethics construes vulnerability as deficient autonomy. It does not take into account that autonomy itself demands appropriate conditions in order to arise, to develop and to be exercised. Vulnerability therefore is misconstrued as an individual attribute; rather it directs attention towards the underlying conditions for human flourishing. Vulnerability is not merely inability or deficiency but most of all ability and opportunity. Vulnerable subjects are not victims in need of protection or dependent on the benevolence or the strong. Human capabilities will develop when inequality and structural violence have been removed, and the appropriate social, cultural, political and economic conditions for human flourishing have been created. Ethics itself has emerged through reflection on the experiences of vulnerability. Human rights based approaches articulate a perspective that is stronger than humanitarianism.

References

Abebe, Allehone Mulugeta. 2011. Special report – human rights in the context of disasters: The special session of the UN Human Rights Council on Haiti. *Journal of Human Rights* 10: 99–111.

Adger, W. Neil. 2006. Vulnerability. *Global Environmental Change* 16: 268–281.

Arbour, Mary Catherine, Kara Murray, Felipe Arriet, Cecilia Moraga, and Miguel Cordero Vega. 2011. Lessons from the Chilean earthquake: How a human rights framework facilitates disaster response. *Health and Human Rights* 13 (1): 62–73.

Bamford, J. 2013. They know much more than you think. *The New York Review of Books* 13: 4–8.

Barnett, Michael, and Peter Walker. 2015. Regime change for humanitarian aid, how to make relief more accountable. *Foreign Affairs* 94 (4): 130–141.

Boo, K. 2012. *Behind the beautiful forevers. Life, death, and hope in a Mumbai undercity*. New York: Random House.

Brookings-Bern Project on Internal Displacement. 2008. Human rights and natural disasters. Operational guidelines and field manual on human rights protection in situations of natural disaster. March 2008. http://www.refworld.org/pdfid/49a2b8f72.pdf. Accessed 6 Dec 2016.

Brown, Tim. 2011. 'Vulnerability is universal': Considering the place of 'security' and 'vulnerability' within contemporary global health discourse. *Social Science & Medicine* 72: 319–326.

Carmalt, Jean. 2014. Prioritizing health: A human rights analysis of disaster, vulnerability and urbanization in New Orleans and Port-au-Prince. *Health and Human Rights Journal* 16 (1): 41–53.

Carver, Richard. 2011. Is there a right to shelter after disaster? *Environmental Hazards* 10: 232–247.

Cox, Robert W. 2002. *The political economy of a plural world: Critical reflections on power, morals and civilization*. London: Routledge.

Da Costa, Karen, and Pulina Pospieszna. 2015. The relationship between human rights and disaster risk reduction revisited: Bringing the legal perspective into the discussion. *Journal of International Humanitarian Legal Studies* 6: 64–86.

Delor, Francois, and Michel Hubert. 2000. Revisiting the concept of 'vulnerability. *Social Science and Medicine* 50: 1557–1570.

Evans, Tony. 2005. *The politics of human rights. A global perspective*. 2nd ed. London/Ann Arbor: Pluto Press.

Fassin, Didier. 2007. Humanitarianism as a politics of life. *Public Culture* 19 (3): 499–520.

Gallopin, Gilberto C. 2006. Linkages between vulnerability, resilience, and adaptive capacity. *Global Environmental Change* 16: 293–303.

Gluchman, Vasil. 2016. Moral theory and natural, or social disasters. *Human Affairs* 26: 3–7.

Gordijn, B., and H.A.M.J. Ten Have. 2014. Future perspectives. In *Handbook of global bioethics*, ed. H.A.M.J. Ten Have and B. Gordijn, vol. II, 829–844. New York: Springer.

Gostin, Lawrence O., and Robert Archer. 2007. The duty of states to assist other states in need: Ethics, human rights, and international law. *The Journal of Law, Medicine & Ethics* 35 (4): 526–533.

Harvey, D. 2005. *A brief history of neoliberalism*. Oxford/New York: Oxford University Press.

Hunt, Lynn. 2007. *Inventing human rights. A history*. New York/London: W.W. Norton & Company.

Hurst, Jessica L. 2010. Establishing human rights protections in postdisaster contexts. *Journal of Emergence Management* 8 (6): 7–14.

Ignatieff, Michael. 2001. *Human rights as politics and idolatry*. Princeton/Oxford: Princeton University Press.
Jaggar, Alison M. 2002. Vulnerable women and neo-liberal globalization: Debt burdens undermine women's health in the global South. *Theoretical Medicine* 23 (6): 425–440.
Jonsen, A.R. 1998. *The birth of bioethics*. New York/Oxford: Oxford University Press.
Kälin, Walter, and Claudine Haenni Dale. 2008. Disaster risk mitigation – why human rights matter. *Forced Migration Review* 31: 38–39.
Kirby, P. 2006. *Vulnerability and violence. The impact of globalization*. London/Ann Arbor: Pluto Press.
Lewis, Hope. 2006. Human rights and natural disaster: The Indian Ocean tsunami. *Human Rights* 33 (4): 12–16.
Lewis, Bridget, Rowena Maguire, Helen Stringer. 2013. Addressing vulnerability and human rights in disaster response mechanism in Oceania. In *Crime, justice and social democracy conference*, ed. Richards, Kelly and Tauri, Juan. 8–11 July, 2013, Queensland University of Technology, Brisbane. http://eprints.qut.edu.au/61243/.
Michell, James K. 2001. Policy forum: human rights to disaster assistance and mitigation. *Environmental Hazards* 3: 123–124.
Miliband, David, and Ravi Gurumurthy. 2015. Improving humanitarian aid. How to make relief more efficient and effective. *Foreign Affairs* 94 (4): 118–129.
O'Mathuna, Donal P., Bert Gordijn, and Mike Clarke, eds. 2014. *Disaster bioethics: Normative issues when nothing is normal*. Dordrecht/Heidelberg/London/New York: Springer.
Oxfam. 2014. *Working for the few*. 178 Oxfam Briefing paper (electronic version). Accessed 13 Dec 2016, via http://www.oxfam.org/sites/www.oxfam.org/files/bp-working-for-few-political-capture-economic-inequality-200114-summ-en.pdf.
Posner, Eric. 2014. *The twilight of human rights*. Oxford: Oxford University Press.
Potter, Van Renselaer. 1988. *Global bioethics. Building on the Leopold legacy*. East Lansing: Michigan State University Press.
Puspita, Natalia Yeti. 2010. *Legal analysis of human rights protection in times of natural disaster and its implementation in Indonesia*. Working paper series no. 013. Asian Law Institute. April 2010. https://law.nus.edu.sg/asli/pdf/WPS013.pdf.
Reid, S. 2014. Iceland's saga. *Foreign Affairs* 93 (1): 142–150.
Robinson, F. 2011. *The ethics of care. A feminist approach to human security*. Philadelphia: Temple University Press.
Steger, M.B. 2009. *Globalisms. The great ideological struggle of the twenty-first century*. Lanham: Rowman & Littlefield Publishers.
ten Have, Henk. 2012. Potter's notion of bioethics. *Kennedy Institute of Ethics Journal* 22 (1): 59–82.
———. 2014. Macro-triage in disaster planning. In *Disaster bioethics: Normative issues when nothing is normal*, ed. Donal P. O'Mathuna, Bert Gordijn, and Mike Clarke, 13–32. Dordrecht/Heidelberg/London/New York: Springer.
———. 2016a. *Global bioethics. An introduction*. London: Routledge.
———. 2016b. *Vulnerability. challenging bioethics*. London: Routledge.
Thomas, C. 2007. Globalization and human security. In *Globalization, development and human security*, ed. A. Mc Grew and N.K. Poku, 107–131. Cambridge, UK/Malden: Polity Press.
Turner, Bryan S. 2006. *Vulnerability and human rights*. University Park: Penn State University Press.
UNDP. 1999. *Human development report 1999*. New York: Oxford University Press.
United Nations. 2015. General assembly, seventieth session. Extreme poverty and human rights, 4 August 2015. https://documents-dds-ny.un.org/doc/UNDOC/GEN/G16/088/20/PDF/G1608820.pdf?OpenElement. Accessed 12 Dec 2017.
Voigt, Lydia, and William E. Thornton. 2015. Disaster-related human rights violations and corruption: A 10-year review of post-hurricane Katrina New Orleans. *American Behavioral Scientist* 59 (10): 1292–1313.

Walker, Peter. 1997. To do the right thing or to do the thing right? Humanitarianism and ethics. *The Ecumenical Review* 49 (1): 78–84.
Watts, Michael J., and Hans G. Bohle. 1993. The space of vulnerability: The causal structure of hunger and famine. *Progress in Human Geography* 93: 43–67.
Zack, Naomi. 2009. *Ethics for disaster*. Lanham: Rowman & Littlefield.
———. 2011. Digging deeper into ethics for disaster. *Review Journal of Political Philosophy* 8 (2): 35–54.
———. 2014. The ethics of disaster and Hurricane Katrina. Human security, Homeland Security, and women's groups. In *Human security and natural disasters*, ed. Christopher Hobson, Paul Bacon, and Robin Cameron, 57–73. London/New York: Routledge.

Chapter 12
Capabilities, Ethics and Disasters

Andrew Crabtree

> *The memory of the Bengal famine of 1943, in which between two and three million people had died, and which I had watched from Santiniketan, was still quite fresh in my mind. I had been struck by its thoroughly class-dependent character. (I knew of no one in my school or among my friends and relations whose family had experienced the slightest problem during the entire famine; it was not a famine that afflicted even the lower middle classes – only people much further down the economic ladder, such as landless rural labourers.) Calcutta itself, despite its immensely rich intellectual and cultural life, provided many constant reminders of the proximity of unbearable economic misery, and not even an elite college could ignore its continuous and close presence.*
>
> *Amartya Sen, Nobel Prize Biographical (1998)*

Abstract The work of Amartya Sen proved breakthrough in our understanding of disasters by shifting the emphasis from the hazard to societal causes of vulnerability. This chapter begins with an outline of Sen's work on famines and its relation to the Disaster Risk Reduction literature. It then goes on to outline the capability approach the development of which Sen played a central role. The approach is contrasted with the view of income as development, utilitarianism and Rawls. Thereafter, taking the case of climate change, the chapter criticises Sen for his inattention to sustainability issues. It is argued that instead of seeing development as increasing people's freedoms to live the lives they value, as Sen does, we should think of sustainable development as increasing legitimate freedoms. Legitimate freedoms are demarcated by drawing on Thomas Scanlon's version of contractualism and the

A. Crabtree (✉)
Department of Management, Society and Communication, Copenhagen Business School, Copenhagen, Denmark
e-mail: ac.msc@cbs.dk

D. P. O'Mathúna et al. (eds.), *Disasters: Core Concepts and Ethical Theories*, Advancing Global Bioethics 11, https://doi.org/10.1007/978-3-319-92722-0_12

notion of reasonable rejection. As climate change is with us, it is argued that we are already living in an unsustainable world.

Keywords Disasters · Ethics · Contractualism · Sen · Capabilities · Climate change · Unsustainability · Legitimate freedoms

12.1 Introduction

Amartya Sen won the Nobel prize for Economics in 1998 for his contribution to welfare economics which includes his work on social choice theory, poverty and famines, and measurers of human development. As he described in his Nobel biography, cited above, his experiencing of the 1943 Bengali famine has had a profound influence on his life's work, the scope of which is unique. Sen completed his PhD in Economics at Cambridge after just 1 year but, because of regulations, had to wait a further 2 years before the PhD could be awarded. During that period, Sen gained a Prize Fellowship at Trinity College which allowed him to study philosophy which, in turn, has played a central role in his development of the capability approach. This chapter begins with an overview of Sen's path-breaking work on famine disasters and thereafter introduces the capability approach. The chapter then moves onto issues of ethics, justice and climate change related disasters.

12.1.1 Sen's Work on Famine Disasters

As the quote above makes clear, there is a strong social dimension to famines. Sen's experience contrasted strongly with the belief that famine is the result of food availability decline (FAD). Together with other authors such as Hewitt (1983) and Wisner et al. (2004), Sen played a decisive role within disaster research in shifting the emphasis on the understanding of disasters from the hazard (drought, flood, earthquake etc.) to the social context in which the hazard occurs (Wisner et al. 2004; Pelling 2011). This shift in the understanding of famines and disasters more generally points to a host of ethical issues which are ignored if one only concentrates on the hazard. As I will argue later in relation to climate change, the philosophical and public debate has not kept up with the disaster literature.

As Sen (2009) argues, famines are relatively easy to prevent, and usually not more than five to ten per cent of a population in any one country are affected. Indeed, there is usually enough food within a country to feed everyone. Even at the time of the Irish potato famine from 1845 to 1852 when approximately one million people died, Ireland was exporting potatoes to England (Sen 1999). More theoretically, in his major work on famines, *Poverty and Famines,* Sen (1981) argued that starvation was not due to a lack of food *per se* but to a lack of entitlements to food. Starving people do not *have* food, rather than there not *being* food. That is, starvation is thus related to ownership and having command over commodities. Consequently, the lack of entitlements, of which Sen distinguishes four being of greatest importance in relation to famines, is paramount:

1. *Trade-based entitlement*: one is entitled to own what one obtains by trading something one owns with a willing party (or, multilaterally, with a willing set of parties);
2. *Production-based entitlement*: one is entitled to own what one gets by arranging production using one's owned resources, or resources hired from willing parties meeting the agreed conditions of trade;
3. *Own-labour entitlement*: one is entitled to one's own labour power, and thus to the trade-based and production-based entitlements related to one's labour power;
4. *Inheritance and transfer entitlement*: one is entitled to own what is willingly given to one by another who legitimately owns it, possibly to take affect after the latter's death (if so specified by him). (Sen 1981, 2).

In the absence of non-entitlement transfers, such as aid or food for work programmes, a person will starve if that person's entitlements cannot be exchanged for sufficient food. A person's entitlements are relative to others. Thus, for example, food decline might lead to increased prices with the consequence that a person's entitlements might decline relative to others or if others become richer, a person's exchange entitlements may decrease because of inflation (Sen 1981).

Whilst Sen's entitlement theory pointed to the importance of different types of ownership and entitlements in different economic systems, a major criticism of Sen's earliest work is that his theory failed to take a much broader range of socio-political and cultural factors into account. Entitlement theory is primarily an economic explanation of famines. It goes some way to explaining why the rich have no problems in famines whilst the poor do, but for the inclusion of other factors, we have to turn to his later work or that of others (Wisner et al. 2004).

Sen has also advanced the thesis that famines never occur in democratic countries (Sen 1999). There has, according to Sen, never been a famine in India since the British left. The logic is quite straightforward: in a democratic country candidates need to secure votes in order to be re-elected. If candidates do nothing to ensure that a famine is avoided, they will not be re-elected and therefore they have an incentive to act. Conversely, the Great Famine in China of 1959–1961, which resulted in the deaths of some 29.5 million people, continued for 3 years without a significant change in policy. As Sen points out, there was an absence of a free press and opposition parties which could place pressures on the government. Whilst, the empirical validity of Sen's claim that there has not been a famine in a democratic country has been questioned in relation to the famines in Bihar (1966), Malawi (2002) and Niger (2005), these criticisms have pointed to other important political factors such as the roles of the International Monetary Fund (IMF) and World Bank in forcing the sale of grain reserves (Rubin 2009). Thus, Sen's arguments have been criticised for not taking other socio-cultural factors into account or not providing a deeper analysis of other socio-cultural factors that affect famines (Wisner et al. 2004). However, while such criticisms call for a more profound understanding of societal relationships, they do not invalidate the underlying thesis that societies rather than hazards are the major causes of disasters. If poverty and vulnerability are part of the causes of disasters, it is important to understand what poverty and vulnerability are and who is responsible for those states.

12.2 Sen, the Capability Approach and Development as Freedom

Although Sen had already begun work on the capability approach in relation to justice in 1979 (Sen 1979), the term 'capability' does not appear in *Poverty and Famines* (1981). For Sen (1999), poverty is conceived as capability deprivation, and development can be seen as a process of increasing the real freedoms (capabilities) people have to live the lives they value and have reason to value. Within the development field, this view contrasts with the view of development seen as an increase in income, which is the approach that had been endorsed by the IMF and World Bank for many years (however, the institutions' approach has now, to some extent, changed partly as a result of Sen's work). The capability approach to development also distinguishes itself from those approaches which concentrate on resources as do the industrialization or modernization approaches or some versions of the basic needs approach. In the present context, it is important to make clear that whilst Sen's work on famines is *explanatory* the capability approach in Sen's version is *primarily* an analysis of the *evaluative space* for well-being. Nonetheless, there are interconnections (Sen 1989) as will be discussed below.

It is important to state that although the capability approach is normative, it does not entail one specific theory of ethics or justice. The leading proponents of the approach, Sen and Martha Nussbaum hold different views about ethics and justice and indeed have different aims. Nussbaum's principle question is "When is a society just?" It is in answering this question that she puts forward and defends a list of ten *central capabilities* that individuals should have, as near as possible, in order for societies to be just. These capabilities provide a threshold of justice for underwriting constitutional guarantees (Nussbaum 2001). Although Nussbaum's work is of considerable importance and highly innovative, it does not claim to go beyond basic social justice. In terms of disasters it only tells us that basic injustices are done and that it is the government's responsibility to change the situation. It does not provide an intricate analysis of the responsibilities involved in disasters. Sen (2009) rejects Nussbaum's basic question which he sees as neither being a good starting point or ending point for a theory of justice. Whilst this chapter concentrates on Sen's version of the capabilities approach rather than Nussbaum's, it should not be read as meaning that Nussbaum's work is of lesser importance.

The basic framework of the capabilities approach is shown schematically in Fig. 12.1 below.

Sen argues for taking capabilities (highlighted in red) as the evaluative space for development by showing the weaknesses of resource-based approaches and end-state approaches, such as utilitarianism, which concentrate on our actual doings and beings (technically called functionings). The resource-based views include the income approach to development and poverty analysis, the basic needs approach and Rawls' theory of justice. According to Sen, resource-based views are problematic as different people need different resources to be able to do the same things. An oft-used example is that someone in a wheelchair needs many more resources to get

Fig. 12.1 The basic framework of the capabilities approach

about (a wheelchair, lifts, etc.) than does an able-bodied person. If we just rely on income or the provision of basic needs as an evaluation of well-being, we miss out on the individual conversion factors (in this example wheelchairs, ramps, etc.) that are needed for people to have the same freedoms. The supporters of the resource-based view might retort that this is not a "knock out argument", it just makes the picture more complicated. A resource-based view could simply factor in the increased number of resources by adding the costs of wheelchairs and so forth. A poverty line of $1.90 a day may be too simplistic if we are to include wheelchairs in the analysis, but in principle one can factor in the relevant costs.

The argument becomes more problematic for resource-based views when we consider conversion factors which relate to human behaviour. For example, in an apartheid regime or the USA prior to the enfranchisement of blacks, certain people were not allowed to vote. Unlike the wheelchair case, blacks would not be able to do the same thing (vote) as whites irrespective of how much more money blacks had. Other forms of discrimination also require changes in behaviour rather than the provision of a more complex set of resources.

The capability approach's criticisms of Rawls are much more complex, and concern Rawls' entire project (Sen 2009; Nussbaum 2006). Essentially, Sen has argued that Rawls tried to provide a transcendental theory of justice which would in principle provide a full, perfect, view of justice. Sen in contrast offers a comparative view of justice in which he claims that we can identify certain manifest injustices without having a perfect theory of justice. For Sen, many questions concerning justice can be decided "and agreed upon reasoned arguments" (Sen 2009, ix). This involves public debate and an appeal to what Adam Smith called the 'impartial spectator'; the idea is that we should not simply think of our own vested interests, but step back and reflect on the situation from the outside (Sen 2009). Surprisingly, Sen never gives us a clear idea of how this reasoning process or public discussion should take place. Nor does he establish when we will know if a particular outcome is correct. It would be strange to deny public discussion any role (and Rawls does not). However, Sen's dependence on public discussion jars with Sen and Jean Drèze's recent book on India *An Uncertain Glory* and their attack on the limits to public debate that result from present day media control in India. Inequalities in voice are sharply criticized by Drèze and Sen (2013). Hence public scrutiny, though vital, is in practice often weak for establishing what is just and unjust.

When one turns to the examples Sen gives (see above), the agreement involved tends to reflect generally accepted criteria (Sen 2009). But these criteria are time-bound and reflect the humanist agenda. It is one thing to reach agreement on fairly obvious injustices of the 'if slavery is not wrong, nothing is wrong' type, but there are many issues relating to justice where the injustices are less clear. There are no 'generally accepted criteria' to answer questions such as 'What do equal opportunities look like?' Or, 'Who should 'pay' for climate change loss and damage resulting from disasters?' Indeed if there were, there would be little need for perusing the debate further. In such cases, one might have expected Sen to offer a method of moving forward, such as a discussion of Rawls' idea of reflective equilibrium; however, Sen does not supply a method beyond public discussion and the impartial spectator. As Shapiro (2011) points out, Sen simply does not show us how his comparative method works in more complex matters.

However, in terms of resources, the argument against Rawls has been aimed at the difference principle which is central to his theory of justice. The guiding insights behind Rawls' theory of justice are that humans are social animals who have to live and work together to have a decent life, and that people place importance on the distribution of goods within a society. For Rawls, co-operation "should be fair to all citizens regarded as free and as equals" (Wenar 2017). These insights lead to two principles:

> First Principle: Each person has the same indefeasible claim to a fully adequate scheme of equal basic liberties, which scheme is compatible with the same scheme of liberties for all;
> Second Principle: Social and economic inequalities are to satisfy two conditions:
>
> (a). They are to be attached to offices and positions open to all under conditions of *fair equality of opportunity*;
> (b). They are to be to the greatest benefit of the least-advantaged members of society (the *difference principle*). (Rawls 2001, 42–43)

The first of these takes precedence over the second and (a) takes precedence over (b). Talk of equal opportunity above might be understood in the same sense as capability freedoms, but this would be mistaken. For Rawls, opportunity here is limited to education and income. The problem of resources arises once again because of conversion factors.

Sen is obviously not saying that resources are unimportant. Rather, they only have instrumental value in respect to capabilities which have both intrinsic value and can have instrumental value in achieving other capabilities. Thus, the capability to swim may have intrinsic value but it can also have the instrumental value of being able to survive in a flood. Not being allowed to learn how to swim may be seen as a capability deprivation and it is one that some women suffer and hence drown in floods. Conversion factors in Fig. 12.1 refer to those different factors which translate resources into capabilities. Examples include norms, social institutions, other people's behaviour, and environmental factors.

If we turn to our actual doings and beings, such as calorie intake or being happy, we again run into evaluative problems. Sen offers the comparison of someone in a famine and Mahatma Gandhi on a hunger strike. The two people may have the same calorie intake but are clearly in different positions. Gandhi made a choice whereas a person in a famine does not. Historically, it is arguable that Gautama Buddha has been the person with the greatest well-being, however on any measure of poverty such as lack of income, shelter, and food Buddha was chronically poor. The capability approach captures the fact that Buddha chose to live the way he did, he exercised his free agency. If we concentrate on functionings alone, we miss out on agency and the real choices people have. Clearly, there may be practical reasons why one would measure actual functionings rather than capabilities, as in a famine.

Similarly, with utilitarianism, whilst Sen is appreciative of the point that the consequences of people's actions are important, utility is the ultimate measure of well-being. In classical utilitarianism, utility is conceived in terms of happiness or pleasure. There is then a sum ranking to calculate the greatest happiness of the greatest number. Conversely, pain should be avoided. This does not entail that all utilitarians follow James Mill's argument that those suffering from the famine during the "summer that never was," which was caused by the eruption of Mount Tambora a year earlier in 1815 and the consequent blocking of the sun, should have their throats cut like pigs to ease their misery (Sen 2009).

Utilitarianism is pervasive within welfare economics. However, philosophical scepticism about the possibility of knowing whether or not other people were happy or gained greater pleasure led welfare economists to concentrate on observable choices. Sen has delivered a number of criticisms against utilitarianism, claiming that it ignores inequalities, rights, freedoms and it fails to take social conditioning or adaptive preferences into consideration. A dutiful housewife may say she is satisfied with her lot because that is what she has been brought up to expect. Furthermore, two people may exhibit the same choice behaviour preferring two kilos of rice to one, but may do so for different reasons. A person with a stomach parasite is in a different situation than someone who does not have one. Again, real freedoms are essential to assessing well-being and development (Sen 1999).

In *Food and Freedom* (1989), Sen draws out some of the connections between development as understood in terms of capabilities, food and ethics. Basic capabilities such as having enough food to eat are clearly fundamental to engaging in ethical activity, and having insufficient food may force individuals into undertaking things "they resent doing" and thus reduce their freedom and others' freedoms. Extreme examples of this include the Great Famine of China in which some parents ate their own children (Branigan 2013). Conversely, a lack of freedom may affect food production. Here Sen points to the policies introduced by Deng Xiao Ping in post-1979 China. These allowed peasants a greater say in the choice of food production as opposed to having it decided centrally by Beijing resulting in a significant increase in output. The lack of political freedoms under authoritarian regimes and colonial powers may also affect food distribution.

The emphasis on freedoms in the capability approach also points to the importance of agency. This again is linked to food and famine prevention for if we see people in famines as agents rather than victims who need charity, one appropriate response to a possible famine is to provide work programs so that people can increase their purchasing power and entitlements. John Stuart Mill argued against taking this approach in Ireland during the potato famine as he thought the Irish were "indolent, unenterprising, careless of the future, doing nothing for themselves, and demanding everything from other people…" (Henry 2016). The Irish, in Mill's opinion, would squander aid. The Irish, in John Stuart Mill's opinion were not active agents.

12.3 Climate Change, Unsustainability and Disasters

Sen has done little work on disasters since the 1980s. Rather his work has concentrated on issues connected with development and justice (Sen 1999, 2009). His efforts have been institutionalised in the form of the Human Development Index (HDI) and the Human Development Reports supported by the United Nations Development Program. Much of the work within the capabilities approach more generally has been on been on specific aspects of these issues, though it must be emphasised that Martha Nussbaum's work on justice cannot be considered a footnote to Sen (see especially Nussbaum 2001, 2006).

Here I wish to concentrate on something of a paradox. Sen has not undertaken much work on sustainability. On the one hand, we might see this as acceptable as we should not expect any author to cover everything and as Sen has said his childhood experiences have greatly influenced the direction of his work – sustainability might appear to be secondary to the more immediate problems surrounding famines and poverty. Yet, Sen's conceptualization of development in terms of increasing the freedoms that people have to live the lives they value raises an obvious and immediate question: do we not have good reason to reject what others may value doing, or others reject what we are doing? Not surprisingly others have raised this issue, to quote Nussbaum for example:

> …it is unclear whether the idea of promoting freedom is even a coherent political project. Some freedoms limit others. The freedom of rich people to make large donations to political campaigns limits the equal worth of the right to vote. The freedom of businesses to pollute the environment limits the freedom of citizens to enjoy an unpolluted environment. The freedom of landowners to keep their land limits projects of land reform that might be argued to be central that might be central to many freedoms for the poor. And so on. Obviously these freedoms are not among those that Sen considers, but he says nothing to limit the account of freedom or to rule out conflicts of this type. (Nussbaum 2003, 44)

With respect to sustainability, the paradox for Sen is that those countries which are most developed in terms of the HDI are all large, per capita, Greenhouse Gas emitters or in the case of Norway dependent on oil exports. If we return to Fig. 12.1, the capability approach's evaluative space concerns capabilities and functionings. Although Sen sees the importance of the consequences of our actions as being part of ethical analysis, the general use of the capability approach tends to be static rather than dynamic, i.e. it does not take the consequences of our actions and the correlative responsibilities into account. The type of development Sen is advocating is one that leads to unsustainability (climate change is already here), part of which is an increase in weather-related disasters. In other words, some freedoms can be reasonably rejected.

To meet this problem, I have argued for a legitimate freedom approach (see also Crabtree 2010, 2012) which defines sustainable development as a process of expanding the real freedoms that people value which are in accordance with principles that cannot be reasonably rejected by others (Crabtree 2013). This combines Sen's concept of development with the idea of reasonable rejection developed by Sen's

Harvard colleague Thomas Scanlon who offers a contractualist approach to ethics (Scanlon 1998; see also Barry 1995; Forst 2007; Parfit 2011). For Scanlon, judgments of right and wrong center on reasonable rejection:

> When I ask myself what reason the fact that an action would be wrong provides me with not to do it, my answer is that such an action would be one that I could not justify to others on grounds I could expect them to accept… judgments of right and wrong by saying that they are judgments about what would be permitted by principles that could not reasonably be rejected, by people who were moved to find principles for the general regulation of behavior that others, similarly motivated, could not reasonably reject. (Scanlon 1998, 4)

Thus, the fundamental idea in Scanlon's approach is that an action (I would add, a lifestyle) is morally wrong if the actor cannot justify his or her action to others in accordance with principles that they could not reasonably reject. The Scanlonian formulation guarantees impartiality by ensuring everyone the right of veto as all can reasonably reject a principle. As Barry (1995) argues, the approach affords a very strong basis for equal rights for "it invites us to ask why anybody should freely consent to being treated less well in respect of rights than anybody else in his society" (Barry 1995, 70), or indeed the world, and can be extended across generations by employing the notion of trusteeship (Crabtree 2013).

In the present context, those who suffer or will suffer from climate change disasters can reasonably reject principles that allow for unmitigated climate change. Even with the Paris agreement, average temperatures are expected to rise over 3 °C by the end of the century. This is not just a problem for future generations as many people alive now will be alive in 2100 (82 years' time). People can reasonably reject a 3 °C world, which will be even warmer in some areas. This would seem to bring us back to utilitarianism and John Stuart Mill's no harm principle, but contractualism rejects the idea that there are criteria, such as harm, outside the contract which can be the basis for establishing principles of right and wrong. Indeed, if there were so there would be no need for contractualism as the criteria would already be established.

Returning to the disaster risk reduction literature, it makes clear there is no pure climate disaster and hence no pure climate change disaster. To repeat, there are two necessary causes of a disaster, namely a hazard and a society. Hence there are two sets of responsibility. This line of thought can lead us to question the dominant philosophical, international, institutional and civil society discourse which sees responsibility for climate change related disasters as being the responsibility of the Greenhouse Gas emitters *alone*. For example we find statements such as 'Climate change kills!' (DARA 2012) and the assertion of the World Health Organization (WHO) that climate change is expected to *cause* approximately 250,000 additional deaths per year between 2030 and 2050 (WHO 2013). The argument can also be found in much of the philosophical literature that discusses the polluter pays principle or principle of Common but Differentiated Responsibilities and climate change (Caney 2009, 2010; Gardiner 2004, 2006; Scruton 2012). This is also the thinking that lies behind the case brought by the Dutch Urgenda Foundation and 886 individual citizens against the Dutch government (Cox 2014). The argument is based on an understanding of vulnerability, primarily in terms of hazards that are caused by the developed countries (Jordan et al. 2013). The main principle within international environmental law relating to climate change is that of Common but Differentiated Responsibilities (CBDR), which states:

> In view of the different contributions to global environmental degradation, States have common but differentiated responsibilities. The developed countries acknowledge the responsibility that they bear in the international pursuit of sustainable development in view of the pressures their societies place on the global environment and of the technologies and financial resources they command. (IPCC 2018)

The idea of legitimate freedoms places ethical limitations on the kind of development that is acceptable. We can also reasonably reject principles that allow inaction and the failure in societies in which disasters occur to take disaster risk reduction measures. In *Famine, Affluence and Morality* Peter Singer argued for Western Aid to developing countries on the basis that:

> If it is in our power to prevent something very bad from happening, without thereby sacrificing anything morally significant, we ought, morally, to do it. An application of this principle would be as follows: if I am walking past a shallow pond and see a child drowning in it, I ought to wade in and pull the child out. This will mean getting my clothes muddy, but this is insignificant, while the death of the child would presumably be a very bad thing. (Singer 1972, 231)

Such arguments do not simply apply to Western aid; they also apply to the societies in which disasters happen. For example, in 1999, approximately 10,000 people died as a result of the super cyclone disaster in Orissa. A similar cyclone in the same area in 2013 left 44 dead (The Hindu 2013). The difference being that approximately 500.000 people were moved out of path of the cyclone. Inaction by the state government could be reasonably rejected. This does not mean that all the negative effects of the cyclones could have been prevented. Disaster risk reduction literature is precisely about reducing risk. It does not claim that risk can be eliminated. There was substantial livelihood loss following both cyclones. The hazard still plays a role in disaster causation.

This raises a further question, for if the society in which a disaster happens has some of the responsibility for the disaster, then the responsibility of the Greenhouse Gas emitting nations is diminished by the actions or inactions of those countries in which the disasters happen (Scanlon 1998; Crabtree 2016). This principle is well known from tort law. If a driver breaks the speed limit and hits a child, then the driver is responsible for the injury to the child. However, if someone who is present, such as a traffic warden, has the duty to ensure that a child goes over the road safely, then the responsibility of the driver is diminished. The question, in relation to climate change, is what responsibilities people have in the affected societies. This varies considerably, and at a variety of levels down to local 'communities' that exclude people and the individual who ignores warnings (Scanlon 1998; Crabtree 2013). Part of the problem here is that responsibility becomes extremely complex such that litigation or the calculation of climate change loss and damage would become almost impossible. This brief discussion does not exhaust the issues involved, but it does show that the complexity of ethical issues is increased when we embrace the shift in understanding of disasters in which Sen played a key role. It is a shift that has been ignored in much of the climate change debate.

The discussion also points to a fundamental problem within the capability approach. We might argue that development can be understood in terms of freedom, but if we are to answer the question, 'Is development sustainable or not?' we need to evaluate what the consequences of our doings and beings are and what is happening to the environment. This expands the evaluative space and brings resources back into the picture, albeit seeing these as broader than income. It would also lead us to reject the HDI as a stand-alone figure which does not relate to the environment.

12.4 Conclusion

Sen's work on famines was path-breaking and a significant achievement in itself. He has had an enormous impact on the field of development studies, policy and practice (through the HDI), and made a significant contribution to the theory of justice both as a critic and protagonist. The sad paradox is that by ignoring sustainability issues, the development Sen envisages will lead to more disasters. Thus while we need to reduce people's vulnerabilities by increasing their freedoms and adapting to climate change, we also need to engage in actions to mitigate climate change and the reduction of hazards more generally. We need to establish which freedoms are legitimate and which can be reasonably rejected.

References

Barry, Brian. 1995. *Justice as impartiality*. Oxford: Clarendon Press.

Branigan, Tania. 2013. China's great famine: The true story. https://www.theguardian.com/world/2013/jan/01/china-great-famine-book-tombstone.

Caney, Simon. 2009. Justice and the distribution of greenhouse gas emissions. *Journal of Global Ethics* 5 (2): 125–146. https://doi.org/10.1080/17449620903110300.

———. 2010. Climate change, human rights, and moral thresholds. In *Climate ethics: Essential readings*, ed. Stephen Gardiner, S. Caney, D. Jamieson, and H. Shue, 163–177. Oxford: Oxford University Press.

Cox, R. 2014. Liability of European states for climate change. *Utrecht Journal of International and European Law* 30 (78): 125–135. https://doi.org/10.5334/ujiel.ci.

Crabtree, Andrew. 2010. Sustainable development, capabilities and the missing case of mental health. In *A new agenda for sustainability*, ed. Nielsen, Klaus, A., Elling, B. Figueroa, M., and E. Jelsoe , 159–176. Aldershot: Ashgate.

Crabtree, A. 2012. A legitimate freedom approach to sustainability: Sen, Scanlon and the inadequacy of the human development index. *International Journal of Social Quality* 2 (1): 24–40. https://doi.org/10.3167/IJSQ.2012.020103.

———. 2013. Sustainable development: Does the capability approach have anything to offer? Outlining a legitimate freedom approach. *Journal of Human Development and Capabilities* 14: 40–57. https://doi.org/10.1080/19452829.2012.748721.

Crabtree, Andrew. 2016. *Sustainability and unsustainability*. Roskilde: Roskilde University.

DARA and the Climate Vulnerable Forum. 2012. Climate vulnerability monitor, 2nd edn. *A guide to the cold calculus of a hot planet.* http://www.daraint.org/wp-content/ uploads/2012/09/ CVM2ndEd-FrontMatter.pdf. Accessed 1 Sept 2016.

Drèze, Jean, and A. Amartya Sen. 2013. *An uncertain glory: The contradictions of modern India*. London: Allen Lane.

Forst, Rainer. 2007. *The right to justification*. New York: Columbia University Press.

Gardiner, Stephen. 2004. Ethics and global climate change. *Ethics* 114: 555–600.

Gardiner, S.M. 2006. A perfect moral storm: Climate change, intergenerational ethics and the problem of moral corruption. *Environmental Values* 15 (3): 397–413. https://doi.org/10.3197/096327106778226293.

Henry. 2016. Liberalism and the Irish famine, http://crookedtimber.org/2016/01/28/millian-liberalism-and-the-irish-famine/ Accessed 12 Jan 2018.

Hewitt, Ken. 1983. *Interpretations of calamity from the viewpoint of human ecology*. Boston: Allen and Unwin.

Intergovernmental Panel on Climate Change. 2018. *Working group III. Mitigation.* http://www.ipcc.ch/ipccreports/tar/wg3/index.php?idp=56. Accessed 12 Jan 2018.

Jordan, A., T. Rayner, H. Schroeder, N. Adger, K. Anderson, A. Bows, and L. Whitmarsh. 2013. Going beyond two degrees? The risks and opportunities of alternative options. *Climate Policy* 13 (6): 751–769. https://doi.org/10.1080/14693062.2013.835705.

Nussbaum, Martha C. 2001. *Women and human development*. Cambridge, UK: Cambridge University Press.

———. 2003. Capabilities as fundamental entitlements: Sen and social justice. *Feminist Economics* 9 (2–3): 33–59.

Nussbaum, Martha. C. 2006. *Frontiers of justice*. Cambridge, MA: Harvard University Press.

Parfit, Derek. 2011. *On what matters*. Vol. 1 and 2. Oxford: Oxford University Press.

Pelling, Mark. 2011. *Adaptation to climate change*. London: Routledge.

Rawls, John. 2001. In *Justice as fairness: A restatement*, ed. E. Kelly. Cambridge, MA: Harvard University Press.

Rubin, Olivier. 2009. The merits of democracy in famine protection-fact or fallacy? *The European Journal of Development Research* 21 (5): 699–717.

Scanlon, Thomas. M. 1998. *What we owe each other*. Cambridge, MA:Harvard University Press.

Scruton, Roger. 2012. *Green philosophy*. London: Atlantic Books.

Sen, Amartya. 1979. Equality of what? Tanner lecture on human values. In *Tanner lectures*. Stanford University. http://hdrnet.org/43/. Accessed 12 Jan 2018.

———. 1981. *Poverty and famines: An essay on entitlement and deprivation*. Oxford: Oxford university press.

———. 1989. Food and freedom. *World Development* 17 (6): 769–781.

———. 1998. Nobel prize biographical. http://www.nobelprize.org/nobel_prizes/economic-sciences/laureates/1998/sen-bio.html. Accessed 12 Jan 2018.

———. 1999. *Development as freedom*. Oxford: Oxford University Press.

———. 2009. *The idea of justice*. London: Allen Lane.

Shapiro, Ian. 2011. Review of the idea of justice by Sen, A. *Journal of Economic Literature* XLIX (December): 1251–1263.

Singer, Peter. 1972. Famine, affluence, and morality. *Philosophy & Public A Airs* 1 (3): 229–243.

The Hindu. 2013. Odisha's death toll after cyclone, floods climbs to 44. http://www.thehindu.com/news/national/other-states/odishas-death-toll-after-cyclone-floods-climbs-to-44/article5247992.ece. Accessed 30 Oct 2013.

Wenar, Leif. 2017. John Rawls. In *The Stanford encyclopedia of philosophy* (Spring 2017 edn), ed. Edward N. Zalta. https://plato.stanford.edu/archives/spr2017/entries/rawls/. Accessed 12 Jan 2018.

Wisner, Ben, P. Blaikie, T. Cannon, and I. Davis. 2004. *At risk: Natural hazards, people's vulnerability and disasters*. London: Routledge.

World Health Organization. 2013. Climate change and health. http://www.who.int/mediacentre/factsheets/fs266/en/. Accessed 12 Jan 2018.

Chapter 13
Disasters and Communitarianism

Paul Voice

Abstract There has not been a sustained application of communitarian ethical theory to the topic of disasters, as far as I am aware. While there is an occasional reference to communitarian ethics in disaster management discussions, this does not amount to a philosophical treatment of either the contribution that communitarian ethics might make to the complex moral problem of disasters, nor does it amount to an examination of its philosophical difficulties and weaknesses. The aim of this chapter is to take a step towards filling this gap in the literature.

Keywords Disasters · Communitarianism · Morality · Justice

13.1 Introduction

There has not been a sustained application of communitarian ethical theory to the topic of disasters, as far as I am aware.[1] While there is an occasional reference to communitarian ethics in disaster management discussions, this does not amount to a philosophical treatment of either the contribution that communitarian ethics might make to the complex moral problem of disasters, nor does it amount to an examination of its philosophical difficulties and weaknesses. The aim of this chapter is to take a step towards filling this gap in the literature.

Disasters challenge ethical theories because they frequently exceed the grasp of our ordinary ways of moral thinking. Disasters pose ethical dilemmas by their scale and their effects. No ethical theory (with the possible problematic exception of act utilitarianism) has a template that neatly fits a disaster and prescribes unambiguously a sure course of action. So, my purpose in this chapter is not to articulate a communitarian ethical template for use in disastrous situations, but to look at the moral landscape that disasters produce from the vantage point of a communitarian

[1] For example, I have been able to find only two works that directly connect ethical communitarianism and the problem of disasters. They are Saban (2016) and Ackerman (2008).

P. Voice (✉)
Philosophy Department, Bennington College, Bennington, VT, USA
e-mail: pvoice@bennington.edu

D. P. O'Mathúna et al. (eds.), *Disasters: Core Concepts and Ethical Theories*, Advancing Global Bioethics 11, https://doi.org/10.1007/978-3-319-92722-0_13

stance. From this view certain features will stand out and call for our ethical attention, features that perhaps other normative approaches miss or do not emphasize.

Additionally, as can be expected, the ethical challenges that disasters occasion serve to emphasize both the base commitments of an ethical theory as well its weaknesses. The critical question that I will pose at the end is whether communitarianism is an attractive moral approach for people grappling with the ethical demands of disasters.

I will first lay out in a somewhat rough fashion the main elements of a communitarian ethics. Secondly, I will discuss the many ways in which the communitarian moral view applies to the various stages of disasters and how this view highlights values that other normative approaches do not. In particular, I will highlight the importance of community in thinking ethically about disaster preparedness, response, and recovery, as well as the implications of the communitarian view for questions concerning distributive justice and disasters, and value conflicts between community disaster victims and non-community responders. Thirdly, at the end of the chapter, I will pose a number of critical questions of the communitarian approach to disasters.

13.2 What Is Communitarianism?

As with any approach to moral thinking and choice, communitarianism cannot be neatly summed up and described without philosophical controversy. Thinkers in the communitarian tradition subscribe to different versions of the theory and emphasize alternative aspects of it. For the classical expression of philosophical communitarianism see Walzer (1984), MacIntyre (2007), Taylor (1992b), and Sandel (1998). The philosophical articulation of the communitarian moral view was, in large part, a critical response to John Rawls's *A Theory of Justice* (1999), first published in 1971, that revitalized political philosophy and that fixed a liberal moral and political view as the dominant normative outlook in political philosophy.[2] In response to Rawls' work, the main themes of ethical communitarianism are articulated in the 1980s, and in later decades a political communitarian literature emerges that is less concerned with the niceties of philosophical debate and more concerned with a critique of Western culture. Consequently, for the purposes of this chapter I have chosen to divide my discussion of communitarianism into two parts. The main one is an account of the philosophical grounds of communitarianism and second part is a brief look at the political version of communitarianism.

[2] For discussions of communitarian critiques of liberalism see, for example, Walzer (1984), Mulhall and Swift (1996), and Avineri and de-Shalit (1992).

13.2.1 Particularism and Partiality

Rawls's *A Theory of Justice* offered an account of justice that was viewed by most readers as a defense of a universalist liberal political philosophy. By this it was understood that his principles of justice prescribed values that were supposed to have application to all persons, regardless of their particular circumstances, their historical period, or their social context.[3] The so-called universalist hypothesis was seen as an essential element of the liberal worldview and was a main target of communitarian critique and shaped communitarian ideas on an alternative particularist social ethics. While Rawls's early work was a prime focus of communitarian criticism, other liberal thinkers who grounded their ethical and political values in universalism were also subject to criticism. For example, the libertarian views of Robert Nozick (2013), the liberal philosophers Brian Barry (1996) and Richard Dworkin (1978), as well as the capability theorists, Martha Nussbaum (2001) and Amartya Sen (2000), were all criticized for their universalist account of the source of moral and political value.[4] More generally, any view that grounded values in a conception that purported to transcend the social and historical traditions and practices of particular communities were subject to criticism from communitarians.

There is a further epistemological dimension to the communitarian criticism of universalist liberalism. Communitarians are skeptical about claims to the authority of Reason, or of human nature, of universal human rights, and so on – each of which purports to ground and justify the universal normative claims of liberalism. Instead of transcendent universalist values, communitarians rather avert to the authority of practice and tradition that is anchored in a particular, historically located community. Hence, the critique of universalism is both that moral and political values are particular to communities and also that knowledge of these values comes from an education in, and participation in, the traditions and practices of a particular community.[5]

A consequence of rejecting transcendent moral and political values is that, on the communitarian view, the source of a person's ethical outlook, her normative view on the world, is anchored in the particular circumstances of her upbringing, and her ties to family and community. These are the values that make sense to her, that, as it were, illuminate the moral landscape for her. It follows from this that it makes no sense to adopt a neutral, *impartial* moral stance – in fact, such a stance is incoherent on the communitarian account. It also follows from this view that there is no Archimedean point from which to make judgments concerning the validity of one's

[3] It should be mentioned that Rawls disputed the communitarian criticisms and interpretation of *A Theory of Justice* and his *Political Liberalism* (Rawls 1996) is, in large part, a response to communitarian concerns.

[4] For a discussion of Sen and Nussbaum's capability approach in the context of disasters see Gardoni and Murphy (2010).

[5] This is not to say that communitarians think that criticism of ethical practices and traditions cannot be made. Instead, it is argued that criticism takes place internally to the culture and community in question.

own moral outlook. Impartiality with respect to moral judgments is thus also rejected by communitarians as a universalist liberal fiction. Moreover, the community out of which particularist values emerge is regarded as itself valuable. In fact, since it is the source of our values, the community acquires a central place in thinking about and addressing moral questions. The community's composition and its continuity are vital as the foundation of moral agency. Instead of moral objectivity or impartiality which are tied to the liberal universalist view, the communitarian calls for and requires an attitude of critical and reflective partiality towards one's own community and its values. This attitude of partiality towards one's own community, its norms and its historical continuity, will be vital to assessing the communitarian contribution to thinking about disasters.

13.2.2 The Communal Self

We have seen how communitarianism, in rejecting liberal universalism and value neutrality, anchors its ethical conception in a particular view of the self and moral agency. For example, Sandel (1998) has argued that Rawls's liberal argument depends on a notion of the self as abstracted from its social, historical, cultural, and ethical context. This "unencumbered self", Sandel argues, is required by Rawls's theory to choose between candidate principles of justice. However, in the absence of a particular social and historical context, Sandal argues that a person *could not* choose moral principles, since she would be stripped of precisely the qualities that make choice possible, namely, an agency embedded in and emerging from a particular community. People grow up *somewhere* and their moral self is the consequence of the practices and beliefs that structure their experiences. The liberal idea of a universal, abstract self thus became a foil against which a communitarian conception of moral agency was developed. Michael Walzer, in his influential *Spheres of Justice* (1984), for example, argues that the problem of justice must begin with the idea that people start out with a particular, inherited relation to goods that they inherit, as an historical fact, from their communities. He says (1984, 8), "Without such a history, which begins at birth, they wouldn't be men and women in any recognizable sense, and they wouldn't have the first notion of how to go about the business of giving, allocating, and exchanging goods."

Charles Taylor (1992a), focusing his critique on Robert Nozick's libertarian individualism, has described the universalist conception of the self as an "atomistic" view in which persons are understood as implausibly disconnected from a particular social context in which they are nurtured and their agency formed. Taylor complains that Nozick's idea of agency is a reduction to the idea of mere choice, choices untethered to a cultural background that would make sense of them. He says (1992a, 47):

> The crucial point here is this: since the free individual can only maintain his identity within a society/culture of a certain kind, he has to be concerned about the shape of this society/culture as a whole. He cannot, following the libertarian anarchist model he sketched, be concerned purely with his individual choices and the associations formed from such choices to the neglect of the matrix in which such choices can be open or closed, rich or meager.

The atomistic self that Taylor criticizes here is not only disconnected from its social background and community but also conceived as essentially acquisitive. The universalist liberal self is presented as rational in the sense of instrumental rationality, i.e. a self that calculates for his own advantage. Thus, the liberal self is not only adrift from community but also regarded by some communitarians as a threat to community by disentangling the individual from the attachments of their social background necessary for forming a robust moral agency.

Therefore, in summary, liberal individualism both as a metaphysical theory and as an account of practical agency is rejected by communitarianism. Instead communitarianism gives normative priority to the community and understands an individual's agency as an emergent property of the social and historical background that forms and shapes a person's scheme of values. It rejects normative justifications that rest on universal claims to epistemic authority and rejects a moral psychology that is grounded in an acquisitive account of moral agency.

13.3 Political Communitarianism

I want to mention briefly a movement in communitarian thought that is less concerned with the intricacies and details of philosophical arguments and more concerned with advancing a politically conservative campaign to undo what it regarded as an erosion of tradition values. Communitarianism as a philosophical theory does not specify which community values and practices are justifiable since, obviously, this will depend on the particular community in question. What I am calling political communitarianism has a particular agenda aimed mainly at Western liberal democracies and laments what it takes to be a loss of "community spirit" that is to be found in traditional conceptions of family, good neighborliness, local autonomy, and self-reliance. Possibly the clearest statement of political communitarianism can be found in the many works of Etzioni, and, in particular, in his book *The Spirit of Community* (1994). Lastly, political communitarianism is particularly skeptical about the value of the state and its agencies and frequently regards the state and government as interfering with local community autonomy. Again, this skepticism will have obvious consequences for the way communitarians think about the role of the state in the preparation for, response to, and recovery from disasters.

13.4 Disasters and Communitarianism

As I mentioned in the introduction, communitarians have written very little on the problem of disasters and even less on the challenges to ethical thinking that disasters represent. For instance, Naomi Zack's book *Ethics for Disaster* (Zack 2009) and her article "Philosophy and Disasters" (Zack 2006) mention a variety of ethical approaches to disasters, but she makes no mention of communitarianism as an option. While there are a couple of communitarian sources that directly engage with disasters, which I will discuss below, we will have to rely largely on a construction of communitarian insights and, hopefully, this will be sufficient to get a general picture of a communitarian perspective on the ethical dilemmas that disasters occasion. For someone sympathetic to this approach to moral thinking there is fertile ground for further thought and writing.

It might strike readers who are familiar with the extensive social science literature on disasters as odd that communitarian ethics is so underrepresented in the philosophical thinking about disasters. After all, the importance of community is a common theme in discussions of disasters. Indeed, it is one of the attractions of the communitarian approach that it places so much importance on the role of the community. Liza Saban, whose recent work offers the clearest and most sustained defense of the value of communitarianism for thinking about disasters, writes (Saban 2016, 61):

> …. An applied communitarian ethics approach in disaster resilience is both normative and a political framework for promoting administrative ethical engagement because of its emphasis on social bonding and participation, and, crucially, its commitment to community values and social meanings of needed goods to guide policies designed to protect and promote them.

She goes on to apply Walzer's communitarian account of social goods to inform her discussion of the role and ethical responsibilities of public administration officials in preparing for and responding to natural disasters.

Robert Ackerman (2008) employs a communitarian political view in his discussion of how to mitigate the effects of disasters. He writes that (2008, 2):

> Communitarians value the role of civil society – the tapestry of voluntary associations such as civic clubs, neighborhood organizations, corporations, labor unions, religious institutions, charitable organizations, educational institutions, and even Robert Putnam's bowling leagues – in stepping forward to meet various needs in time of disaster.

It is this community network that ought to be the first line of defense when disaster strikes and what people rely on rather than immediately turning to outside agencies such as the government to meet their post-disaster needs.

Both Saban and Ackerman thus premise their communitarian approach to disasters on the central place of communities in the preparation for, response to, and recovery from disasters. It seems natural that an ethical theory that places a supremely high value on communities would resonate with those concerned with the moral challenges of disasters, where the role of community is so central to a successful response to calamity.

However, it is important to keep in mind that *any* ethical approach to disasters will value the contribution that community can play in ameliorating the consequences of disasters, but each approach will value community for different reasons. What we need to be clear about here is the specifically communitarian reasons for valuing community. In other words, we have to focus on moral particularism, ethical partiality and the notion of the communal self, and how these ideas inform the communitarian concept of community in the face of disaster. The value of the communitarian approach depends not on how much attention it gives to the role of the community, but on the specific reasons it advances for the normative importance of community.

To get an idea of the distinctiveness of the communitarian approach we can begin by asking: What is bad about a disaster for a communitarian? The question may sound odd because its usual answer is so obvious that it does not often need mentioning. For most normative approaches, what is bad when a disaster occurs is the harm caused to the persons affected by it. Natural and non-natural disasters massively diminish victims' well-being, their life prospects, and their ability to function as citizens and moral agents. In most instances it is the aggregate of these harms that contributes to our calling an event a disaster in the first place. An earthquake in a remote and uninhabited region is not a disaster and an event that harms a few individuals is likewise a misfortune for those affected, but not usually counted as a disaster. The point being that what is bad about a disaster is usually understood as a summing of the direct and indirect harm that befalls individuals.

It is important to recognize that the communitarian approach goes beyond this focus on individuals and this is a major part of what would be distinctive about the communitarian approach. As we have already seen, the community itself has moral standing for the communitarian. Its moral worth is not merely its instrumental value to the individuals who compose it. It has value independently of its members. The values, practices, and traditions of a community have ethical standing and so what is bad about a disaster is not only that its occurrence harms some number of individuals, but that it threatens the existence of the community itself. For the communitarian, the calculation of the amount of harm occasioned by a disaster thus extends to the possible loss of the community itself. So, part of what is bad about a disaster is the threat of the disappearance of the independent good that the existence of an ongoing community represents.

The displacement of victims after Hurricane Katrina's flooding destroyed long-standing neighborhoods in New Orleans and is an example of a loss of community and also an example of the consequences for people who lose the anchoring sense of place and values that communities provide. Thus the measurement of their loss must go beyond their individual suffering and their loss of property to include also their loss of community. But still further, the fact of this latter loss is itself something ethically bad and not merely an aggregate of individuals' feelings about the destruction of their community life.

Beyond a concern with the preservation of community, communitarians are also advocates of the value of community in addressing and confronting problems such as disasters. In this they resist what they take to be the atomistic individualist view that, for example, a template of human rights captures the full range of moral problems and remedies. If the community is not only the source and anchor of a person's values, but also the necessary and binding connection that gives purpose and meaning to an individual's existence, then the community is the ethical lens through which disasters must be addressed. Therefore, once a disaster strikes, in addition to the threat a disaster poses to the existence of a community, it is the community that structures the ethical response to the disaster.

The communitarian view that the community is best placed to address the challenges of disaster is best understood from the perspective of the opposite view which is well-articulated in the philosophical literature and a view that is frequently aired by the press in post-disaster situations. On the philosophical front, Naomi Zack has argued at length that disasters create what she calls a "second state of nature". She writes (2006, 76):

> Disasters may block or delay and disrupt the distribution of necessities. Civilians' inability to create in a short period of time a useful social condition that will sustain their lives means that some will lie, steal, and kill to get what they need to protect themselves. As a result, the second state of nature may more resemble a brutal Hobbesian condition than a peaceful, cooperative, and productive Lockean community. Such conditions of social disorganization require central authority for efficient reorganization and repair and for keeping the peace.

Disasters are *second* states of nature because the condition into which people are thrown by a disaster is temporary and does not provide grounds for the establishment of a new social contract. More relevant to our discussion though are Zack's notions that, firstly, disasters destroy social bonds, secondly, that the ethical restraints of society are likewise destroyed, leading victims to "lie, steal, and kill," and thirdly, that the proper agency of response to disasters is "the government". Communitarians challenge each of these claims.

While the empirical evidence is, of course, mixed, there is plenty of research that points to community resilience in the face of disaster and, indeed, points to the value of social bonds in the aftermath of calamity. Rather than destroying community ties, disasters have often been shown to demonstrate the depth and value of existing social bonds. Nancy Rosenblum, for example, writes that (2016, 202): "Disasters bring to bear neighbors' local knowledge, their experiences of reciprocity among 'decent folk,' of spontaneous rallying and improvised collective action." Chris Gilligan (2008, 311)argues that awareness of the basic communitarian premise of the primacy of the community is "stifled by the formal routines of everyday life," and that the ethical value of community is most clearly demonstrated precisely on those occasions when disaster strikes. He goes on to say (2008, 312): "In this sense disasters, perhaps more than any other kind of event, reveal that elusive phenomenon that Etzioni refers to as a 'spirit of community'."

These claims directly challenge Zack's Hobbesian-like definition of disasters. Rather than throwing victims into a state of nature where their innate selfishness is revealed, disasters serve to reveal the precise opposite, namely, the fundamental social bonds that anchor a person's values in a network of reciprocity based on a shared ethical outlook. Zack's view is often rehearsed in a less sophisticated way by the media. However, there is evidence that "lying, killing, and stealing" (and, in particular, looting) is not the dominant note in post-disaster situations. For instance, Rodriguez, Trainor, and Quarantelli (Rodriguez et al. 2007) have argued that in the case of Hurricane Katrina, emergent prosocial behavior was the norm rather than the general criminality and looting that was widely reported by the media. They conclude their study by stating that (2007, 100): "The various social systems and the people in them rose to the demanding challenges of a catastrophe. Equally important, the behaviors that did appear were overwhelmingly prosocial, making the anti-social behavior seem relatively minor in terms of frequency and significance."[6]

Finally, political communitarians, in concert with the above ethical points, argue that the proper, and often actual, first response to disasters is the community, in its various formal and informal organizational structures, rather than the government. They go further and make the argument that the state's response sometimes not only interferes with, but also actively opposes the community's spontaneous, ethically based aid for neighbors. John P. Clark, for example, argues (2013, 201) that during the Katrina crisis, "the state wreaked havoc not only by its exclusion of citizens from the city and its failure to deliver aid to storm victims, but also through its active persecution of those citizens who sought to save and rebuild their communities." This attitude is part of political communitarian's general antagonism towards, and skepticism concerning the value of, the government and the state. Political communitarians would thus argue that the local community is best placed to respond to disasters, at least initially, and that the state should provide assistance, where necessary, in accord with the community's expressed wishes and values.

One could argue that these examples speak in favor of the general communitarian proposition that the community, understood as the primary source of ethical values, is the proper lens for understanding and addressing the moral difficulties of disasters and catastrophes. It could then be argued that both the importance of community in mitigating the effects of disasters and communitarianism's unique placement of the community at the center of ethical concern together support taking communitarianism seriously as an approach to understanding the moral dimensions of disasters. In the final section I will challenge this argument by claiming that the inference from the centrality of community in disaster mitigation to the adoption of a communitarian perspective is weak, at least as far as the limited arguments currently available in the philosophical literature.

13.5 Disasters and Communitarian Justice

13.5.1 Distributive Justice Between Communities

In this section I want to move on from how the larger questions concerning what makes disasters ethically bad for communitarians and why communitarians take themselves to be correct in placing the community at the center of their ethical concerns regarding disasters, to the consequences of this view for the practice of disaster prevention, response, and mitigation. While, as I have said, very little has been written on the topics addressed in this chapter, what follows is necessarily a construction of the kinds of things an advocate of communitarianism *would* say on these issues. This fact opens up an area for research since, as we will notice below, communitarianism

[6] On this topic also see Sandin and Wester (2009).

has much to add to important debates concerning the role of the government, first responders, public health administrators, and the medical profession in dealing with the practical issues of addressing the consequences of disasters.

I first want to look at the consequences of the communitarian commitment to particularism and partiality. In the broader scheme of philosophical and political debate, this commitment raises questions about the distribution of resources following a disaster. There are two dimensions to this issue. The first is the extent to which non-affected communities are morally obligated to provide aid and support to communities affected by disaster and catastrophe. Moral universalism with its foundational commitment to impartial moral judgment that does not distinguish between the ethical needs of persons based on their membership of a community, has no difficulty on this score. The distribution of resources following disaster should be based on need, combined with considerations of efficiency. The clearest example of this kind of moral reasoning is to be found among utilitarians.[7] On the political side, liberal cosmopolitans likewise subscribe to impartiality when assessing the obligations of persons and states in addressing needs.[8]

The first issue above asked about the obligations of non-affected communities towards affected communities; the second issue asks about the obligations of communities affected by disaster towards other communities also affected. Once again, the universalist impartialist position on this matter is quite clear, at least in the abstract – partiality towards or favoring one's own community *merely* because it is one's own community is morally arbitrary and thus a moral fault. I should note here that there are universalist impartialist grounds for partiality in cases, for instance, where attention to one's own community is the most *efficient* way of meeting the most need. But, once again, *mere* membership of a particular community is not, on its own, grounds for moral partiality. A further caveat should be noted before I get to the main issue of distributive justice in cases of disaster for communitarianism. It is quite possible to be a liberal communitarian – that is, someone who defends traditional liberal values but from a particularist and partialist standpoint. In other words, a liberal communitarian would, in most cases, make the same moral and political choices as a universalist liberal, but for very different reasons. This caveat is important because what follows is a discussion of the moral implications of the communitarian position on partiality rather than a description of the moral choices that communitarians may make in practice.

On topics closely related to these two issues, particularists have argued, in the context of a defense of national partiality and defenses of patriotism, that community membership extends or intensifies the degree and type of obligation that members have towards one another. For example, David Miller has argued that (1988, 647): "The duties we owe to our compatriots may be more extensive than the duties we owe to strangers, simply because they are compatriots." If we translate this into the context of a disaster, then it follows that, for a communitarian, a just distribution of resources for preparing for and mitigating the effects of a disaster could favor members of one's own community. In other words, partiality towards one's fellow community members

[7] For a classic expression of this view see Singer (1972).

[8] For a classical expression of this view see Pogge (1994).

can be justified and morally required on particularist grounds. Of course, this matters only in circumstances where there is a scarcity of resources or obstacles to distribution. However, the point to emphasize here is that the particularist and partialist premises of the communitarian position have important consequences for how to think about questions of distributive justice in the context of disasters. This is an area of inquiry and research that has not been developed in the literature.

13.5.2 Disaster Interventions and Community Goods

The ethical guidelines that inform the decisions and actions of state agencies charged with disaster preparedness, first responders, and those responsible for disaster recovery, are often expressed in the universalist language of human rights. This approach makes the assumption that there is a concordance between the ethical views of victims, state agencies, and rescuers in terms of their moral priorities. In other words, there is often a general assumption that the hierarchy of goods that one side subscribes to is mirrored on the other side. The communitarian view challenges this assumption and this has important consequences for how to think about disaster interventions all along the scale of preparedness, response, and recovery. If what counts as ethically good, as well as the arrangement of a community's moral priorities, is particular to its traditions and practices, then an argument can be made that outside agencies should calibrate their disaster inventions in alignment with those goods and priorities. The communitarian thus demands more than the usual community consultation in disaster planning and response but seeks a genuine comprehension of the particular ethical stance of a community and that disaster planning and response be appropriately tailored to the ethical needs of the community. In my view, this is the most obvious area in which a communitarian approach to the discussion of the ethical challenges of disasters can make an important contribution. Adopting a communitarian ethical view here would have significant practical consequences for disaster management that go well beyond the more abstract philosophical issues that have been addressed in this chapter. A detailed working out of this aspect of communitarianism in relation to disasters would be a welcome addition to the literature.[9]

13.6 Criticisms

There are numerous criticisms of communitarian ethics and I will not rehearse them here in any detail.[10] However, I will consider a few issues that have particular relevance to thinking about disasters.

Firstly, perhaps the most pressing issue for the existing literature is its assumption that a concern with community and an emphasis on the needs of community

[9] Liza Saban's (2016) work here is a useful start in this direction.

[10] For a representative example, see Carney (1992).

members is *in itself* an argument for the communitarian position. As I have mentioned several times, universalist liberals have good reason to focus on the importance of communities. The evidence strongly suggests that engaging with communities, and sensitivity to their perceived needs, makes disaster inventions more efficient and effective. Another reason that a universalist liberal may place community at the center of their concern is out of respect for the traditions and practices of its members. However, these two reasons, efficiency and respect, are not communitarian reasons for privileging community. Therefore, merely pointing out that community is important in disaster management is not enough on its own to make the case for communitarianism. The case needs to be made by anchoring the importance of community in the premises of a communitarian ethics. At present, this has not been done in detail and counts as a deficiency in the existing literature.

Secondly, it is not obvious that placing the community at the center of ethical concern is always the right approach to the challenges of disasters. There is a persistent problem of defining the meaning of "community," beyond abstract philosophical definitions that have limited practical use. This is more pressing in modern pluralistic societies where individuals often have multiple connections across a variety of often loosely defined associations. Capturing these kinds of associations under the label of "community" threatens to severely dilute the meaning of "community" and thus reduce its practical and ethical significance. On the other hand, maintaining a deeper conception of community that requires more embedded ties and connections between members threatens to limit the scope of the communitarian approach to more traditional societies and exclude modern pluralistic societies altogether. While it is true that many philosophical and political communitarians are critical of modern pluralistic societies for their lack of traditional community values, the immediate ethical problems that disasters pose demand a response to societies as they are and not how they ought to be.

Thirdly, even if the notion of community could be defined in a satisfactory way, community membership is a crucial practical problem for disaster management. In particular, questions arise of who is included and who is excluded from membership? And who decides this question? If disaster preparedness and response is supposed to align with community values then whose understanding of these values counts? Who counts as a member thus takes on a great importance since it determines whose voice should be listened to. Furthermore, hierarchical communities, for example, traditional patriarchal societies, where power is invested in a few members, and many community members are excluded from power, pose a pressing ethical challenge for outsiders.

Fourthly, following on from the point made above, non-community members involved in disaster planning and rescue may face considerable ethical quandaries when their own ethical standards conflict with those of a community. In such instances, whose ethical viewpoint should prevail? While a communitarian argument for the ethical autonomy of communities may seem persuasive to some, it does not follow from this that non-community members ought to sacrifice their own ethical viewpoint in the morally fraught circumstances that disasters inevitably present. An additional argument would need to be made here and it would have to be a particularly strong argument to obligate someone to act in a way that they believed to be unethical. Once again, there are numerous interesting and important arguments to be made here both for and against the communitarian position in the context of disasters.

Lastly, disasters are extreme events and expose ethical theories to apparent contradictions, conceptual confusions, and difficulties. Communitarianism is not immune to these challenges. For example, the sorts of community virtues that are championed by communitarians, in particular political communitarians, such as good neighborliness, family support, and community togetherness, are, in some extreme circumstances likely to lead to worse rather then better outcomes.[11] It would be a service to the literature for a communitarian position on these kinds of extreme circumstances to be fully articulated and defended.

13.7 Conclusion

In this chapter I have explained the normative commitments of communitarianism and discussed a communitarian approach to thinking ethically about disasters. I also noted the limited philosophical literature on this topic. While a communitarian approach to disaster theory is initially attractive because of its emphasis on the role community in preparing for, and mitigating the consequences of, disasters, much more philosophical work needs to be done to fully articulate a communitarian approach and to respond to the several criticisms I raised above.

References

Ackerman, Robert. 2008. Mitigating disaster: A communitarian response. *Cardozo Journal of Conflict Resolution* 283: 1–13.

Avineri, Shlomo, and Avner de Shalit, eds. 1992. *Communitarianism and individualism*. 1st ed. Oxford/New York: Oxford University Press.

Barry, Brian. 1996. *Justice as impartiality*. Revised ed. Oxford: Clarendon Press.

Carney, Simon. 1992. Liberalism and communitarianism: A misconceived debate. *Political Studies* 40 (2): 273–289.

Clark, John P. 2013. *The impossible community: Realizing communitarian anarchism*. New York: Bloomsbury Academic.

Dworkin, Ronald. 1978. *Taking rights seriously*. Fifth Printing ed. Cambridge, MA: Harvard University Press.

Etzioni, Amitai. 1994. *Spirit of community*. Touchstone ed. New York: Touchstone.

Gardoni, Paolo, and Colleen Murphy. 2010. Gauging the societal impacts of natural disasters using a capability approach. *Disasters* 34 (3): 619–636.

Gilligan, Christopher. 2008. Community responses to disaster: Northern Ireland 1969 as a case study. In *Handbook of community movements and local organizations*, 311–328. New York: Springer.

Kipnis, Kenneth. 2013. Disasters, catastrophes, and worse: A scalar taxonomy. *Cambridge Quarterly of Healthcare Ethics* 22: 297–307.

[11] The ways in which communities may become obstacles to good outcomes in disaster situations are discussed in Kipnis (2013) and Kodama (2015)).

Kodama, Satoshi. 2015. Tsunami-Tendeko and morality in disasters. *Journal of Medical Ethics* 41: 361–363.
MacIntyre, Alasdair. 2007. *After virtue: A study in moral theory*. 3rd ed. Notre Dame: University of Notre Dame Press.
Miller, D. 1988. The ethical significance of nationality. *Ethics* 98 (4): 647–662.
Mulhall, Stephen, and Adam Swift. 1996. *Liberals and communitarians*. 2nd ed. Oxford/Cambridge, MA: Wiley-Blackwell.
Nozick, Robert. 2013. *Anarchy, state, and Utopia*. Reprint ed. New York: Basic Books.
Nussbaum, Martha C. 2001. *Women and human development: The capabilities approach*. Cambridge: Cambridge University Press.
Pogge, T.W. 1994. An egalitarian law of peoples. *Philosophy & Public Affairs* 23 (3): 195–224.
Rawls, J. 1996. *Political liberalism*. 2nd ed. New York: Columbia University Press.
———. 1999. *A theory of justice. Revised*. Cambridge, MA: Harvard University Press.
Rodriguez, H., E.L. Quarantelli, and R.R. Dynes. 2007. *The handbook of disaster research*. New York: Springer.
Rosenblum, Nancy L. 2016. *Good neighbors: The democracy of everyday life in America*. Princeton: Princeton University Press.
Saban, Liza Ireni. 2016. *International disaster management ethics*. Albany: State University of New York Press.
Sandel, Michael J. 1998. *Liberalism and the limits of justice*. 2nd ed. Cambridge/New York: Cambridge University Press.
Sandin, Per, and Misse Wester. 2009. The moral black hole. *Ethical Theory and Moral Practice* 12 (3): 291–301. https://doi.org/10.1007/s10677-009-9152-z.
Sen, Amartya. 2000. *Development as freedom*. Reprint ed. New York: Anchor.
Singer, P. 1972. Famine, affluence and morality. *Philosophy & Public Affairs* 1: 229–243.
Taylor, Charles 1992a. Atomism. In *Communitarianism and individualism*, ed. Shlomo Avineri and Shalit de Avner, 29–50. Oxford: Oxford University Press.
———. 1992b. *Sources of the self: The making of the modern identity*. Cambridge, MA: Harvard University Press.
Walzer, Michael. 1984. *Spheres of justice: A defense of pluralism and equality*. Reprint ed. New York: Basic Books.
Zack, Naomi. 2006. Philosophy and disaster. *Homeland Security Affairs* 2 (1): 1. http://search.proquest.com/openview/8788717540c8238a7d140800d618c9cc/1?pq-origsite=gscholar&cbl=1336360.
———. 2009. *Ethics for disaster*. New York: Rowman and Littlefield.

Chapter 14
Virtue Ethics and Disasters

Lars Löfquist

Abstract Virtue ethics studies the character traits of good persons. This includes analysis of how ordinary persons can emulate moral role models in order to improve their moral character. This chapter investigates the link between virtues and disasters by relating classic and contemporary virtue ethical thinking to the character traits of humanity and resilience. The article finds ample support for the claim that these two character traits can be analysed as virtues and that classical virtue theorists can help us articulate the content of these traits. The contemporary discourse about virtues and disasters includes the long-standing analysis of the role of reason and emotions in virtues but the discourse also considers what kind of virtues that are relevant in disaster situations. Two important examples of the latter are the virtues of humanitarian workers and the virtues of those who suffer disasters. The chapter conclude that that future research should consider how training can strengthen individual resilience and how the pursuit of moral excellence can be included in the humanitarian field as a complement to minimum standards.

Keywords Virtues · Ethics · Humanitarianism · Disasters · Humanity · Resilience

14.1 Introduction

Many philosophers have not been interested primarily in analysing the moral rightness of individual acts but instead focused on how a human life should be lead. This involves an analysis of what kind of personal characteristics are essential parts of a good life. Such personal characteristics can be categorized into those traits or qualities that are good, virtues, and those that are negative and harmful, vices. Virtue ethics in general is the study of these character traits.

Compared to consequentialist and deontological ethical theories, virtue ethics provide a distinct refocus on an actor's habits and motivation in general instead of

L. Löfquist (✉)
Theology Department, Uppsala University, Uppsala, Sweden
e-mail: lars.lofquist@teol.uu.se

D. P. O'Mathúna et al. (eds.), *Disasters: Core Concepts and Ethical Theories*, Advancing Global Bioethics 11, https://doi.org/10.1007/978-3-319-92722-0_14

his or her deliberation and acts on a single occasion. Virtue ethical theories often share a teleological character with consequentialism. Virtues are good for something, for living a good, full or flourishing human life. Even if there is much disagreement about the specific definitions of all character traits, it seems that a good life according to a virtue perspective should include development of character traits like bravery, industry, benevolence, integrity and friendship. But as with deontological theories, virtue ethics does not presume that ethics foremost concerns maximization of the good. Instead, the good life also might include protection of some values against other values.

The recent revival of the virtue ethical tradition adds a distinctive and thought-provoking perspective on disasters, whether natural or man-made. Authors such as Anscombe (1958) and MacIntrye (1985) have stressed that virtue ethics provides us with another understanding of human moral relations that is less reductionist than the alternatives. This chapter will provide a short introduction to non-religious Western virtue ethics, a historical overview of the relations between virtues and disasters, an analysis of the current debate and point towards several areas that are in need of further analysis.

14.2 Virtue Ethics

It is natural to start with Aristotle (384–322 BC) because he is perhaps the most famous of all philosophers who have thought about virtue ethics. His most famous work on ethics, *The Nicomachean Ethics,* provides a rich understanding about what a good life might be and how virtues figure as parts of this life.

All of Aristotle's thinking about virtues builds upon his philosophical anthropology about the nature of human beings. As a starting point Aristotle presumes that there are better and worse ways to live a human life. All things have a final end, a telos. This is true of knives and other tools, but is likewise true for human beings. The telos is what is the specific character of an entity. For a knife the characteristic is cutting. A good knife is then characterized as being good to cut with. Humans too have a characteristic trait, our capacity to reason. A good human life must therefore include the use of reason (Aristotle 2004, 1197b20–1098a1-20). Aristotle's analogy is plagued with strong assumptions that are not easy to accept. The knife is obviously made but that is not obviously true of human beings.

Aristotle claims that a good life is a life governed by reason, which is a distinguishing human ability and our highest faculty. This has two dimensions. First, that the best life is a life spent in continuous contemplation since that is the primary activity associated with reason. Contemplation is an activity we can practice by ourselves and it has its own value (Aristotle 2004, 1177a). Second, living in accordance with reason includes acting in a way that is appropriate to the situation at hand by using our intellectual capacity for *practical reason* (Aristotle 2004, 1140a25–1140b30). What is characteristic of a virtuous person is that he or she has a disposition to act appropriately in different situations. The person who has the virtue of bravery can avoid acting rashly but also avoid acting cowardly (Aristotle

2004, 1107a1–10). A virtuous person who possesses practical reason will also be able to give the right response to different situations; this can include emotional responses where it is fitting. For example, anger can be justified when a person is treated without due respect.

Another important thinker in the virtue ethical tradition is David Hume (1711–1776). In Hume's central work, *An Enquiry concerning the Principles of Morals* (1751), he provides an account of virtues that shares some similar traits with Aristotle, specifically the importance of emotions and the social utility of virtues.

Hume's thinking on virtues is shaped by his general empiricist methodology in which he seeks the explanation of different phenomena, including morality. This means that Hume too sees emotions as a significant part of morality, even more fundamental than reason. Morality is not a matter of true of false nor reasonable or unreasonable; it is a matter of proper motivation, which can only be provided by emotions (Hume 1998, 1:6–8). Hume's core idea is that human beings are to a large extent governed by a wish to do good for others (Hume 1998, 2:5). In Hume's complex moral psychology, humans are driven by both egoism and sympathy to each other, but it is the latter that holds moral importance. This can be noted by the fact that we can even praise the virtuous character of an enemy (Hume 1998, 5:8).

It is noteworthy that Hume also sees a practical function for emotions. Hume claims that a virtue is a character trait which humans find agreeable or useful (Hume 1998, 7:19–25). A counter-argument is that humans might have different emotional responses to different character traits, and thus Hume's argument seems to lead to relativism. Instead of accepting this outcome, Hume argues that humans in general tend to like and dislike the same moral character traits. This *moral sense* is a feature common to all normal human beings even if not all have developed it to the full extent. He also claims that we tend to praise those character traits which in the long run are useful for both society in general and individuals in particular (Hume 1998, 2:22). Thus, Hume and Aristotle share the idea that virtue is beneficial and that a morally good life is the best way to live. This puts them in contrast to a common experience that acting virtuously is often not as successful as deceiving and maximizing one's egoistic benefits.

A modern day virtue ethicist in the Aristotelian tradition, Alistair MacIntyre (b. 1929), also describes virtue in relation to a good life. In his seminal work, *After Virtue: A Study in Moral Theory,* MacIntyre argues that a virtue must be conceived as:

> ...acquired human quality the possession and exercise of which tends to enable us to achieve those goods which are internal to practices and the lack of which effectively prevents us from achieving any such goods. (MacIntyre 1985, p. 191)

As such one cannot define a virtue without looking closer to a practice. Practices include many different forms of shared human activities that are identified by having internal standards of excellence; an example would be the game of chess. A good chess player has the virtues that makes it possible to excel in this practice. An excellent chess player gains goods that are internal to the game, for example strategic thinking and patience. In addition, the player might gain external goods such as money and fame. There can be a tension between these goods. In practice, internal goods might inhibit our ability to gain external goods (MacIntrye 1985, pp. 191–196).

In considering a good life, MacIntyre argues that one can only discern the content of this life in relation to the overall narrative (or moral tradition), which provides meaning for individuals (MacIntyre 1985, pp. 204–225). A person living in Athens 400 BC has another moral tradition than a seventeenth century New England farmer. This means that the virtues in respective traditions can be different (MacIntyre 1985, p. 220). Compared to Aristotle, MacIntyre does not present a specific teleological view of human existence and is open to different ideas of the good life. Different cultures can have different ideas about the good life, which makes it impossible to *a priori* identify the content of a specific virtue such as bravery.

Michael Slote (b. 1941) has elaborated Hume's ethics further. In *Morals from Motives* (2001) Slote defends Hume's, and others, case that the feeling of sympathy to others is a fundamental part of morality. He claims that benevolence as a moral ideal can provide the foundation for an understanding of virtues that is distinctively non-Aristotelian which also avoids the utilitarian focus on consequences (Slote 2001, p. viii). This position includes the idea that virtue ethics primary content is how our motivation for actions relate to excellence (Slote 2001, p. 4f). Cases such as the Good Samaritan show what ethical excellence mean by being paradigm and praiseworthy examples of benevolence (Slote 2001, p. 35f).

A reoccurring idea in the history of virtue ethical thinking is that human beings are not morally static creatures but can develop their moral virtues. Aristotle stressed the importance of proper moral teaching (Aristotle 2004, 1179b20–1180a30). Hume claimed that the natural virtue of fellow feeling can be strengthened with education (Hume 1998, 5:3–4). MacIntyre too identifies the importance of learning the internal rules of excellence in a tradition (MacIntyre 1985, p. 216) and Slote argues for extending our sympathy to others by moral education (Slote 2007, p. 290f). The idea of moral development has an important implication. We cannot be content with the current state of our moral capacity. We might be brave, just and humane but we have not achieved the final stage of these virtues. There is always room for improvement. Aristotle, Hume, MacIntyre and Slote all stress that it is only by learning from those who achieved a higher stage of virtue that we can become better persons.

Turning to the connection between virtues and disasters, we can note that disasters, in the sense of unforeseen radical events with significant negative impacts on many people, are linked to the idea of virtues in two ways. First, what is a morally excellent response to those disasters we ourselves might face? Second, what is a morally excellent response to disasters that others face?[1] I will discuss these two themes as representing two different virtues, first the virtue of resilience and second, the virtue of humanity. The main discussion partners will be classical virtue ethical thinkers. I will return to contemporaries in the section on the current state of virtue ethical research and disasters.

[1] This distinction between two types of virtues is methodological and not ontological. One can follow Aristotle and argue that a person who possess the virtue of practical reason also possess all other virtues (Aristotle 2004, 1145a0–5). The idea of "the unity of virtue" does not preclude that each virtue can be analysed in itself separated from the other virtues.

14.2.1 The Virtue of Resilience

Human life always has been, and still is, weak and vulnerable, it is to be expected that we can suffer in this life. Most humans have not had the tools or knowledge to do much about this vulnerability. Thus, suffering was simply considered to be a part of life. The primary philosophical question was not how to avoid suffering but how to relate to it. Should a proper response to this human condition be defeatism, fatalism and horror or self-control and gratitude for the fleeing moments we have? Resilience is one term that describes the later kind of response. Excellence in responding to disasters can be described as possessing the virtue of resilience.[2]

The Stoic intellectual tradition is popularly thought of as propagating an unflinching response to human hardship. The original sources do support this popular account. In his *Meditations*, the Roman emperor and Stoic philosopher Marcus Aurelius (121–180) contemplates the following:

> 'It is my bad luck that this has happened to me.' No, you should rather say: 'It is my good luck that, although this has happened to me, I can bear it without pain, neither crushed by the present nor fearful of the future.' Because such a thing could have happened to any man, but not every man could have borne it without pain. (Aurelius 2006, 4:49)

Aurelius accepts suffering as a human constant but instead of falling back to fatalism he argues that bad luck gives us the chance of developing and showing excellent character traits. This is not an attempt to redefine disasters – they are still something negative – but an acknowledgement that disasters make it possible to show sides of our humanity that are of moral worth.

The right response to disasters can also be discussed from the perspective of Aristotle. He wrote about disasters in his reasoning about bravery. He notes that a brave person governed by practical reason would not be broken down by the events nor would he or she simply shrug it off. Instead, the virtuous person would acknowledge the horrors of the disaster but would not dwell upon it forever (Aristotle 2004, 1115a5–1115b6). Compared to Aurelius, Aristotle's perspective is more in tune with the idea that some situations require a substantial emotional response, which is something that Aurelius rejects (Aristotle 2004, 1108a32–1108b6).

Hume also identifies the moral importance of perseverance and associated virtues such as resilience. He claims that there are four distinct categories of personal character qualities. There are those qualities that are agreeable for ourselves, those that are useful for ourselves, those that are agreeable to others and those that are useful for others. Perseverance (and resilience) then is something that humans in general approve of as a character quality that is obviously useful for ourselves and therefore a virtue (Hume 1998, 6:21).

---

[2] Fortitude is an alternative term. The term resilience is more inclusive since it can include both how a person withstands difficulties and how he or she recovers from them. Both groups and individuals can be resilient. However, since virtues are individual traits, I will focus on how a person relate to extreme circumstances such as disasters.

One can also argue that individuals with these qualities are useful for society as a whole since they can help rebuild the community after disaster has struck. However, for Hume this quality would fall under the more general virtue of humanity, which itself is useful to society. This makes Hume's position different compared to Aurelius' and Aristotle' who do not directly consider whether resilience has a good beyond the individual possessor.

14.2.2 The Virtue of Humanity

The other dimension of the human response to disasters that connects with virtue ethics is how to respond to the suffering of others. The primary focus for this response is helping other human beings in need, and doing good for fellow men. This disposition for doing good is referred to with many different terms such as beneficence, benevolence and fellow feeling. Humanity is part of doing good in general with the specific emphasis on helping those in need.

The idea that a good person will assist others is fundamental for all classical thinkers on virtue. For example, both Aristotle and Aurelius claimed that helping others was the key to the good life. Aristotle's analysis of friendship includes a detailed analysis of the relations between friends. A proper friendship involves appreciating one another because of each friend's inner character and not only the fact that both feel good in each other's company (Aristotle 2004, 1169b3–1170b20). In Aurelius's case, the emperor shows disdain for other humans but also keeps referring to the need to help his fellow humans (Aurelius 2006, 4:12) and strive to love them (e.g. Aurelius 2006, 6: 39).

That a virtuous person practices goodness towards his or her friends is not controversial. Humanity as a specific virtue, though, is not restricted to friendship but extends care to a much larger group, which in its most abstract form includes the whole of humanity. The determining factor becomes who is human and who is not, which can be restricted to one's own social group or universalized to include all members of *Homo sapiens sapiens*.

Both Greek and Roman philosophical traditions include such a universal idea of humanity. It is again relevant to consider a Stoic thinker. Marcus Tillus Cicero (106–43 BC) argued for the moral commonality between mankind. In his influential work, *On the Laws,* Cicero states:

> ...what nation does not cherish kindness, benevolence, or a soul that is grateful for and mindful of a benefit? What nation does not despise, does not hate the haughty, the nefarious, the cruel, the ungrateful? Since from these things it may be understood that the whole race of human beings has been united among themselves, the final result is that knowledge of living correctly makes persons better. (Cicero 2013, 1:32, p. 140)

According to Cicero this moral unity provides a foundation for extending humanity to cover every human in need. Hume also notes the universal aspect of humanity. He too stressed the centrality of helping other persons and made the capacity for beneficence a central part of his philosophical analysis of virtue. Humans appreciate those character traits that motivate people to help others in need:

> ...no qualities are more entitled to the general good-will and approbation of mankind, than beneficence and humanity, friendship and gratitude, natural affection and public spirit, or whatever proceeds from a tender sympathy with others, and a generous concern for our kind and species. (Hume 1998, 2:5)

Since such different thinkers as Aristotle, Cicero and Hume, who all lived in different times and different cultures, have found grounds to claim that humanity is a good character trait we have reasons to believe that this is an important part of a good human life.

14.3 The Current State of Virtue Ethics and Disasters

A quick survey of the general research field of virtue ethics shows that the number of texts that explicitly discuss virtues and disasters are limited. But one can identify three specific research themes. The first theme involves general writings on the connection between virtue ethics and disasters. The second theme concerns the professional virtues of humanitarian workers, and the third theme concerns the virtues of those suffering a disaster.

14.3.1 General Writings on the Connection Between Virtue Ethics and Disasters

There are several examples of research that includes a general analysis of the relation between virtues and disasters. Slote (2007) argues for a virtue ethics based on Hume and Hutcheson as a response to the ethical challenges expressed by Peter Singer. Singer claims that the suffering of those with lesser means requires a significant transfer of resources of wealthy countries to poorer countries (Singer 1972). As a response to Singer, Slote points to the human feeling for empathy with other human beings. Empathy is directed to specific persons and cannot be understood as having humanity at large as its object. Instead, Slote claims that empathy is directed towards those we have a relation with, and this reduces the moral demand of helping all. A person who extends his or her empathy to include distant others simply extends this virtue more than is possible for most persons. Slote also argues that our empathy can be trained to include more and more people and that we have moral reasons to conduct such training (Slote 2007, p. 290f).

Naomi Zack (2009) discusses virtue ethics in relation to disasters and makes a detailed comparison between different ways of relating to disasters. She contrasts the character traits of such fictional reckless heroes such as Achilles and the modern day agent Mitch Rapp with the bonds between the boy and father in the novel *The Road*

(2006) and the real life description of Ernest Shackleton in his failed expedition to Antarctica. Zack argues that it is not the traditional heroic virtues such as fast thinking and bravery that are needed in facing disasters. Instead it is the virtues of integrity and diligence that makes it possible to rise to the occasion (Zack 2009, p. 52f). One of the chief points of integrity as a virtue involves staying away from the slippery slope of justifying extreme actions because they are unique (Zack 2009, 60f).

Zack notices how Shackleton rose to the occasion as a leader. When he and his crew got stranded in Antarctica, he took the lead in a situation of extreme hardship and became an example of a moral role model. Shackleton showed integrity in all small details ranging from food distribution to caring of the sick. Moreover, Zack also notices that Shackleton as an explorer went searching for challenges, which is an important difference compared to the life of many contemporaries. This raises the wider issue of how virtues and disasters should be interpreted from a political and institutional perspective (Zack 2009, pp. 61–64).

Sara Kathleen Geale provides an example of a more applied approach to virtues and disasters (2012). She argues that disaster management includes a wide variety of virtues such as prudence, courage and resilience. She also notices that it is difficult to formulate a finished list of virtues and that disaster response is an ongoing work process (Geale 2012, p. 460). This implies that new situations could accentuate other character traits of those who respond. Another issue she analyses is the virtue of justice and how a disaster can raise the need for applying a triage in resource allocation. This can be considered problematic for those who believe medical care is a right and will require that all people receive fair treatment. It is part of a virtuous response to balance these demands (Geale 2012, p. 450f).

14.3.2 Professional Virtues of Humanitarian Workers

Numerous authors have studied professional virtues. For example, the specific virtues associated with physicians has been analysed by Oakley and Cocking (2001) and the virtues of nurses and social workers by Banks and Gallagher (2009). Others have focused on the virtues of disaster relief workers, humanitarian workers, and how they need to be prepared to act in relation to moral dilemmas where every alternative action might include harming some persons or values.

Perhaps the most prolific current writer on humanitarian ethics is Hugo Slim (1997, 2015). Slim provides a broad discussion about the moral challenges for relief professionals and the ethical resources available to meet these challenges. He argues explicitly that virtue ethics provides the most integrated account of morality since it gives due weight to both reason and emotions. Moreover, Slim notes that ethical principles are just one limited part of ethics. An appropriate ethical response will often require good personal character traits, which can only be developed by experience (Slim 2015, pp. 126–133).

Slim also provide a list of possible professional virtues for a humanitarian worker. This includes the virtues of humanity, impartiality, neutrality, and independence which builds upon the established ethical principles of the ICRC and is supplanted by key parts of the *Code of Conduct for the International Red Cross and Red Crescent Movement and Non-Governmental Organizations (NGOs) in Disaster Relief* (IFRC and ICRC 1994). The professional virtues should be complemented with everyday virtues such as courage and practical wisdom (Slim 2015, pp. 241–247). Slim also makes a compelling case for the importance of role models. Role models can be found in both international and local relief organizations and Slim argues for a larger role of non-western role models (Slim 1997, p. 255f).

A possible tension in Slim's account is the degree to which a good humanitarian relief worker must be a good person. For Aristotle, it was clear that a person could excel in technical skills such as shoemaking but fail to excel in goodness, in virtue. Similarly, must one be morally good to excel in disaster relief? The answer is not obvious since we can think of professions such as engineering and surgery where the professional virtues are distinct from the personal moral virtues. MacIntyre's perspective can offer support to Slim's. One can argue that there are internal goods in humanitarian work that can only be obtained by practicing certain moral virtues. Thus, in order for a relief worker to be good, he or she must show proper attitudes and actions, including humanity, towards people in need.

Other researchers have also noted the possible implications of a virtue perspective for professional humanitarian workers. Matthew Hunt (2011) analyses the different medical ethical frameworks that can help relief workers in morally challenging situations. Besides medical ethical codes, he too supports the importance of good role models but he does not provide a longer elaboration of what this means from a virtue perspective.

Eva Wortel (2009) makes a detailed analysis of different humanitarian principles such as humanity and impartiality and argues that these principles can be understood also as values and virtues. Wortel refers to Aristotle, Jean Pictet, and Thomas Aquinas, and defends the idea that humanity includes an emotional motivation to help those in need, which requires experience and practical wisdom. Trying to reduce both humanity and other ethical principles into a doctrine would then be a misinterpretation of their ethical meaning (Wortel 2009, p. 790). Wortel's analysis shows how the different humanitarian principles can be interpreted in different ways and demonstrates the need for a clear articulation of such interpretations.

Finally, I have analysed the implications of professional codes for relief workers from a virtue perspective (Löfquist 2016). Some of the findings are the need to retain experienced staff as role models, initiating training programs that support development of virtues and the need for an open discourse about the final aims of relief work professions.

14.3.3 Virtues of Those Suffering a Disaster

A third research theme that concerns the relation between virtues and disasters is the resilience discourse. Resilience, the ability to bounce back from a disaster, involves a broad discourse including sociological, economic and ecological dimensions.

Resilience as an ethical virtue focuses on what character traits is required to face, manage and overcome the shock, fear and effects of a disaster.

An example of resilience research relevant for a virtue perspective is provided by Alice Gritti. She studies resilience of individual aid workers and their organizational context from a psychosocial perspective. Noticing the difference in how women and men experienced stress she also identifies the institutional factors that reduce or increase stress. She argues for an increased focus on stress training for aid workers and claims that:

> ... resilience is not only about static personality traits owned by specific individuals; on the contrary, resilience comprises a continuum of qualities that can be possessed to varying degrees, and that can be built and enhanced by training. (Gritti 2015, p. 452)

From a virtue perspective it is relevant to discern that Gritti treats resilience as a good personal trait that can be supported and developed. Although she presents her work in the language of stress management and not philosophical ethics, this is a highly relevant insight. As with other virtues, resilience can be learned and can best be learned in a supporting context.

There are also examples of explicit analyses of resilience as a virtue. Craig Steven Titus (2006) is an example of a current researcher who relates psychosocial research on resilience to virtue ethical thinking. Titus argues that contemporary empirical findings on the human ability to adapt to disasters can be related to philosophical anthropology. He also provides a substantial definition of resilience:

> First, resilience is the ability to cope in adverse conditions; it endures, minimizes, or overcomes hardship. Second, it consists in resisting destructive pressures on the human person's physiological, psychosocial, and spiritual life; that is, it maintains capacities in the face of challenges, threats, and loss. Third, resilience creatively constructs and adapts after adversity; it implies recovering with maturity, confidence, and wisdom to lead a meaningful and productive life. (Titus 2006, p. 29)

The rest of Titus's work focuses on fleshing out what Aquinas adds to the resilience discussion and what resources that discussion can supply in order to reinterpret Aquinas. He notes that Aquinas provides a rich analysis of human nature, which provides for both reason and emotions (Titus 2006, p. 84). Titus relates Aquinas' virtues of fortitude, initiative and endurance to the concept of resilience and suggests several insights for the analysis. One interesting idea from Aquinas is that hope provides a powerful foundation for daring activities in face of fear and disaster (Titus 2006, p. 198ff).

14.4 Towards the Future of Virtue Ethics and Disasters

After this short survey of the field it is time to identify a few themes that can be the focus of future research. At least two issues about virtues and disasters stand out as requiring further discussion.

1. *Teaching resilience*

Conceiving resilience as a virtue is fruitful since it stresses human capacity for personal development. Instead of looking at resilience as a personal quality that is static and stable, one can see it as dynamic. Resilience training is obviously relevant for all those who face unsecure living conditions including both natural and man-made disasters. But when one looks at historical thinkers such as Aristotle and Hume it is clear that they do not believe that resilience is just a virtue for those who regularly face disasters. Instead resilience is part of a good human life in general since the lack of this virtue will have negative effects and make it more difficult for us to lead our life. Aurelius is one interesting example of a person who despite secure living conditions saw the benefits of learning to face adversity. Further research can provide greater insights into how the virtue of resilience can be taught as well as its relationship to other virtues such as bravery.

There is also room for caution in treating resilience as a virtue. Any focus on individual resilience risks devaluing the real suffering of those who face disasters. Despite the ideas of Stoics such as Aurelius, most of those who exhibit significant resilience would be better off avoiding the experience altogether. Making resilience an individual affair could place unjust responsibility on individuals and make them more responsible for their recovery than they should be. Aristotle claimed that a virtue is an ability to respond appropriately to different situations. One can therefore argue that a resilient person who had faced extreme horrors will need time to reconnect to everyday life. Resilience would need to include the strength and permanence of the recovery in addition to its speed.

2. *Ethical excellence in professional ethics for relief workers*

It is a challenge for the humanitarian profession to move beyond lists of ethical principles and systematically consider how such lists should function in the strive towards ethical excellence. Despite Slim's efforts, a significant part of humanitarian ethics is still about listing and analysing ethical principles. Documents such as *Code of Conduct for the International Red Cross and Red Crescent Movement and Non-Governmental Organizations (NGOs) in Disaster Relief* (IFRC and ICRC 1994) and the *Humanitarian Charter* (The Sphere Project 2011) both list different ethical principles that should guide relief workers. The obvious benefit with the quasi-legalistic framework is that it can be adapted to project evaluations and the interests of different donor institutions. This can help donors, organizations and beneficiaries to accomplish more ethical relief operations and avoid doing harm to people in need. Viewed as a minimum standard the principles are fruitful but we must be aware of their limitations.

Virtuous behaviour is about moral excellence, and meeting minimum standards simply fails to achieve this goal. In the virtue ethical tradition, an individual is understood as a person in the process of becoming morally better. For example, to be "good enough" simply does not make sense from an Aristotelian idea of the good person. The risk with minimum standards is that one can believe that the quest for moral improvement can be relaxed when one has achieved this standard. One can see this in the case of how humanitarian workers relate the idea of accountability to recipients. Is it enough to include the disaster-struck people's views in a needs assessment? From the perspective of minimum standards this might be adequate, but the virtue of humanity might demand a constant striving to find better ways to show accountability to those in need.

From this background, the humanitarian discourse would benefit from an ongoing explicit discussion of what excellence means. One can, for example, ask in what way partnerships with local humanitarian actors mean only that they should accept the priorities of the international organizations (and their donors)? Or does it mean that the international organizations accept revisions and even total reorientations based on the concerns of the local organization? The search for ethical excellence can have deep effects on the power between local and international humanitarian actors, which needs to be explored further.

14.5 Conclusion

From this short descriptive investigation it is clear that virtue ethics is an untapped philosophical resource for the analysis of human responses to disasters. A virtue ethical perspective can identify several promising paths for future research. Resilience is of general importance for a good life since every person would benefit in being able to come back to everyday life after an extreme experience. It is also clear that virtue perspective provides a more stringent moral ideal than traditional professional ethical codes. Virtues are not about meeting minimum standards but about actively pursuing excellence in moral matters. There is no room for complacency in such an ideal. Ethical standards will therefore need to be understood as pedagogical tools in the pursuit of excellence or to be set so high that they are seldom or ever achieved. The ancient and contemporary thinkers who analyse virtues does not believe that such moral excellence is beyond human ability. However, they do acknowledge that morality make strong demands on us and a general benefit of virtue ethics is to make this demand explicit.

References

Anscombe, Elizabeth. 1958. Modern moral philosophy. *Philosophy* 33: 1–19.

Aristotle. 2004. *The Nicomachean ethics*. London: Penguin Books.

Aurelius, Marcus. 2006. *Meditations*. London: Penguin Books.

Banks, Sarah, and Ann Gallagher. 2009. *Ethics in professional life: Virtues for health and social care*. Basingstoke: Palgrave Macmillan.

Cicero, Marcus Tullius. 2013. *On the Republic and on the laws* Trans: D. Fott. London: Cornell University Press.

Geale, Sara Kathleen. 2012. The ethics of disaster management. *Disaster Prevention and Management: An International Journal* 21: 445–463.
Gritti, Alice. 2015. Building aid workers' resilience: Why a gendered approach is needed. *Gender and Development* 23: 449–462.
Hume, David. 1998. In *An enquiry concerning the principles of morals*, ed. T.L. Beauchamp. Oxford: Oxford University Press.
Hunt, Matthew. 2011. Establishing moral bearings: Ethics and expatriate health care professionals in humanitarian work. *Disasters* 35: 606–622.
International Federation of the Red Cross and Red Crescent societies and International Committee of the Red Cross. 1994. Code of conduct for the International Red Cross and Red Crescent Movement and Non-Governmental Organizations (NGOs) in disaster relief. http://www.ifrc.org/Global/Publications/disasters/code-of-conduct/code-english.pdf. Accessed 26 Apr 2018.
Löfquist, Lars. 2016. Virtues and humanitarian ethics. *Disasters* 41: 41–54.
MacIntyre, Allistar. 1985. *After virtue: A study in moral theory*. London: Duckworth.
Oakley, Justin, and Dean Cocking. 2001. *Virtue ethics and professional roles*. Cambridge: Cambridge University Press.
Singer, Peter. 1972. Famine, affluence, and morality. *Philosophy and Public Affairs* 1: 229–243.
Slim, Hugo. 1997. Doing the right thing: Relief agencies, moral dilemmas and moral responsibility in political emergencies and war. *Disasters* 21: 244–257.
———. 2015. *Humanitarian ethics: A guide to the morality and aid in war and disaster*. London: Hurst Company.
Slote, Michael. 2001. *Morals from motives*. Oxford: Oxford University Press.
———. 2007. Famine, affluence, and virtue. In *Working virtue: Virtue ethics and contemporary moral problems*, ed. Rebecca Walker and Philip Ivanhoe. London: Clarendon Press.
The Sphere Project. 2011. *The Sphere handbook: Humanitarian charter and minimum standards in humanitarian response*. Geneva: The Sphere Project.
Titus, Craig Steven. 2006. *Resilience and the virtue of fortitude: Aquinas in dialogue with the psychosocial sciences*. Washington, DC: The Catholic University of America Press.
Wortel, Eva. 2009. Humanitarians and their moral stance in war: The underlying values. *International Review of the Red Cross* 91: 779–802.
Zack, Naomi. 2009. *Ethics for disaster*. New York: Rowman Littlefield Publishers.

Chapter 15
Kantian Virtue Ethics Approaches

Eleni Kalokairinou

Abstract Various disasters have been affecting our societies for the last few decades, ranging from earthquakes, floods and tsunamis to economic crises, terrorism and migration. When a disaster strikes, it upsets the normal way of life of the society and leaves behind hundreds of thousands of victims and casualties. The questions that arise automatically are first, how one is going to conceive and understand the disasters that occur and, secondly, in what way one is going to intervene, especially after these disasters have struck, and help those affected and injured. What obviously concerns us here is to track down the ethical account which will enable us to consider the disaster theoretically and will guide us to intervene on the field when the actual disaster has occurred. A number of different ethical approaches to dealing with disasters have been propounded by philosophers, among which are notably two, utilitarianism and Kant's deontology. However, even though these two ethical theories seem to be the "ideal" theories for dealing with the problematic situations arising from disasters, it is argued that they are not ideal at all, as they overlook and do not take into account the particular features of the problematic situations and the feelings of both, the victims and the workers. However, on a more careful examination, it turns out that Kant's deontological account is not just the formal distanced ethical theory that first appears to be. It also possesses an empirical account, the ethical account of virtues, which can be directly applied to the problems caused by disasters in the real world. Especially, by presenting us with an elaborate analysis of the duty of justice and the duty of beneficence, Kant succeeds in bringing out the practical relevance that his theory of virtues has for disasters.

Keywords Disaster · Utilitarianism · Deontology · Kant · Virtue · Duty · Autonomy · End · Justice · Beneficence

---

E. Kalokairinou (✉)
Department of Philosophy and Education, Aristotle University of Thessaloniki, Thessaloniki, Greece
e-mail: ekalo@edlit.auth.gr

D. P. O'Mathúna et al. (eds.), *Disasters: Core Concepts and Ethical Theories*, Advancing Global Bioethics 11, https://doi.org/10.1007/978-3-319-92722-0_15

15.1 Ethical Theories and Disasters

The bioethical problems that arise in everyday life are of a fairly complex character. They range from simple questions of personal choice to rather complicated issues of social, political and economic policy (Kalokairinou 2016). If the dilemmas which are encountered under normal everyday circumstances are complex, then one can very easily imagine how much more complicated are the bioethical problems one comes across in disaster settings.

Disasters may be of a great variety. They may include natural disasters like, for instance, earthquakes, floods, and tsunamis, which explode unexpectedly and affect badly usually underdeveloped or developing countries. They may include social disasters, caused mainly by men, like accidents in industry and transportation, wars, terrorism and migration. Or, there may be a third, mixed kind of disasters which include both natural and human causes like, for instance, various kinds of pandemics, pests and plagues (O'Mathúna et al. 2014).

What characterizes all these kinds of disasters is the sudden loss of normality that follows directly the occurrence of the disaster. A sense of normality that has prevailed so far in society is suddenly lost, as a number of people die unexpectedly, hundreds of them get badly injured, and thousands of others are made homeless (Kalokairinou 2016). The notion of normality is necessary for human society, for it helps men safeguard their stability and their security, both necessary conditions for developing their abilities and for flourishing in life. It would seem therefore that disasters, both natural and man-related, threaten human society deep inside, because they break what holds it together and controls it. Disasters on the whole put at risk the tissue that holds people and societies together and makes their lives secure, eudaimonious and worth living.

If so much is at stake in cases of disasters, it is quite understandable that bioethical problems and dilemmas in disasters have been engaging philosophers so much recently. Philosophers have been studying the ethical dilemmas we face in disaster settings not only with a view to offering practical assistance. Prior to this, their aim was theoretical: to explore those moral concepts which will enable us to analyze and conceive better what has been going on in disasters and, therefore, decide how to respond to them.

Disaster Bioethics is a fairly new discipline. As a consequence, the relevant literature has only recently started to appear, especially under the influence of research on other related fields, such as public health, global health, famine relief and world poverty. Philosophers, under the stress of the global problems that plague humanity, have been dealing systematically with these issues for the last 20–30 years. As O'Mathúna points out, there are on the one hand the philosophers who claim that a form of utilitarianism is the appropriate theory for dealing with the problems of public health, famine relief and disasters; there are on the other hand the scholars who contend that deontological accounts like, for instance, Kant's deontological theory, are the ideal types of accounts for considering these dilemmas (O'Mathúna 2016; Singer 1972; O'Neill 1993).

15.2 Utilitarianism and Deontology

However, as O'Mathúna has argued, neither the utilitarian nor the deontological accounts are the appropriate theories for dealing with the bioethical problems which arise on a world scale (O'Mathúna 2016). In particular, on a utilitarian account ethical dilemmas are solved on the basis of the principle of utility, that is on the basis of the action which is calculated in advance to maximize the greater happiness of the greater number. On this account, to mention O'Mathúna's example, if there is only one oxygen tank, using it for a number of people who need it short-term has better consequences and is likely to increase the happiness of more people than using it for a person who needs it long-term (O'Mathúna 2016). However, utilitarian accounts face a lot of difficulties, when applied to the ethical problems which arise on a global stage. Even on a theoretical level it is quite difficult in many cases to calculate in advance and to predict what is the right thing to do, which is the policy which is likely to increase the pleasure or happiness of more people. Furthermore, even if this is feasible in some cases, it need not imply necessarily that it is the right, ethical or just thing to do. By increasing the greatest happiness of the greatest number at the expense of the happiness of minorities and individuals, utilitarianism sacrifices overtly the individual rights to the altar of the majorities and the big authorities (O'Mathúna 2016).

In an analogous manner, deontological accounts place an emphasis on duties. In particular, according to Kantian deontology, our fundamental duty is to respect the other person and to treat him not merely as a means but at the same time as an end. On this account, we do not only have duties to ourselves but also to other people. In a situation of need and destitution we would not want to remain helpless and deserted by other people. In the same way that we cannot want to leave the other people without help, when they find themselves in circumstances of need. The Universal Law of Nature, therefore, prescribes that we help others when they are in difficult circumstances like, for instance, disease, poverty, or disaster, as it also prescribes that the other people help us when we find ourselves in circumstances as difficult as these (Kant 1997, § 4:423). However, the circumstances that crises responders find themselves in are not always clear and straightforward. Should a military medical unit, for instance, give priority to civilian casualties or to recently arrived severely injured soldiers, when they cannot treat both at the same time? What is their duty to do? (O'Mathúna 2016). If the soldiers respond on the basis of their duty and give priority to treating the injured soldiers, it may not be necessarily the right thing to do (O'Mathúna 2016).

Consequently, as O'Mathúna has brought out, neither of these two ideal moral theories can help us deal fully with the ethical dilemmas encountered in disaster settings (O'Mathúna 2016). As pointed out, disaster responders often come across devastating, complex situations which involve a lot of human suffering and pain which neither of these two types of moral theories can account for adequately (O'Mathúna 2016). Both utilitarianism and Kantian deontology seem to offer us "the ideal solution" for every ethical dilemma we encounter in disasters, however it is very far from capturing reality and the feelings of those directly involved in the disasters, whether victims or disaster responders. O'Mathúna mentions the decisions taken under triage circumstances in disaster fields according to which the most serious cases are treated first, while other equally or less critical cases are treated second or left untreated (O'Mathúna 2016). O'Mathúna holds that in this kind of situations neither utilitarianism nor deontological accounts seem to be able to provide us with an ideal solution. Most obviously, this is because there is no ideal solution. Moreover, disaster responders who have come back from disaster fields in which they had to take such strenuous decisions, often claim that they considered their experience of working under these circumstances as a good opportunity to rethink and reassess their moral values and "deepen their relationships with co-workers and others" (O'Mathúna 2016, 9).

As a consequence, different approaches have been sought recently for dealing with the ethical dilemmas we come across in public health, world poverty and disaster settings. Traditionally, along with the rationalistic theories, like utilitarianism and the deontological accounts which claim to have the ideal solution for all kinds of disaster dilemmas, there are also the so-called nonideal moral theories, which tend to concentrate on the specific characteristics of each situation. Care ethics, feminist ethics, narrative ethics or the Aristotelian *phronesis* are cases in point. However, things may not be exactly so simple. For, there have been moral accounts which have attempted to bring out and combine what is best in each of these two types of moral approaches. R. M. Hare, the famous British moral philosopher of the twentieth century, for instance, has devoted a lot of time and space to arguing that a rationalist account, like his Universal Prescriptivism, need not imply necessarily that it overlooks the relevant specific features of the situation. The moral principle, "One ought never to make false statements to one's wife" (Hare 1963, 3.4), is more specific than the moral principle, "One ought never to make false statements" (Hare 1963, 3.4). But both of them are universal. The opposite of "specific" is "general". And the opposite of "universal" is "singular". A moral principle may be so specific as to defy formulation, but it remains universal, as long as it does not contain any particular reference to an individual, country or jurisdiction. This is why, according to Hare, the legal judgement, "It is illegal to torture one's children in England or according to the English law" is not a proper universalizable judgement, because it contains a particular reference to the individual "England". On the other hand, the judgement, "One ought not to torture one's children" is universalizable in the proper sense because it does not involve a particular reference to an individual or jurisdiction (Kalokairinou 2011, 53; Hare 1963, 3.4). The conclusion, therefore, that Hare reaches is that, given the logical feature of universalizability that all moral judgements possess, a moral judgement may be as specific as possible and at the same time be universalizable, as long as it does not contain any reference to a particular individual, country or jurisdiction.

15.3 Kantian Ethics

As a consequence, unlike those who conceive the debate between ideal and nonideal moral theories as a kind of disconnect, Hare has paved the way for showing that ideal theories may be compatible with nonideal moral theories (O'Mathúna 2016). However, 200 years before him, the German philosopher Immanuel Kant reached a similar conclusion, though through a different route. In his *Groundwork* he argues that ethics like physics has an empirical as well as an *a priori* part (Kant 1997). As he states in the preface of his brief treatise, his project is to start from ordinary morality and proceed to philosophical morality, that is the knowledge of moral principles. However, this knowledge cannot be founded on experience but must be *a priori*. It can only be justified by reference to a *Metaphysics of Morals*, as Kant calls the *a priori* part of ethics. So far Kant presents us with an ideal or a formal type of ethical theory. But after he has justified the knowledge of moral principles by virtue of a *Metaphysics of Morals*, Kant proceeds to clarify these principles and to make them concrete and applicable in the real world. Kant devotes his two ethical books, *The Metaphysics of Morals* and *Anthropology from a pragmatic point of view* to do precisely this (Kant 1996a, b). In this way, he supplements his initial ideal ethical account with a nonideal ethical theory.

My claim, therefore, in the present paper will be that all those ethical theorists who classify Kant's deontological account among the ideal ethical theories obviously misunderstand it and misrepresent it, because they leave out the nonideal part of it. As pointed out above, and as will become clear in what follows, Kant's ideal ethical account would have been incomplete without its nonideal part. Those who criticize Kantian deontology on the grounds that it is a formal, ideal ethical theory which overlooks the specific features of the dilemmas we encounter in public health, world hunger or disaster settings simply miss or ignore Kant's nonideal part of his ethical account, his theory of virtues (O'Mathúna 2016). From this point of view, even his renowned successor Hegel made the same mistake, when he accused him of having propounded a formalistic ethical theory which fails to take into account the complex features of the situations we come across in life (Hegel 1977, § 431). Quite to the contrary, as we will realize, Kant succeeds in putting forward an ethical theory which, though subject to the Universal moral law, is sensitive to the specific characteristics of the situations we encounter.

15.4 Kantian Virtues and Disasters

In his ethical writings Kant quite often puts forward the claim that we have a moral obligation to help those in need and in poor conditions. In the *Groundwork,* when he tests the Formula of the Universal Law of Nature against particular examples, Kant mentions the case of the man who, even though he is in a position to help and support those in need, prefers to live in comfortable conditions and indulge in pleasures (Kant 1997, § 4: 423). Kant recognizes that there is nothing wrong if one decides to behave in this way, as long as one also abstains from harming those in need. However, this person cannot will that his maxim become a Universal Law of Nature, because in that case the Universal Law would involve a contradiction of the will. For, there may be cases in which he may find himself in situations of need and despair, and "by such a law of nature arisen from his own will, he would rob himself of all hope of the assistance he wishes for himself" (Kant 1997, § 4: 423).

He also speaks about the duty of beneficence we have to other people in several parts of *The Metaphysics of Morals* (Kant 1996a). In particular, he argues about the duties of love we have to other human beings, which in turn he divides into duties of beneficence, duties of gratitude and duties of sympathy (Kant 1996a, §§ 6: 448–6: 452). But he also speaks about the duty of beneficence in the context of civil society. The wealthy have an obligation to the state, because, by having submitted their will to the protection of the state, they owe their existence and their wealth to it (Kant 1996a, § 6: 326). The state therefore has the right to contribute part of their wealth to their poor fellow citizens. The way to do this will be either by imposing taxes on the property and the income of the wealthy citizens or by establishing funds and supporting social institutions and organizations (Kant 1996a, § 6: 326).

Put in this way, it would seem that the duty of beneficence which is realized by the state in the context of the civil society is a duty of justice. However, the duty of beneficence which makes sense regardless and independently of the commonwealth is a duty of virtue. Quite understandably, one may wonder whether Kant's virtue ethics approach has to tell us something about famine relief, poverty and disasters on a global stage.

According to certain Kantian scholars, these two duties constitute the core of Kantian ethics (O'Neill 1993). The core of Kantian ethics, to remind the reader, is provided by the Formula of the End in itself: "So act that you use humanity, whether in your own person or in the person of any other, always at the same time as an end, never merely as a means" (Kant 1997, § 4: 429). But the requirements of each duty are entirely different. The duty of justice requires that we guide our behavior on the maxim that we never harm or cause anything wrong to others. The duty of beneficence, on the other hand, requires that we act in ways that foster and promote the other persons' ends (O'Neill 1993).

O'Neill, for sure, provides us with a deeper understanding of the Formula of the End in itself, when she analyzes it by virtue of the duty of justice and the duty of beneficence (O'Neill 1993). To use a person as a mere means, and not at the same time as an End in itself, implies that I treat her in a way or in ways to which she has not given her free, informed consent. If she has not given her free consent to my treating her in the way I do, this means that she has been coerced. If, on the other hand, she has consented to it, while she was kept in ignorance, then she has been deceived.

Of course, in our everyday dealings with other people, we may often use one another as a mere means. I may use, for instance, my students during my lectures and my tutorials, as a kind of guinea-pig, in order to test how they respond to the very controversial philosophical ideas I propound. But they also use me as a mere means, when they exhaust me mentally in the effort they make to cultivate their intellectual capacities and their critical thinking. But I am pretty aware of this and I consent to it, as they are also aware of the educational procedure that has been going on and agreed on it. As long as both parties have freely consented to entering a kind of dealing in the frame of a social and cooperative scheme, there is no deception or coercion involved one way or another.

There may be cases, however, in which one party may have been deceived into consenting to something to which he would not have consented, if he had known. Thus, if someone gives a promise with the intention of not keeping it, he is behaving on a maxim that the person to whom the promise is made, cannot have known. As a consequence, he is agreeing to something to which he would not have agreed, if he had known the promisor's actual maxim. According to Kant's ethical theory, the person who has in this way been driven to consent to something to which he would not have consented, if he had known the other party's maxim of behavior, has been deceived and coerced; in one word, he has become a victim of injustice (O'Neill 2016, 40).

But, as already mentioned, in addition to the duty of justice, the Formula of the End in itself also involves the duty of beneficence (O'Neill 1993). This implies that we do not violate the Formula only when we deceive, coerce or do injustice to a person. We also treat the other as a mere means, and so violate the Formula, when we refuse at least some of the times to foster the others' ends like our own, especially when the others are in situations of famine, poverty and disasters.

In this kind of reading of Kant's ethical theory, a person fails to be treated as an End in itself, and so she is treated as a mere means, not only when she is made a victim of deception, coercion or injustice. A person is also treated as a mere means, when she has lost the capacity to foster and develop his own ends. One usually becomes incapable of promoting one's own ends in cases of serious diseases, in cases of famine or extreme poverty or even in cases of sudden and unexpected natural and/or social disasters. In such cases of extreme abnormality, it is not so much that the others cannot have their own ends; it is rather that the idea of adopting one's own ends becomes meaningless. What actually lacks in people who manage to survive in such abnormal circumstances is their capacity to foster any end whatever. People who find themselves in this sort of vulnerable condition have limited drastically their "possibilities for autonomous action" (O'Neill 1993, 102).

It would seem therefore that, if the duty of justice safeguards that each person retains his ability to consent, after he has known all the relevant facts of the situation, and so keeps his autonomy, the duty of beneficence appears after the capacity for making autonomous choices and performing free actions has weakened, and its aim is to foster one's capacity of setting one's ends and to recover one's capacity for autonomy. But while in the case of the duty of justice, autonomy is something that all people possess, and they should act in ways that do not violate it; in the case of the duty of beneficence, autonomy is seriously threatened by external, natural or man-related factors. The duty of beneficence consists precisely in this: to help those in need and disasters recover the capacity of autonomy which under the circumstances they have lost, and so enable them to promote and develop their own ends

(O'Neill 2016, 40–41). Sometimes helping the other recover his autonomy may be difficult or may take time. This is why the duty of beneficence is primarily concerned with fostering the others' ends as if they are our own, until the others acquire the capacity to promote and develop their ends themselves.

Unlike the duty of justice, which aims at preserving the autonomy of others, the duty of beneficence is, in Aristotelian terms, *corrective* (Aristotle 1990, 1131 a 1). It makes sense in contexts in which the capacity of autonomy has been badly affected and in which its aim is "to correct", i.e. to recover the lost capacity.

Nevertheless, the duty of beneficence holds a central position in Kant's virtue ethics account. Together with the duty of gratitude and the duty of sympathy, it constitutes the expression of the duty of love we have to other human beings. It promotes the happiness of others, i.e. the one of the two moral ends the lawgiving reason sets against the influence of human inclinations which tempt us to adopt their own immoral ends. The second of these two moral ends being my own perfection (Kant 1996a, b, § 6: 381).

The duty of beneficence, therefore, is a duty of virtue. The duties of virtue are adapted to certain ends (i.e. my own perfection and the happiness of others) and not to specific actions. In the duty of beneficence we only need to specify the maxim of actions upon which we will behave, not the particular acts, since there are many different actions by virtue of which we can promote the happiness of others. Kant, further, distinguishes the duty of beneficence, and by and large the duties of virtue, into those which are *meritorious* and those which *are owed* (Kant 1996a, § 6: 448). Meritorious duties are the duties the other people do not have a right to claim, which however if you perform, your action acquires merit and you are praiseworthy. If you do not perform them, you do not lack in virtue, since nobody is wronged. Duties that are owed, on the other hand, are duties that the others have a right or a lawful claim to, which however is not enforced by a law or some other kind of external means. To perform duties that are owed is to accomplish the others' lawful claim and do what is required. If one fails to perform duties that are owed, on the other hand, one violates the others' right, i.e. their autonomy, and so exhibits signs of an immoral character.

According to Kant, the duties of (practical) love and respect in the practical sense are two good examples of the above two types of duties. The duty of love (in which the duty of beneficence is included) is to be understood as the duty "to make others' *ends* my own (provided only that these are not immoral)" (Kant 1996a, § 6: 450). The duty of beneficence is a meritorious duty. The duty of respect for my neighbor, on the other hand, involves fostering "the maxim of limiting our self-esteem by the dignity of humanity in another person" (Kant 1996a, § 6: 449). Or, in another formulation, it implies that I adopt the maxim "not to degrade any other to a mere means to my ends (not to demand that another throw himself away in order to slave for my end)" (Kant 1996a, § 6: 450). The duty of respect, therefore, is a duty that is owed.

Furthermore, to the extent that the duty of beneficence implies fostering the ends of others as if they are our own, it is also a *wide, positive* duty. It does not specify the actions we ought to perform but only the maxim upon which we should act. The duty of respect, on the other hand, is a *negative* duty. It operates on the maxim that prescribes us to limit our self-esteem in the name of the dignity of humanity in another person. It is therefore *restrictive* and *narrow* (Kant 1996a, §§ 6: 449,450).

As we realize, Kant has developed a fairly complex system of virtues. The duty of virtue whose end is to promote the happiness of others involves a great number of virtues, ranging from the duty of love to the duty of respect. (Interestingly enough, according to Kant, these two duties are intimately united in friendship). In all these duties we foster the other persons' ends in the attempt we make to promote their happiness. Of course, not all the ends that persons have are equally required, if they wish to promote their happiness. Or, even better, to put it negatively, while fostering or failing to foster certain ends will not make any difference at all to the promotion of the persons' happiness, failing to sustain and develop some other ends may affect seriously the chances certain persons have to achieve their happiness. Thus, while living in Lesvos and not in Berlin as a refugee, after he has escaped the horrors of the Syrian war, may not make any tremendous difference to the promotion of his happiness, having been captivated, tortured or sent to jail will have destroyed completely any chances he might have for achieving happiness.

Kant knows very well that among the various ends people adopt in their life, only very few are essential and contribute to the promotion of their happiness. As might have been understood, Kant in fact considers that there is one end the preservation and the development of which is a necessary condition for the promotion of our happiness. This is the capacity to set and pursue ends, i.e. the capacity to be autonomous.

As the persons' various ends contribute to different degrees to the promotion of their happiness, in an analogous manner Kant has developed a rather sophisticated account of duties. All duties we have to other human beings are duties of love; all make the other persons' ends our own in the attempt we make to promote the other persons' happiness. But as the other persons' ends may contribute to varying degrees to their happiness, in a similar way the duties of love and beneficence we have to other human beings oblige us to a smaller or greater degree to adopt their ends as if they are our own. When the ends we foster simply enrich the autonomy that the other persons already possess, then the duty of love or beneficence is *meritorious*, since it enhances the capacity that the other persons already have to set their own ends. If we fail to perform a duty of beneficence in this case, we do not do injustice to anyone and so we are not blameworthy.

Quite often, however, especially in the refugee crises, like the one that is going on in the Mediterranean, or in the economic crises that are taking place in many parts of the world, what is at stake is our capacity to set and pursue our ends. Refugees who are, most of the time, on the run, or persons who live in total poverty, have lost any capacity for autonomy. They *cannot* be autonomous beings, like the rest of us. And this "cannot", we must underline, is both logical and psychological. In such cases, Kant claims, the duty of beneficence, in the particular form of the duty of respect, obliges us that we do not "exalt ourselves above the others" (Kant 1996a, § 6: 449). Furthermore, it prescribes that we foster their ends as if they are our own, and that we help them recover their lost capacity for autonomy. In this situation, the duty of respect is not just meritorious but, instead, a duty that *is owed.* People who have found themselves in the condition of a refugee or a misplaced, or in an absolute poverty situation lay a lawful claim on us, have a right to claim a decent and peaceful life, even though this right is not enforced by any law; not enforced yet. Even so, Kant acknowledges that we owe them some basics, at least their ability to think and determine their ends freely. And to the extent that we do not help them to regain their autonomy, "we degrade them to a mere means to our ends", we harm them, and we make them victims of injustice (Kant 1996a, § 6: 450). In arguing in this manner, there is no doubt that Kant's ethical account of virtues has paved the way for an international legislature which will provide for the basic claims and rights of all those who are in conditions of famine, absolute poverty and other forms of disasters.

15.5 Conclusion

In this chapter I argue that Kant's deontological account and, in particular, his theory of virtues, is the appropriate ethical account for dealing with disasters, famine and world poverty. I take sides with O'Mathúna in claiming that, contrary to what certain philosophers have supported, utilitarianism and Kant's deontological formal account are far from "ideal" theories, when dealing with disasters, as they leave out the particular features of the situation, the feelings and the intentions of those involved, whether victims or healthcare workers. However, as I then point out, Kant's deontological account, apart from its formal part, also includes an empirical part, which renders his ethical theory applicable in the concrete circumstances of the real world. I then devote the remainder of this chapter to bringing out Kant's account of virtues and to analyzing his two duties of virtue, i.e. the duty of justice and the duty of beneficence. The conclusion reached is that Kant's account of these two duties of virtue is so carefully worked-out that leaves no doubt that it is the right one for dealing with disasters.

References

Aristotle. 1990. *Nicomachean ethics.* Trans H. Rackham. Cambridge, MA: The Loeb Classical Library, Harvard University Press.

Hare, R.M. 1963. *Freedom and reason.* Oxford: Oxford University Press.

Hegel, G.W.F. 1977. *Phenomenology of spirit.* Trans. A. V. Miller. Oxford: Oxford University Press.

Kalokairinou, Eleni. 2011. *From meta-ethics to ethics. An overview of R. M. Hare's moral philosophy.* Frankfurt am Main: Peter Lang.

Kalokairinou, Eleni M. 2016. Why helping the victims of disasters makes me a better person? Towards an anthropological theory of humanitarian action. *Human Affairs* 26: 26–33.

Kant, Immanuel. 1996a. *The metaphysics of morals*. In Mary Gregor, ed. and Roger J. Sullivan (Introd.). Cambridge: Cambridge University Press.
———. 1996b. *Anthropology from a pragmatic point of view*. Victor Lyle Dowdell (transl.), Frederick p. Van De Pitte (Introd.). Carbondale/Edwardsville: Southern Illinois University Press.
———. 1997. *Groundwork of the metaphysics of morals*. In Mary Gregor, ed. and Christine M. Korsgaard (Introd.). Cambridge: Cambridge University Press.
O'Mathúna, Donal. 2016. Ideal and nonideal moral theory for disaster bioethics. *Human Affairs* 26: 8–17.
O'Mathúna, D.P., Bert Gordijn, and Mike Clarke. 2014. Disaster bioethics: An introduction. In *Disaster bioethics: Normative issues when nothing is normal*, ed. D.P. O'Mathúna, Bert Gordijn, and Mike Clarke. Dordrecht: Springer.
O'Neill, Onora. 1993. Ending world hunger. In *Matters of life and death*, ed. Tom Regan, 3rd ed., 85–112. New York: McGraw-Hill.
———. 2016. Rights, obligations and world hunger. In *Justice across boundaries. Whose obligations?* ed. Onora O'Neill, 29–42. Cambridge: Cambridge University Press.
Singer, Peter. 1972. Famine, affluence and morality. *Philosophy and public affairs* 1 (1): 229–243.

Chapter 16
The Loss of Deontology on the Road to Apathy: Examples of Homelessness and IVF Now, with Disaster to Follow

Veselin Mitrović and Naomi Zack

Abstract Vulnerable groups, from contemporary homeless people to IVF embryos may fall between the cracks of otherwise good social values, such as government welfare programs and individual autonomy. These present and slow disasters are in principle no different from more immediate catastrophes resulting from natural events or wars that harm civilians. The failure to respond with indignation and demands for change constitutes apathy, which is also an absence of deontology. We begin with concrete examples of social apathy, in Part 1. Our examples are homelessness and IVF, neither of which are usually considered disasters but both of which are in fact ongoing disasters within normal society. Part 2. is a discussion of theoretical and practical deontology that is lacking in these examples.

Keywords Vulnerability · Social values · Resilience · Homelessness · In vitro fertilization (IVF) · Deontology · Apathy

16.1 Introduction

Vulnerable groups, from contemporary homeless people to IVF embryos may fall between the cracks of otherwise good social values, such as government welfare programs and individual autonomy. These present and slow disasters are in principle no different from more immediate catastrophes resulting from natural events or wars that harm civilians. The failure to respond with indignation and demands for change constitutes apathy, which is also an absence of deontology. We begin with concrete examples of social apathy, in Part I. Our examples are homelessness and IVF, neither of which are usually considered disasters but both of which are in fact

V. Mitrović (✉)
Faculty of Philosophy, University of Belgrade, Belgrade, Serbia

N. Zack
Philosophy Department, University of Oregon, Eugene, OR, USA
e-mail: nzack@uoregon.edu

D. P. O'Mathúna et al. (eds.), *Disasters: Core Concepts and Ethical Theories*, Advancing Global Bioethics 11, https://doi.org/10.1007/978-3-319-92722-0_16

ongoing disasters within normal society. Part II is a discussion of theoretical and practical deontology that is lacking in these examples.

16.2 Part 1: Homelessness and IVF Sacrifice

We present two case studies. The first paints a picture of social apathy and loss of care through social and linguistic transformation of one of the most at risk and non-resilient social groups: the homeless. "Resilience is understood as the capacity to act voluntarily in the interest of enhancing one's own life conditions (e.g. anticipation and capacity for planning)" (Mitrović 2015a, b, 187). When resilience is lacking within a group in society, or by society at large in interacting with that group, the group's vulnerability increases.

Our second case study derives from one personal story of ten former patients of an IVF (in vitro fertilization) procedure. The subjects in this study possessed a strong will for having offspring. Apathy and the loss of care on a broader social and institutional level, combined with the desire for offspring at any cost, forces the clinical subjects who want to become parents to disavow their own freedom, ultimately rendering them more apathetic than they would otherwise be. Gradually, these actors cross from a group with some prospects into the non-resilient group. In other words, these individuals consider that the state/institutions can compensate for the lack of altruism and solidarity. Altruism is here understood as CD Batson defined it, a "motivational state with the ultimate goal of increasing another's welfare" (Batson 2011, 20). With that in mind, solidarity as a social value could be taken to be "a degree of altruism in competitive social systems, e.g., mutual support in social reproduction, providing basic rights, social protection, and concern throughout the main channels of social mobility in a given community" (Mitrović 2016, 49). Both the prospective parents and their sacrificed embryos are examples of disaster victims. The parents are victims of moral disaster, the sacrificed embryos of loss of life.

The premise of these case studies is that the transformation of solidarity into state altruism leads individuals and groups to think that they cannot help themselves or others in need, even their close family members whose lives might be in their hands. In catastrophic situations, this state of affairs would mean greater susceptibility to risk, in addition to rendering rescue operations more difficult.

Both of our case studies include a personal view of the sovereign or good life. What kind of autonomy represents the true internal choice of actors, informed by the idea one has of the good life? This question is of particular importance in borderline cases, as well as for the prevention of eugenic choices when making decisions regarding the lives of others (especially the marginalized) in the course of catastrophes.

16.3 Case 1[1]: How the Clochards Became the Homeless

The total number of individuals in Serbia today who have plans to enhance their life conditions in the coming 1–2 years is 50.3%. In this study, we call them people with non-damaged resilience. In contrast, 49.7% of the population (non-resilient) has no such life plans (Mitrović 2015a, b).[2]

One group of people belonging to the non-resilient are the homeless. The word "homeless" as it is used today did not exist in the social vocabulary of Yugoslavia. In a small town in north-eastern Bosnia (when Bosnia and Herzegovina was one of the six federal republics in Yugoslavia) where one of the authors (Mitrović) grew up in the 1970s, there were two persons who could vaguely be seen as *klošar*. The official terminology of the time termed these persons "socially endangered," but they were colloquially known as *klošar*, that is, hobos.

The Serbian *klošar* comes from French *clochard*, meaning a person who limps, an etymology relevant for this article. To call one "a hobo" had a bohemian, almost sympathetic sound. However, what exactly is the background of the word "hobo"? As "Hobo" means poor, alcoholic, artistic soul, lacking permanent residence. But on top of this, a hobo is either physically or socially "lame" or "limping." Were such persons born "lame" or did they become part of the "lame" (hobo) social group, on an individual basis or simply through social assignment? How does one become recognized as a "lame, marginalized" person? In order to answer these questions, we will have to look beyond the veil of personal and collective memory to a country that held promise, yet is now dead.

The two men known in the small town in the 1970s did have homes, usually provided by the community, although they were unemployed. One of them sold candy apples in the yard of a local elementary school. The other of the two "marginals" worked as a seasonal laborer. Regardless of their meager incomes, consisting in part of occasional jobs and small scale trading, and in part their social benefits, the local office for social protection ensured basic material means of subsistence for these men and their families. Part of their social welfare was free healthcare and treatment, as was the norm and legally guaranteed practice for all citizens.

One of the basic social values in the socialist system was solidarity. In addition to the state policy of free education and social and health protection, solidarity was, in one way or another, the basis of communal life. In that sense, these two men were part of the community, while also leading independent lives. They took advantage

---

[1] This case study is a shortened and adapted version of an article by Veselin Mitrović (2015a). How *Klošar* Became the Homeless Upon the Dissolution of Yugoslavia. *Homelessness and Home,* Community Philosophy Institute, Philosophy Department, University of Oregon. http://homelessness.philosophy.uoregon.edu/narratives-of-homelessness/ Accessed 24 July, 2016.

[2] The presented data are from Mitrović's research of apathy in Serbian society, published in cited reference. This research is done in the frame of the wider scientific project "The Challenges of the New Social Integration: Concepts and Agents." (nr.179035) granted by the Serbian Ministry of Education, Science and Technological Development.

of their right to basic material necessities: a roof over their heads, minimum income, healthcare and education for their children, and so forth.

A homeless person, in the social and linguistic sense, assumed relevance in the last decade of the twentieth century, during the painful and bitter dissolution of socialist Yugoslavia. Quickly, if unoriginally, politicians, along with a section of the intellectual elite, coined a term for these people: losers of the post-socialist transition. While deeply opposed to a term that characterizes individuals and groups as "losers" at a given historical moment, we find citing this phrase an apt way to present the reader with a picture that society (or the majority) can form of someone who has lost everything but his or her life. The tragic loss of basic civil rights, not to mention the overnight disappearance of guaranteed benefits, was justified by way of a new "loser or winner ethics" due to some evolutionary, well-nigh eugenic, understanding of the incompatibility of some individuals and groups to a specific social programme. It was as if the power of culture and yesterday's basic values, such as solidarity and tolerance, completely disappeared with the dissolution of a way of life, wiping out a promised better future in the (nearly) ethnically clean former Yugoslav republics. In the course of the wars at the end of the twentieth century, the region of the west Balkans faced hundreds of thousands of refugees. They became homeless, even though they were now placed in collective centers, ghettoized from the rest of the "domestic" population. Thus the social and political transformation, begun in the late eighties, and the wars of independence in the nineties, created fertile ground for homelessness in the contemporary sense of the word.

What happened to the old, exotic image of the hobo? Did he disappear or has the homeless person (who is one of the losers of the transition) acquired one of the hobo's faces, the socially "lame" person? How, we might ask, does one today become a hobo or a socially "lame" person in this region?

Complementing the sketch above of the hobo from the 1970s, before the breakdown of socialist Yugoslavia, we offer a specific example of Belgrade homelessness to describe what homelessness means today. After a domestic tragedy, such as a violent breakup of a family, an average member of the middle class ends up in prison where he may spend a third of his life. He has lost his house, family, and, of course, his employment, the guarantor of middle class status. After a while, he ends up on the street, in the city center, near the place of work of his son, who has practically grown up without either parent. He can be seen today, three sheets to the wind, slumped on the pavement in front of the offices of the most important Serbian daily, *Politika*, and the building of Radio Belgrade. More than one journalist, on more than one occasion, has tried, and some have even succeeded, in coaxing out of him his story and explanation of homelessness (*se non è vero, è ben trovato* – even if not true, it is well conceived). He told them that by choosing a life in the open, imbibing copious amounts of alcohol, he has chosen a sort of slow death. One particularly cold winter, he loses several toes and is left literally limping. He becomes recognizable socially and medically as lame, homeless, alcoholic, an ex-con, etcetera. Even so, some of his acquaintances still bring him warm meals and others even alcoholic beverages in front of *Politika's* offices. Obviously, certain people still regard him as a member of the community and accept his self-identification as a homeless person who is not seeking to survive in the long run, but rather dissipate his life towards a slow death.

A few years later, Belgrade gets a homeless shelter, which usually happens to be full in the winter months. On several significant occasions at the shelter, this homeless man attempts to die his slow death. He looks quite old and weak, but is protected (*nolens volens*) in the cold winter months. The institutionalization of homelessness that occurred with the social changes that followed the dissolution of socialism not only limited the way of life, but also the way in which a homeless person wished to die. In post-socialist, *post-bellum* circumstances, the poor socioeconomic conditions of life, combined with individual acts of protection, could create an image of a "caring" or "altruistic" society, one that cares about its members, regardless of their social status. However, the basic social value of solidarity seems to have vanished along with the old political system and former state, leaving behind a vacuum to be filled by the invisible hand of state altruism. In other words, what was once a matter of right is now a matter of government charity. What lurks beneath the image of an altruistic society? Is there a dark side to the "altruism" that regulates not only the way of life but also the way of death?

Social history and psychology remind us of the possibility of measuring authoritarian behavior. Government policy that removes the homeless from the streets and eyes of the majority, regardless of altruistic explanations, can be valued as a caring activity in poor European countries, where around half the population possesses no short term plans for improvement of their life conditions. However, strict regulation that at first sight may appear altruistic can be easily upended into a totalitarian type of ordering the daily life of citizens, regardless of whether they do or do not have a roof over their heads.

There is a thin line between sympathy with government policy that prohibits one's ways of living and dying, and cultural complicity with the state determining who lives and dies. The social and linguistic metamorphosis of the erstwhile Yugoslav hobo into a homeless person could be a social bellwether for much wider future socioeconomic and political change in this area of the world. The collapse of an old ossified political system, taking place in the midst of the creation and harmonization of European Union regulation, also transforms former social and health security into a new type of "altruism." Yet does such altruism carry more worry for the most precarious social groups? The answer to that question depends on the balance between the way in which, on the one hand, the majority sees its rights and achievements, and, on the other, the sympathy with the actions of government altruism that influences the lives of the homeless and other marginalized groups. In other words, the answer is in the sociological imagination of today's "altruism" in the most developed countries.

Social sympathies with some limits on how members of marginal groups will die, open not only the possibilities that the majority or the state decides who and when someone will die – above all the marginalized – but also the further step of social and ethical justification of measures that allow the majority its inertness and apathy in a situation that requires taking action.

16.4 Case 2[3]: False Autonomy. The Story of Participant P8: How Good a Mother Can I Be?

The Serbian health care system provides the possibility of free treatment for infertility, recognized as an illness, allowing for the fulfillment of the social role of parenthood. The system ensures medical, legal, and social conditions for conception through Assisted Reproductive Technology (ART) for partners and single women with diagnosed infertility. From this perspective, altruism refers to one organism enhancing the reproductive advantage of another, especially at a cost to itself. This poses the question of "whether the state can personify a characteristic such as reproductive or procreative altruism" (Mitrović 2016, 49).

The fact that institutions in Serbia did not have a bio-repository is one of the most frequent elements that fuels dilemmas regarding the patient-physician relationship. The most frequent response shows how this situation induces potential misunderstandings in medical treatments. According to Participant P8, "Through hyperstimulation I had 30 healthy eggs. So, I had to ask myself what happened with them, because I didn't freeze my eggs, so where are they?" Given that egg preservation was not possible in Serbia until recently, the patient never asked outright what really happened with her eggs. Participant P8 is a highly educated woman, in her late 30s, married, fully employed, and an atheist. She showed complete unwillingness to accept or donate generative cells or embryo for any purpose whatever. "I didn't use donated eggs or semen, nor would I, because I want to know who the father of my child is, and at the same time, I want to be the biological mother of that infant. Of course, objectively, that is not important when the child grows up" (P8).

Participant P8 would agree to the possible donation of her husband's semen, adding, however, that it would be physiologically "not easily acceptable for the purposes of donation" (P8). She chose to undergo in vitro fertilization at a private clinic, outside the government run health care system, for better expediency due to her age. After examining the rules for the free infertility program, the participant P8 decided to bypass "the paperwork": "I saw on the internet how much paperwork we needed for free *in vitro*... I knew that this was impossible if one works from 9 to 6" (P8).

Participant P8 and her husband were never asked what they wished to do with the remaining ovum/semen cells or embryos in Serbian private hospitals. All participants agreed that regardless of the health or normal development of these cells or embryos, patients should be asked about their fate. Further, like nearly all the other participants, P8 wished to preserve her own embryos, even if it meant preserving embryos with irregular cellular differentiation.

In addition to the difficulties of conception, this story is characterized by the use of medical technologies to control the number of children and the time of their birth. Participant P8 had a pregnancy terminated a few years prior to her decision to

[3]This portion of the article is an adapted version of an article by Veselin Mitrović (2014). Procreative Ethics of Care in the Process of IVF in Serbia: A Culture of Giving or a Crisis of Altruism? *Teme* 1: 193–211 (Serbian).

undergo IVF. The termination was motivated by the fact that she had become pregnant with a different man. Her general attitude towards termination was positive, because she could choose the man with whom to have a child. After obtaining one child through in vitro fertilization, she was asked how many embryos had been returned to her and whether the number of children was her choice. The answer was that the doctors reached the legal maximum and in order to increase her chances of conception returned three embryos. However, none of the doctors asked her nor informed her regarding this number during the course of the procedure. Regarding this, she responded: "I think that it is not necessary to know everything about these procedures, because the doctor is the specialist and he knows what he should do" (P8).

During Participant P8's early pregnancy, one of three embryos in the womb did not continue to differentiate (which is not uncommon), while the other two developed normally. In the interest of her view of the good life, participant P8 chose to remove one of the remaining healthy embryos, that is, to perform an *embryo reduction*. She explained her decision briefly, by saying that she knows herself: "I decided on my own because I know myself. After a few weeks of thinking about twins, I realized that I am not capable of carrying this through properly and that I could deal with one child, but not two. I know that I will need help and I do not have it. Given how I am, one child is what I can do" (P8).

When asked whether she regards embryo reduction as an abortion, she answered affirmatively. She was further asked whether she did this because she was afraid that a twin pregnancy could cause premature delivery. The answer was similar to the previous one: "Yes, I was afraid of that too, and in the end it turned out that had I not done so, I would not have had any children! But I couldn't have known that at the time. I decided based only on knowing myself" (P8). Interestingly, P8's husband was in favor of adopting a child, which she absolutely opposed. The reason, much like her previous position, lay precisely in connecting aspects of her personality with her idea of a good life. Here is how she describes this connection: "I know myself, and I know my relation towards others' children, children that are not mine. So I was convinced that I would not manage that properly" (P8).

This example shows how an ideal understanding of the role and motivation of parenthood may contrast with an idea of a good life. In particular, it seems that the responsible and autonomous aspect of the mother's identity are emphasized. That is, by controlling biotechnological activity, the mother also entirely controls the idea of the good life. P8 would in that regard be prepared to resort to genetic engineering to enhance the capacity of the child: "If possible, I would enhance the intelligence of the children through genetic engineering; why be stupid if it can be smart" (P8).

Yet given such a clear idea of personhood and the good life, what remains unclear is P8's unwillingness to bring about the good life of other persons in a similar situation. Of course, with the limit of research assumptions, this article can do no more than suppose that the potential incongruence in the ethics of care lies precisely in that portion of the individual that characterizes the self. This aspect of personality in this case is understood in its most narrow sense. It is in direct connection with the idea of the good life of the parent – the feeling of self-actualization through birthing, regardless of the origin of generative cells. Another detail from the case study testifies to this narrow view of the self. Participant P8 offered one of the most interesting affirmative answers to the question whether participants would genetically determine their child to be an altruist. Despite choosing altruism for her child, P8 particularly emphasized that she would never choose that for herself, on the contrary. Therefore, we could conclude that her insecurity regarding her role as a parent within the idea of the good life lies in a narrowly understood selfhood. Although the autonomous aspect of identity is emphasized in this case study through the decisive and different actions of control of having a child, the truth may in fact be completely different.

Everyone is free to control their procreative potentials in seeking the good life. However, the analysis also shows that that responsibility is understood as a kind of prohibition in procreation of using anything that does not biologically come from one's partner, as well as oneself. Such an idea of responsibility has a much broader reflection on the type of genetic altruism already mentioned.

Participant P8's readiness to genetically determine her child as an altruist, while also having no willingness to be so determined herself, issues from the prohibition to help another when this damages the idea of the self. In that sense, this narrow understanding of the self allows the prohibitions to overshadow freedoms, even if at first sight it might seem just the opposite. Her answers that deferred to doctors, justified by their expertise, reveals the scope of internal prohibitions to further act on potential and free choice. Thus, such acts lead to personal disavowal of altruism and solidarity. Still, such actors think that others ought to be altruistic.

16.4.1 Part 2: Theoretical Moral Considerations: Deontology Behind Glass

The cases examined in Part 1 share a deferral of altruistic responsibility, in the former hobo case, from community to the state, and in the IVF case, from parent to child. In the former hobo case, the plight of those who cannot adapt to societal change by securing meaningful paid employment is to perform a slow death in public view. The homeless in Belgrade are legitimate members of society, but in full view as social outcasts. No one would say that they ought to be denied food and shelter, or for that matter, employment. But neither is there a strong, explicit articulation or practice of an obligation to provide them with such fundamental goods of human life. Participant P8 choses one twin embryo over the other for her own convenience. She does not know or apparently care what will happen to her and her husband's reproductive material that is unused by them. Thus, Participant 8 does not seek to have a child out of what is ideally understood to be parental love, with a willingness to endure personal sacrifice for the good of another. Indeed, altruism is a value she recognizes as a desirable trait for her child to have, but not a trait that she is committed to living out for herself.

Both the former hobo and IVF cases display recognitions of altruism as a virtue for others. There is no subjective obligation for individual actors. This renders altruism a form of deontology "behind glass." Anyone may value altruism as something practiced by other people and this separates moral action from moral subjects. Potential practitioners of altruism who observe such cases apathetically thus experience no obligation to perform their own duties of helping others. There is no visceral tug or heart-felt inclination to perform those duties. If the state has a duty to take care of residents but does not fulfill basic needs with adequate public shelter, this is evidence of an official failure to fulfill obligations. But not only are social duties of care deferred by the community to the state, there is no public outcry in response to state failure to fulfill its deferred obligations. This lack of indignation is what is meant by "apathy." Apathy is the result of indifference to deferred duty that is not performed and it makes sense to imagine that it would not result if *solidarity* were present, that is, if members of the community felt a common cause with those who are homeless.

A woman has a right to choose whether or not to continue with a pregnancy, whether it is conceived within her, or as in the case of Participant P8, in vitro. No one has what Immanuel Kant would have called a "perfect duty" to parent all children whom one is in a position to parent and able to parent. But we may have an imperfect duty to parent some of them and a perfect duty to use fair standards in choosing (Schaller 1987).[4] So Participant 8 has a moral right to 'reduce' some embryos but probably not solely on the grounds of what is convenient for her personally.[5]

Moral consideration of the plight of vulnerable groups requires that we choose fundamental principles that will guide us to what we will recognize as kind, compassionate, or just results if those principles are applied to concrete situations. This sounds like a rigged procedure because we are choosing a moral system, not because it is right, but because we approve of the outcome. However, that may be the best we can do, insofar as moral systems have the epistemological structure of scientific theories. We choose or construct a system that provides a satisfactory account of our aspirations and experience and is capable of generating new explanations and predictions in new situations.[6] For example, suppose we chose Autonomous Egoism as

[4] According to Kant, a perfect duty admits of no exceptions to what we are required to do in circumstances when we could perform it. An imperfect duty allows for choice or autonomy in the performance of what would otherwise be perfect duties. The example usually given is charitable donations: One has a duty to make some charitable donations, but not necessarily this one.

[5] In her famous argument defending a woman's right to choose whether or not to continue with a pregnancy, Judith Jarvis Thompson distinguishes between cases where a woman chooses to abort to preserve her own basic well-being versus making that choice because continuing with a pregnancy would interfere with her planned trip (Thomson 1971, 66).

[6] Even John Rawls referred to the theoretical nature of moral systems in his explanation of his project in *A Theory of Justice*:

> I want to stress that a theory of justice is precisely that, namely a theory. It is a theory of the moral sentiments (to recall an eighteenth century title) setting out the principles governing our moral powers, or, more specifically, our sense of justice. There is a definite if limited class of facts against which conjectured principles can be checked, namely, our considered judgments in reflective equilibrium. A theory of justice is subject to the same rules of method as other theories (1971, 50–51). For discussion and further explication, see Zack 2016, 9–34

a moral system and perceive after applying it that some autonomous acts of self-interest are morally repugnant. That perception would work as a disconfirmation of the moral system applied.

Along similar lines, utilitarianism and virtue ethics may be judged inadequate when applied to extreme situations or conditions in which some die—quickly or slowly—when they could otherwise be saved. We might find that instead of lauding heroes who "save the greatest number" in a catastrophe, what we require morally is a principle according to which all who can be saved, fairly, are saved (Zack 2009).

There are at least two well-known formulations of Kant's categorical imperative: Act so that the maxim of your action can be willed by you to be a universal law; treat everyone, including yourself, as an end, rather than a means. The second formulation has been most influential in humanitarian plans and projects, since the end of World War II. There is a broad, albeit somewhat and sometimes vague, consensus that all human lives are intrinsically valuable, principally because, as Kant thought, they are subjectively valuable to those whose lives they are (Johnson and Cureton 2016).

The second universal intrinsic worth formulation of the categorical imperative evokes a humanitarian response when suffering occurs that is not prevented by positive law. This is the nature of moral objection to the slow death of former hobos in Belgrade and the shocking nature of reproductive autonomy without altruistic constraint or imperative. But the humanitarian objection from a deontological perspective is more than acknowledging the rightness or moral correctness of the principle that all human life (at least) is intrinsically valuable. The objection is also a focus on what happens when deontology is no longer a motivational force in people's lives. If the state is supposed (obligated) to take care of homeless people and fails to do so and members of the community accept that situation, deontology, no matter how much lip service may be given to it, has been placed behind glass. Apathy replaces dutiful action. If a prospective mother chooses altruism for her future child, but not for herself, apathy has again replaced duty (deontology).

Indeed, grim as it sounds, deontology is duty-based ethics and it may be our best moral theory as a formal expression of solidarity with others. Deontological values and principles can be taught, but we do not know as yet how to instill motivations to act from duty towards those whose suffering we know is bad, but who are not sufficiently close to or coincidental with what Kant called "the dear self:"

> We cannot better serve the wishes of those who ridicule all morality as a mere chimera of human imagination over stepping itself from vanity, than by conceding to them that notions of duty must be drawn only from experience (as from indolence, people are ready to think is also the case with all other notions); for or is to prepare for them a certain triumph. I am willing to admit out of love of humanity that even most of our actions are correct, but if we look closer at them we everywhere come upon the dear self which is always prominent, and it is this they have in view and not the strict command of duty which would often require self-denial. (Kant 2014)

In other words, according to Kant, partiality to the dear self is not a component of morality, much less a moral system. The dear self is an obstacle to morality. If members of a community are apathetic when the state does not correct the homelessness of those who lack personal relations to help them, or a parent choses altruism as a trait for her child, but not for her dear self, deontology has been obstructed. Also, according to Kant, deontology cannot be derived from social experience alone. This would certainly seem to be the case in a society dominated by the interests of dear selves. Aristotle's insistence that virtuous individuals require a virtuous state to flourish also comes to mind.

To maintain healthy optimism, we need to move from regretful longing for past types of communities that now seem more caring than the present. Instead, it is necessary to look ahead to more and better moral education and the development of communal practices of solidarity to initiate and institute new forms of social deontology. The first step is to take seriously the force of deontology to bridge the gap between what people fail to do and their recognition of what they are obligated (duty bound) to do. This is not an easy task from within a post-modern ethos that is neither strongly religious nor paternalistically statist. But taking deontology seriously is itself an imperfect duty and it can be discharged for multiple issues in multiple ways: activist organizing, inspirational speaking and speaking out, and engaging in progressive intellectual and academic discourses.

References

Batson, Daniel C. 2011. *Altruism in humans*. New York: Oxford University Press.

Johnson, Robert and Adam Cureton. 2016. Kant's moral philosophy. In *The Stanford encyclopedia of philosophy*, ed. Edward N. Zalta. http://plato.stanford.edu/archives/fall2016/entries/kant-moral/. Accessed 20 Jul 2016.

Kant, Immanuel. 2014. Second section: Transition from popular moral philosophy to the metaphysics of morals. In *Fundamental principles of the metaphysics of morals*. Trans. Thomas Kingsmill Abbott, e-books at University of Adelaide, paragraph 3. https://ebooks.adelaide.edu.au/k/kant/immanuel/k16prm/index.html. Accessed 20 Jul 2016.

Mitrović, Veselin. 2014. Procreative ethics of care in the process of IVF in Serbia: A culture of giving or a crisis of altruism? Temenos 1: 193–211.

———. 2015a. Resilience: Detecting vulnerability in marginal groups. *Disaster Prevention and Management* 2: 185–200.

———. 2015b. How *Klošar* became homeless upon the dissolution of Yugoslavia. In *Homelessness and home*. University of Oregon. http://homelessness.philosophy.uoregon.edu/narratives-of-homelessness/. Accessed 24 Jul 2016.

———. 2016. Parents' religious and secular perspectives on IVF planning in Serbia. *Journal for the Study of Religions and Ideologies* 43: 48–81.

Rawls, John. 1971. *A theory of justice*. Cambridge, MA: Harvard University Press.

Schaller, Walter E. 1987. Kant's architectonic of duties. *Philosophy and Phenomenological Research* 2: 299–314.

Thomson, Judith Jarvis. 1971. A defense of abortion, Philosophy & Public Affairs 1: 47–66. http://www.unige.ch/lettres/baumgartner/docs/geda/Thomson_abortion.pdf. Accessed 20 Jul 2016.
Zack, Naomi. 2009. Ethics of disaster planning. In *Ethics of crisis*, Philosophy of Management, Special Issue, ed. Per Sandin, vol. 2, 53–64. Lanham: Rowman and Littlefield.
———. 2016. *Applicative justice: A pragmatic empirical approach to racial injustice*. Lanham: Rowman and Littlefield.

Index

D. P. O'Mathúna et al. (eds.), *Disasters: Core Concepts and Ethical Theories*, Advancing Global Bioethics 11, https://doi.org/10.1007/978-3-319-92722-0

The manufacturer's authorised representative in the EU is Springer Nature Customer Service Centre GmbH, Europaplatz 3, 69115 Heidelberg, Germany. If you have any concerns regarding our products, please contact ProductSafety@springernature.com

Printed and bound by CPI Group (UK) Ltd, Croydon, CR0 4YY

30/09/2026

02225601-0010